CULTURAL AND TRADITIONAL HISTORY OF INDIA

CULTURAL AND TRADITIONAL HISTORY OF INDIA

Manohar Bhardwaj

2008

CYBER TECH PUBLICATIONS
4264/3, Ansari Road, Daryaganj, New Delhi-110002 (India)
Ph.: 011-23244078. Fax: 011-23280028
E-Mail: cyberpublicationsdelhi@yahoo.com

CULTURAL AND TRADITIONAL HISTORY OF INDIA

Manohar Bhardwaj

First Edition 2008

Published by :

G.S. Rawat for **Cyber Tech Publications**
4264/3, Ansari Road, Daryaganj, New Delhi-110002 (India)
Ph.: 011-23244078. Fax: 011-23280028
E-Mail: cyberpublicationsdelhi@yahoo.com

Printed at : **Amit Enterprises**, Maujpur, Delhi, (9810878184)

Preface

The culture of India was moulded throughout various eras of history, all the while absorbing customs, traditions and ideas from both invaders and immigrants. Many cultural practices, languages, customs and monuments are examples of this co-mingling over centuries.

In modern India, there is remarkable cultural and religious diversity throughout the country. This has been influenced by the various regions of India, namely South, North, and North-East, have their own distinct identities and almost every state has carved out its own cultural niche. In spite of this unique cultural diversity, the whole country is bound as a civilization due to its common history, thereby preserving the national identity. India was the birth place of religious systems such as Hinduism, Sikhism, Buddhism and Jainism, which have a strong influence not only over India, but also the whole world.

Following the Islamic invasions and the subsequent foreign domination from the tenth century onwards, the culture of India was influenced by the foreign cultures, particularly Persian, Arabic and Turkish cultures. Their influence comes in the form of religion, language and dress. In turn, the various religions and the multihued traditions of India have influenced South East Asia (and to a minimal extent, East Asia).

Indian culture can be classified into many varied form which are existent in their totality throughout the territory of India. The culture of India has been influenced by various religions and customs of the world, which resulted in the mingling of religious values, folk idioms and art forms. While the religious influence is quite evident in the "classical" Indian culture mostly found in smaller towns and villages, the urban India is now widely influenced by globalization.

—Author

Contents

1

INDIAN PHILOSOPHY AND RELIGION

INTRODUCTION

Indian philosophy includes Hindu philosophy. They contain elements of nonmaterial pursuits, whereas another school of thought from India, Carvaka, preached the enjoyment of material world. Confucianism and Taoism, both of which originated in China have had pervasive influence on both religious and philosophical traditions, as well as statecraft and the arts throughout Asia. Philosophy and religion are often closely interwoven in Eastern thought. Many Asian religious and philosophical traditions originated in India and China and spread across Asia through cultural diffusion and the migration of peoples.

Hinduism is the wellspring of Buddhism, the Mahâyâna branch of which spread north and eastwards from India into Tibet, China, Mongolia, Japan and Korea and south from China into Vietnam. Theravâda Buddhism spread throughout Southeast Asia, including Sri Lanka, parts of southwest China, Cambodia, Laos, Myanmar, and Thailand.

During the 20th century, in the two most populous countries of Asia, two dramatically different political philosophies took shape. Gandhi gave a new meaning to Ahimsa, a core belief of both Hinduism and Jainism, and redefined the concepts of nonviolence and nonresistance. During the same period, Mao Zedong's communist philosophy became a powerful secular belief system in China.

Folk Religions

Folk religions practiced by tribal groups are common in Asia, Africa and the Americas. Their influence can be considerable; may pervade the culture and even become the state religion, as with Shintoism. Like the other major religions, folk religion answers human needs for reassurance in times of trouble, healing, averting misfortune and providing rituals that address the major passages and transitions in human life.

The "American Dream"

The American Dream is a faith, held by many in the United States, that, through hard work, courage, and self-determination, regardless of social class, a person can gain a better life. This notion is rooted in the belief that the United States is a "city upon a hill, a light unto the nations," which were values held by many early European settlers and maintained by subsequent generations.

Marriage

Most Christian churches give some form of blessing to a marriage; the wedding ceremony typically includes some sort of pledge by the community to support the couple's relationship. In marriage, Christians of the relationship between Jesus Christ and His Church. The Roman Catholic Church believes it is morally wrong to divorce, and divorcées cannot remarry in a church marriage.

Cultural Studies

Cultural studies developed in the late 20th century, in part through the re-introduction of Marxist thought into sociology, and in part through the articulation of sociology and other academic disciplines such as literary criticism. This movement aimed to focus on the analysis of subcultures in capitalist societies.

Following the non-anthropological tradition, cultural studies generally focus on the study of consumption goods (such as fashion, art, and literature). Because the 18th-and 19th-century distinction between "high" and "low" culture seems inappropriate to apply to the mass-produced and mass-marketed consumption goods which cultural studies analyses, these scholars refer instead to "popular culture".

Today, some anthropologists have joined the project of cultural studies. Most, however, reject the identification of culture with consumption goods. Furthermore, many now reject the notion of culture as bounded, and consequently reject the notion of subculture. Instead, they culture as a complex of shifting patterns that link people in different locales and that link social formations of different scales.

According to this view, any group can construct its own cultural identity. Currently, a debate is underway regarding whether or not culture can actually change fundamental human cognition. Researchers are divided on the question.

Cultural Change

Cultures, by predisposition, both embrace and resist change, depending on culture traits. For example, men and women have complementary roles in many cultures. One gender might desire changes that affect the other, as happened in the second half of the 20th century in western cultures. Thus there are both dynamic influences that encourage acceptance of new things, and conservative forces that resist change.

Three kinds of influence cause both change and resistance to it:

1. forces at work within a society
2. contact between societies
3. changes in the natural environment.

Cultural change can come about due to the environment, to inventions (and other internal influences), and to contact with other cultures. For example, the end of the last ice age helped lead to the invention of agriculture, which in its turn brought about many cultural innovations. In diffusion, the form of something (though not necessarily its meaning) moves from one culture to another.

For example, hamburgers, mundane in the United States, seemed exotic when introduced into China. "Stimulus diffusion" refers to an element of one culture leading to an invention in another. Diffusion of innovations theory presents a research-based model of why and when individuals and cultures adopt new ideas, practices, and products.

"Acculturation" has different meanings, but in this context refers to replacement of the traits of one culture with those of another, such as happened to certain Native American tribes and to many indigenous peoples across the globe during the process of colonization. Related processes on an individual level include assimilation (adoption of a different culture by an individual) and transculturation.

Cultural invention has come to mean any innovation that is new and found to be useful to a group of people and expressed in their behaviour but which does not exist as a physical object. Humanity is in a global "accelerating culture change period", driven by the expansion of international commerce, the mass media, and above all, the human population explosion, among other factors. The world's population now doubles in less than years.

Culture change is complex and has far-ranging effects. Sociologists and anthropologists believe that a holistic approach to the study of cultures and their environments is needed to understand all of the various aspects of change. Human existence may best be looked at as a "multifaceted whole." Only from this vantage can one grasp the realities of culture change.

CULTURE OF INDIA

The culture of India was moulded throughout various eras of history, all the while absorbing customs, traditions and ideas from both invaders and immigrants. Many cultural practices, languages, customs and monuments are examples of this co-mingling over centuries.

In modern India, there is remarkable cultural and religious diversity throughout the country. This has been influenced by the various regions of India, namely South, North, and North-East, have their own distinct identities and almost every state has carved out its own cultural niche. In spite of this unique cultural diversity, the whole country is bound as a civilization due to its common history, thereby preserving the national identity.

India was the birth place of religious systems such as Hinduism, Sikhism, Buddhism and Jainism, which have a strong influence not only over India, but also the whole world.

Following the Islamic invasions and the subsequent foreign domination from the tenth century onwards, the culture of India was influenced by the foreign cultures, particularly Persian, Arabic and Turkish cultures. Their influence comes in the form of religion, language and dress. In turn, the various religions and the multihued traditions of India have influenced South East Asia (and to a minimal extent, East Asia).

Overview

Regions: Indian culture can be classified into many varied form which are existent in their totality throughout the territory of India. The culture of India has been influenced by various religions and customs of the world, which resulted in the mingling of religious values, folk idioms and art forms. While the religious influence is quite evident in the "classical" Indian culture mostly found in smaller towns and villages, the urban India is now widely influenced by globalization.

Language: As well as regional diversity, languages have created diverse traditions of culture in India. There are a large number of languages in India; 216 of them are spoken by a group of 10,000 persons or more. The two major families of languages are those of the Indo-Aryan languages and those of the Dravidian languages, the former largely confined to the North India and the latter to the South India. The Constitution of India has stipulated the usage of Hindi and English to be the two official languages of communication for the national government.

A further 22 languages are scheduled for official use, mainly by state governments. Sanskrit has served as a classical language of India and South-Eastern Asia, and is equated in importance to Latin or Greek in Europe. It is studied as far away as Japan and the West due its cultural and religious significance. The classical language of the Dravidian family is regarded to be old Tamil. The number of speakers of state languages and dialects is very high.

Cultural Policy

The cultural policy of the Government of India has three major objectives. One of them is to preserve the cultural heritage of India; to inculcate Indian art consciousness amongst countrymen and to promote high standards in creative and performing arts fields.

Literature

The earliest literary traditions were mostly oral and passed through descendants by the citizens. They were later transcribed. Most of these spring from Hindu tradition and are represented by sacred works like the Vedas, the epics of the Mahabharata and Ramayana. Tamil Sangam literature represents some of India's oldest secular traditions. Many Buddhist and Jain works are in Prakrit languages like Pali. The classical works of playwright Kalidasa even today exert an important influence on Indian litterateurs.

Upon the arrival of Mughal dynasty, Islamic culture also influenced the medieval Indian literature. This was due to the spreading influence of Persian and the rise of famous poets such as Amir Khusro. Colonial rule prepared the stage for modern literature exemplified by the works of Rabindranath Tagore, Bankim Chandra Chattopadhyay, Michael Madhusudan Dutt, Munshi Premchand, Devaki Nandan Khatri, among many others. Indian writers in modern times, like R. K. Narayan, Vaikom Muhammad Basheer,Mahasweta Devi, Amrita Pritam, Arundhati Roy, Vikram Seth, Khushwant Singh, Salman Rushdie have been the cynosures of wide acclaim, both in Indian languages and English.

Poetry

India has strong traditions of poetry, as well as prose writing. This is often closely related to musical traditions, and most poetry can be attributed to religious movements. Writers and philosophers were often also skilled poets.

In modern times, poetry served as an important non-violent tool of nationalism during the Indian freedom movement. A famous modern example of this tradition can be found in such figures as Rabindranath Tagore in modern times and poets such as Kabir in medieval times, as well as the epics of ancient times. Two examples of poetry from Tagore's Gitanjali serve as the national anthems of both India and Bangladesh.

Performing Arts

Music: The music of India includes multiples varieties of folk, popular, pop, and classical music. India's classical music tradition, including Carnatic and Hindustani music, noted for the use of several Raga, has a history spanning millennia and, developed over several eras, remains instrumental to the religious inspiration, cultural expression and pure entertainment. Alongside distinctly subcontinental forms there are major influences from Persian, Arab, and British music. Indian genres like filmi and bhangra have become popular throughout the United Kingdom, South and East Asia, and around the world.

Dance: India offers a number of Classical Indian dance forms, each of which can be traced to different parts of the country. Each form represents the culture and ethos of a particular region or a group of people. The eight main styles are Bharata Natyam, Kathak, Odissi, Kuchipudi, Mohiniattam, Bhangra, Manipuri and Kathakali. Besides, there are several forms of Indian folk dances, and special dances observed in regional festivals.

Drama and Theatre

Indian drama and theatre is perhaps as old as its music and dance. Kalidas' plays like Shakuntala and Meghadoot are some of the oldest plays from literary traditions. The tradition of folk theatre is alive in nearly all the linguistic regions of the country. In addition, there is a rich tradition of puppet theatre in rural India. Group Theatre is also thriving in the cities, initiated by the likes of Utpal Dutt, Khwaja Ahmad Abbas and still maintained by groups like Nandikar and Prithvi Theatre.

Visual Arts

Painting: The earliest Indian paintings were the rock paintings of pre-historic times, the petroglyphs as found in places like Bhimbetka, and some of them are older than 5500 BC. Ancient texts outline theories of darragh and anecdotal accounts suggesting that it was common for households to paint their doorways or indoor rooms where guests resided.

Cave paintings from Ajanta, Bagh, Ellora and Sittanavasal and temple paintings testify to a love of naturalism and God. Most rock art in India is Hindu or Buddhist. A freshly made coloured flour design (Rangoli) everyday is still a common sight outside the doorstep of many (mostly South Indian) Indian homes.

Madhubani painting, Rajput painting, Tanjore painting, Mughal painting are some notable Genres of Indian Art; while Raja Ravi Varma, Nandalal Bose, Jamini Roy are some modern painters. Jehangir Art Gallery, Mumbai, has on display several good Indian paintings.

Sculpture: The first sculptures in India date back to the Indus Valley civilization, where stone and bronze carvings have been discovered. This is one of the earliest instances of sculpture in the world. Later, as Hinduism, Buddhism and Jainism developed further, India produced some of the most intricate bronzes in the world, as well as unrivalled temple carvings. Some huge shrines, such as the one at Ellora were not actually constructed using blocks, but instead carved out of solid rock, making them perhaps the largest and most intricate sculptures in the world.

The pink sandstone sculptures of Mathura evolved during the Gupta period (4th to 6th century) to reach a very high fineness of execution and delicacy in the modelling. Newer sculptures in northwest, in stucco, schist or clay, display very strong blending of Indian post-Gupta mannerism and Classical influence, Hellenistic or possibly even Greco-Roman. Meanwhile, elsewhere in India, less anatomically accurate styles of human representation evolved leading to the classical art that the world is now familiar with and contributing to Buddhist and Hindu sculpture throughout Asia.

Architecture: Indian architecture is that vast tapestry of production of the Indian Subcontinent that encompasses a multitude of expressions over space and time, transformed by the forces of history considered unique to the sub-continent, sometimes destroying, but most of the time absorbing new ideas. The result is an evolving range of architectural production that none the less retains a certain amount of continuity across history. The earliest production in the Indus Valley Civilization was characterised by well planned cities and houses where religion did not seem to play an active role, but which demonstrated world-famous city planning.

During the reign of the Gupta and Maurya empires, several Buddhist architectural examples like caves of Ajanta and Ellora and the monumental Sanchi Stupa were built. South India contains several Hindu temples like Brihadeeswara Temple, Thanjavur, the Sun Temple, Konark, Sri Ranganathaswamy Temple at Srirangam, and the Buddha stupa (Chinna Lanja dibba and Vikramarka kota dibba) at Bhattiprolu. Angkor Wat and other Buddhist and Hindu temples carry the evidence of Indian influence on South East Asian architecture, as they are built in styles almost identical to traditional Indian temple building.

With the advent of Islamic influence from the west, the erstwhile Indian architecture was slightly adapted to allow the traditions of the new religion. Fatehpur Sikri, Taj Mahal, Gol Gumbaz, Qutub Minar, Red Fort of Delhi are the creations of this era, and are often used as the stereotypical symbols of India, despite the greater antiquity and originality of traditional architecture.

The colonial rule of the British Indian Empire saw the development of Indo-Saracenic style, and mixing of several other styles, such as European gothic. Victoria Memorial, Victoria Terminus are notable examples. Recent creations such as Lotus Temple, and the various modern urban developments of India, are also notable.

The traditional system of Vaastu Shastra serves as India's version of Feng Shui, influencing town planning, architecture, and ergonomics. It is unclear which system is older, but they contain many similarities. Though Vastu is conceptually similar to Feng Shui in that it also tries to harmonize the flow of energy, (also called life-force or Prana in Sanskrit and Chi/Ki in Chinese/Japanese), through the house, it differs in the details, such as the exact directions in which various objects, rooms, materials etc are to be placed.

Indian architecture has influence the world, especially eastern Asia, due to the spread of ideas with Buddhism. A number of Indian architectural features such as the temple mound or stupa, temple spire or sikhara, temple tower or pagoda and temple gate or torana, have become famous symbols of Asian culture, used extensively in East Asia and South East Asia. The central spire is also sometimes called a vimanam. The variant southern temple gate, or gopuram is noted for its intricacy and majesty. The arch, a cornerstone of world architecture, was first developed by the Indus Valley civilization and would later be a staple of Indian architecture.

Recreation and Sports

In the area of recreation and sports India had evolved a number of games. The modern eastern martial arts originated as ancient games and martial arts in India and it was from here that these games were transmitted to foreign countries, where they were further modernized. Additionally, a few games introduced during the British Raj have grown quite popular in India, field hockey, football (soccer) and especially cricket.

Although field hockey is India's official national sport, cricket is by far the most popular sport not only in India, but the entire subcontinent, thriving recreationally and professionally. Cricket has even been used recently as a forum for diplomatic relations between India and long-standing rival, Pakistan. The two nations' cricket teams face off annually and such contests are quite impassioned on both sides. Traditional indigenous sports include kabaddi and gilli-danda, which are played in most parts of the country. Indoor and outdoor games like Chess, Snakes and Ladders, Playing cards, Polo, Carrom, Badminton are popular.

Cuisine

The earliest Indians, the Harappans, probably ate mainly wheat, rice and lentils, and occasionally meats such as pork, lamb, goat and chicken. Some believe that vegetarianism became popular with the arrival of Buddhism and Jainism that emphasised ahimsa (non-violence).

The cuisine of Modern India has great variety and each region has its own distinctive flavours. The staple cereals are rice and wheat. North Indian staple meals consist of *chapatis* or *rotis*, wheat based and rice as staples, eaten with a wide variety of side dishes like dals, curries, yogurt, chutney and *achars*. South India staple dishes consist of rice, sambhar, rasam, yoghurt and curries being important side dishes.

Another important ingredient in south Indian food is coconut and most popular snacks like idli dosa are also rice-based. Fish is popular in coastal states, especially West Bengal, Orissa and Kerala. Several kind of street foods like Panipuri, Vada pav, Bhelpuri, samosa, vada are popular, though they are known by different names in different regions. Indian Chinese cuisine, an Indianized version of the Chinese cuisine is also popular,especially among youngsters in Mumbai. This cuisine is supposed to have originated from east of India generally and Darjeeling specifically. Tea like other Asian countries, enjoys heavy popularity, while coffee is quite popular in South India. Nimbu pani (lemonade), lassi, and coconut milk are also popular, while India also has many indigenous alcoholic beverages like Fenny and Indian beer.

Dress

Indian costume is full of variations. Every region and state has its distinct style. In cities and towns, men mostly wear collared shirts and cotton trousers with shoes or sandals. A three-quarter-length coat called *achkan,* buttoned all the way up the front and topped with a short, stiff collar, is worn as the official Indian costume on formal occasions. Urban women mostly women wear the shalwar: free-flowing pants topped by a long shirt, often worn with a scarf draped around the neck.

The tradional garments worn by men is *dhoti,* a four-to five-yard white cotton cloth wrapped around the waist and tucked between the legs. There are variations in its drape, length, texture, and quality of border adornment. In Bengal one end hangs loose in front, while in Maharashtra both ends are passed between the legs and tucked into the back waistband. In the Punjab loose-fitting pajamas called *shalwar* are worn. Most Indian women wear the *sari,* a bordered length of cloth from six to nine yards long, which is draped loosely around the entire body and frequently covers the head as well. The sari is wrapped around the waist several times, making pleats in front, and then thrown across the chest and shoulders. Either a full blouse or a short, halterlike garment called a *choli* is worn on the upper body.

Footwear for both men and women consists usually of sandals, though shoes worn in Western countries are beginning to become more popular for women (heels, wedges, etc.). For men distinctive styles of headdress indicate regional affiliation, religious community, or social class. However, only certain cultures of India, such as the Panjabi or Sikh culture, involve the wearing of turbans.

Aside from the many ways of wrapping the turban, special headwear includes the traditional Parsi hat of shiny starched black alpaca in the shape of a rimless bowler; the Muslim hat, preferably of angora wool; and the Gandhi cap, an unadorned visorless cap that originally denoted membership in the Congress party. Women usually wear no headdress other than a shawl or the end of the sari, if even that.

Courtesies

Greetings: The *Namaste* is India's traditional greeting. One presses the palms together (fingers up) below the chin and says *Namaste* (in the south, *Namaskaram*). Muslims might greet each other with *Salaam* or *Adaab*. Traditionally men and women don't shake hands with each other but it is accepeted norm these days in urban india. "Hello" and "Hi" are acceptable greetings among equals, but people address superiors with more formal terms such as "Good morning" or its equivalent. It is considered polite to use titles such as *Professor, Doctor, Mr., Shri* (for men), *Shreemati* (married women), *Kumari* (unmarried women), or the suffix-*ji* with a last name to show respect. Indians usually ask permission before taking leave of others.

Gestures: Excessive hand gestures or verbal articulation is considered impolite. People beckon with the palm turned down; they often point with the chin. It is impolite to sniff or handle flowers displayed at bazaars. Grasping one's own ears expresses repentance or sincerity. One's feet or shoes should not touch another person, and if they do, an immediate apology is necessary. Whistling is considered impolite at public places but is acceptable in informal atmosphere. Too much public displays of affection is considered inappropriate but holding hands is now mostly accepted. Footwear is removed before entering a temple, mosque, or Sikh shrine. When entering a Sikh shrine or mosque, all people cover their heads.

Visiting: Visits in the home between friends or family are often unannounced. The need for prior arrangements is increasing in large cities. It is impolite to say "no" to an invitation; if one cannot attend, one more likely says, "I'll try." At certain gatherings, guests adorned with a garland of flowers remove and carry them as an expression of humility. Guests repay hosts' hospitality by giving gifts, such as flowers, specialty foods (fruits, sweets) from other areas of the country, or something for their children.

Most Indians do not wear shoes inside the home. Most guests at least remove shoes before entering the living room. Hosts offer their guests water, tea or coffee, and fruits or sweets. It is polite for a guest initially to refuse these refreshments but eventually to accept them. Visitors often indicate they are ready to leave by saying *Namaste*.

Eating: Eating habits vary sharply between traditional and modern settings. Many families eat their food with the right hand instead of relying on spoon and fork. Most of families have dinner togather where faimly memebers discuss any issues and decisions.

Popular Media

Cinema: Bollywood is the informal name given to the popular Mumbai-based film industry in India. Bollywood and the other major cinematic hubs (Bengali, Kannada, Malayalam, Tamil, Telugu) constitute the broader Indian film industry, whose output is considered to be the largest in the world in terms of number of films produced and, possibly, number of tickets sold. Bollywood films are usually musicals, though not in the Western sense of the word. Indian movies have a regular plot, with songs and dances interspersed to add to the entertainment value of the movie. Few movies are made without at least one song-and-dance number. Indian audiences expect full value for their money; they want songs and dances, love interest, comedy and dare-devil thrills, all mixed up in a three hour long extravaganza with intermission.

Such movies are called *masala* movies, after the Indian spice mixture *masala*. Like *masala*, these movies are a mixture of many things. Approximately, 95% of Bollywood movies are this type of movie, because Indians enjoy this type of movie very much. Plots tend to be melodramatic. They frequently employ formulaic ingredients such as star-crossed lovers and angry parents, corrupt politicians, kidnappers, conniving villains, courtesans with hearts of gold, long-lost relatives and siblings separated by fate, dramatic reversals of fortune, and convenient coincidences, and even movies with tri polar changes that can turn a movie and its plot upside down. Bollywood is becoming increasingly popular in other countries including several places in Europe and the U.S. Some Bollywood actors have adapted to more Hollywood-type films in movies like Bend It Like Beckham and Bride and Prejudice. Bollywood's fame is increasing internationally as more and more people across the globe are exposed to its style.

Besides the regular *masala* film, India has also produced many critically acclaimed cinema-makers like Satyajit Ray, Ritwik Ghatak, Adoor Gopalakrishnan,Ram Gopal Varma, Mani Ratnam, G. Aravindan etc. In fact, with the opening up of the economy in the recent years & consequent exposure to world cinema, audience tastes have been changing. Indian commercial movies have also started following authentic, real world themes with a lower amount of melodrama & some do not even contain songs. In addition, multiplexes have mushroomed in most cities, changing the revenue patterns & allowing film makers greater liberty & scope for executing bold & innovative ideas which would not have been possible even a decade ago.

Television: Indian television started off in 1959 in New Delhi with tests for educational telecasts. Indian small screen programming started off in the early 1980s. At that time there was only one national channel Doordarshan, which was government owned. The Ramayana and Mahabharat were some among the popular television series produced. By the late 1980s more and more people started to own television sets. Though there was a single channel, television programming had reached saturation. Hence the government opened up another channel which had part national programming and part regional. This channel was known as DD 2 later DD Metro. Both channels were broadcasted terrestrially.

In 1994, the government liberated its markets, opening them up to cable television. Since then, there has been a spurt in the number of channels available. Today, Indian silver screen is a huge industry by itself, and has thousands of programmes in all the states of India. The small screen has produced numerous celebrities of their own kind some even attaining national fame. TV soaps are extremely popular with housewives as well as working women, and even men of all kinds. Some small time actors have made it big in Bollywood. Indian TV has evolved to be similar to Western TV, including stations such as Cartoon Network, Nikelodeon, and Indian MTV.

Radio: Radio broadcasting began in India in 1927, with two privately-owned transmitters at Mumbai and Calcutta. These were nationalised in 1930 and operated under the name "Indian Broadcasting Service" until 1936, when it was renamed All India Radio (AIR). Although officially renamed again to *Akashwani* in 1957, it is still popularly known as All India Radio. All India Radio is a division of Prasar Bharati (Broadcasting Corporation of India), an autonomous corporation of the Ministry of Information and Broadcasting, Government of India. It is the sister service of Prasar Bharati's Doordarshan, the national television broadcaster.

Religion and Philosophy

Philosophy: Indian philosophy throughout the ages has had a tremendous impact on world thought, especially in the east. Various theistic schools of philosophy, such as the many schools of Buddhism and Hinduism, have has huge influences, but also, India produced some of the longest and most influential secular traditions of logic, rationalism, science, mathematics, materialism, atheism, agnosticism, etc, which are often overlooked due to popular conception that India is a 'mystical' country. Many of the complex scientific and mathematical concepts such as the idea of zero, found their way to Europe via Arab intermediaries. The most famous school of Indian atheism, is Carvaka, considered by some to be the oldest materialistic school of thought in the world, composed around the same time as the Hindu Upanishads, as well as the philosophy of Buddhism and Jainism.

This period around 600-400 BCE marked a huge leap in both Indian philosophy and world philosophy in general, with contemporary Greek schools emerging simultaneously. Some philosophical concepts from India were introduced to the Greeks, especially during the campaigns of Alexander the Great, and vis a vis, leading some schools of classical Greek philosophy to be almost identical to prior Indian schools. In addition to the unbroken high emphasis placed on philosophy in India, which has existed since ancient times, modern India has produced some of the world's most influential philosophers of modern times, who have written both in their native languages, and often English. During the British occupation of India, various thinkers, both secular and religious, achieved a new level of recognition across the world as both ancient Indian texts, and the work of contemporary Indian philosophers was translated into English, German and other languages.

Swami Vivekananda travelled to America and participated in the 1893 World Parliament of Religions, impressing delegates with a groundbreaking speech that for the first time gave access to eastern, Indian, Hindu and dharmic philosophy to western intellectuals. As well as various religious thinkers Mahatma Gandhi, Rabindranath Tagore and other members of the Indian freedom movement, generated political philosophy, and formed the basis of modern Indian democracy, secularism and liberalism. Today, economists such as Amartya Sen, who won Asia's first Nobel Prize in economics, continue to give India a reputation as an important contributor to world thought.

Religion: The Dharmic religions, one of the two main families of world religion (the other being the Abrahamic), originated in India. Every dharmic religion originated in India, including Hinduism, Buddhism, Sikhism, Jainism and other schools. Today, Hinduism and Buddhism are the world's third and fourth largest religions respectively, with a collective 1.4 billion followers, despite being free of any evangelistic traditions. Unlike the sectarianism that has often marked differences among the Abrahamic schools, the philosophical-like treatment of these religions has generally made the idea of rivalry and conversion alien, leading to extremely close relationships between these faiths.

India is one of the most religiously diverse nations in the world, with one of the most deeply religious societies and cultures. Religion plays a central and definitive role in the life of the country and most of its people. The religion of more than 80.4% of the people is Hinduism, considered the world's oldest religious and philosophical system. Islam is practiced by around 13.4% of all Indians. Sikhism,Buddhism and Jainism are systems that are strong and influential not only in India but across the world. Christianity, Zoroastrianism, Judaism and the Bahá'í Faith are also influential but their numbers are smaller. Despite the strong role of religion in Indian life, atheism and agnostics are also visible influences.

CULTURE

The word *culture*, from the Latin *colo,-ere*, with its root meaning "to cultivate", generally refers to patterns of human activity and the symbolic structures that give such activity significance. Different definitions of "culture" reflect different theoretical bases for understanding, or criteria for evaluating, human activity. Anthropologists most commonly use the term "culture" to refer to the universal human capacity to classify, codify and communicate their experiences symbolically. This capacity is long been taken as a defining feature of the genus *Homo*. However, primatologists such as Jane Goodall have identified aspects of culture among our closest relatives in the animal kingdom. Similarly, it has recently been determined that the Orca pods have culture specific vocalizations and tastes for food. Orcas used in theme parks are exclusively from pods that only feed on fish.

Defining "Culture"

Culture has been called "the way of life for an entire society." As such, it includes codes of manners, dress, language, religion, rituals, norms of behaviour and systems of belief. Various definitions of culture reflect differing theories for understanding — or criteria for evaluating— human activity. Sir Edward B.

Tylor writing from the perspective of social anthropology in the UK in 1871 described culture in the following way: "Culture or civilization, taken in its wide ethnographic sense, is that complex whole which includes knowledge, belief, art, morals, law, custom, and any other capabilities and habits acquired by man as a member of society."

More recently, the United Nations Educational, Scientific and Cultural Organization UNESCO (2002) described culture as follows: "... culture should be regarded as the set of distinctive spiritual, material, intellectual and emotional features of society or a social group, and that it encompasses, in addition to art and literature, lifestyles, ways of living together, value systems, traditions and beliefs". While these two definitions cover a range of meaning, they do not exhaust the many uses of the term "culture." In 1952, Alfred Kroeber and Clyde Kluckhohn compiled a list of more than 200 definitions of "culture" in *Culture: A Critical Review of Concepts and Definitions*.

These definitions, and many others, provide a catalog of the elements of culture. The items catalogued (*e.g.*, a law, a stone tool, a marriage) each have an existence and life-line of their own. They come into space-time at one set of coordinates and go out of it another. While here, they change, so that one may speak of the evolution of the law or the tool.

A culture, then, is by definition at least, a set of cultural objects. Anthropologist Leslie White asked: "What sort of objects are they? Are they physical objects? Mental objects? Both? Metaphors? Symbols? Reifications?" In *Science of Culture* (1949), he concluded that they are objects "*sui generis*"; that is, of their own kind. In trying to define that kind, he hit upon a previously unrealized aspect of symbolization, which he called "the symbolate"—an object created by the act of symbolization. He thus defined culture as "symbolates understood in an extra-somatic context." The key to this definition is the discovery of the symbolate.

Values comprise ideas about what in life seems important. They guide the rest of the culture. Norms consist of expectations of how people will behave in various situations. Each culture has methods, called *sanctions*, of enforcing its norms. Sanctions vary with the importance of the norm; norms that a society enforces formally have the status of *laws*. Institutions are the structures of a society within which values and norms are transmitted. Artifacts—things, or aspects of material culture—derive from a culture's values and norms.

Julian Huxley gives a slightly different division, into inter-related "mentifacts", "socifacts" and "artifacts", for ideological, sociological, and technological subsystems respectively. Socialization, in Huxley's view, depends on the belief subsystem. The sociological subsystem governs interaction between people. Material objects and their use make up the technological subsystem.

As a rule, archaeologists focus on material culture, whereas cultural anthropologists focus on symbolic culture, although ultimately both groups maintain interests in the relationships between these two dimensions. Moreover, anthropologists understand "culture" to refer not only to consumption goods, but to the general processes which produce such goods and give them meaning, and to the social relationships and practices in which such objects and processes become embedded.

Culture as Civilization

Many people today have an idea of "culture" that developed in Europe during the 18th and early 19th centuries. This notion of culture reflected inequalities within European societies, and between European powers and their colonies around the world. It identifies "culture" with "civilization" and contrasts it with "nature." According to this way of thinking, one can classify some countries as more civilized than others, and some people as more cultured than others. Some cultural theorists have thus tried to eliminate popular or mass culture from the definition of culture. Theorists such as Matthew Arnold (1822-1888) or the Leavises regard culture as simply the result of "the best that has been thought and said in the world" Arnold contrasted culture with social chaos or anarchy. On this account, culture links closely with social cultivation: the progressive refinement of human behavior. Arnold consistently uses the word this way: "... culture being a pursuit of our total perfection by means of getting to know, on all the matters which most concern us, the best which has been thought and said in the world".

In practice, *culture* referred to elite goods and activities such as *haute cuisine*, high fashion or *haute couture*, museum-caliber art and classical music, and the word *cultured* described people who knew about, and took part in, these activities. For example, someone who used 'culture' in the sense of 'cultivation' might argue that classical music is more refined than music produced by working-class people, such as punk rock or the indigenous music traditions of aboriginal peoples of Australia.

People who use the term "culture" in this way tend not to use it in the plural as "cultures". They do not believe that distinct cultures exist, each with their own internal logic and values; but rather that only a single standard of refinement suffices, against which one can measure all groups. Thus, according to this worldview, people with different customs from those who regard themselves as cultured do not usually count as "having a different culture," but are classed as "uncultured." People lacking "culture" often seemed more "natural," and observers often defended (or criticized) elements of high culture for repressing "human nature".

From the 18th century onwards, some social critics have accepted this contrast between cultured and uncultured, but have stressed the interpretation of refinement and of sophistication as corrupting and unnatural developments that obscure and distort people's essential nature. On this account, folk music (as produced by working-class people) honestly expresses a natural way of life, and classical music seems superficial and decadent. Equally, this view often portrays Indigenous peoples as 'noble savages' living authentic unblemished lives, uncomplicated and uncorrupted by the highly-stratified capitalist systems of the West. Today most social scientists reject the monadic conception of culture, and the opposition of culture to nature. They recognize non-elites as just as cultured as élites (and non-Westerners as just as civilized)—simply regarding them as just cultured in a different way. Thus social observers contrast the *"high" culture* of élites to *"popular" or pop culture*, meaning goods and activities produced for, and consumed by the masses. (Note that some classifications relegate both high and low cultures to the status of subcultures.)

Culture as Worldview

During the Romantic era, scholars in Germany, especially those concerned with nationalist movements — such as the nationalist struggle to create a "Germany" out of diverse principalities, and the nationalist struggles by ethnic minorities against the Austro-Hungarian Empire — developed a more inclusive notion of culture as "worldview." In this mode of thought, a distinct and incommensurable world view characterizes each ethnic group. Although more inclusive than earlier views, this approach to culture still allowed for distinctions between "civilized" and "primitive" or "tribal" cultures.

By the late 19th century, anthropologists had adopted and adapted the term *culture* to a broader definition that they could apply to a wider variety of societies. Attentive to the theory of evolution, they assumed that all human beings evolved equally, and that the fact that all humans have cultures must in some way result from human evolution. They also showed some reluctance to use biological evolution to explain differences between specific cultures — an approach that either exemplified a form of, or segment of society *vis a vis* other segments and the society as a whole, they often reveal processes of domination and resistance.

In the 1950s, subcultures—groups with distinctive characteristics within a larger culture—began to be the subject of study by sociologists. The 20th century also saw the popularization of the idea of corporate culture—distinct and malleable within the context of an employing organization or a workplace.

Culture as Symbols

The symbolic view of culture, the legacy of Clifford Geertz (1973) and Victor Turner (1967), holds symbols to be both the practices of social actors and the context that gives such practices meaning. Anthony P. Cohen (1985) writes of the "symbolic gloss" which allows social actors to use common symbols to communicate and understand each other while still imbuing these symbols with personal significance and meanings. Symbols provide the limits of cultured thought. Members of a culture rely on these symbols to frame their thoughts and expressions in intelligible terms. In short, symbols make culture possible, reproducible and readable. They are the "webs of significance" in Weber's sense that, to quote Pierre Bourdieu (1977), "give regularity, unity and systematicity to the practices of a group."

Culture as a Stabilizing Mechanism

Modern cultural theory also considers the possibility that (a) culture itself is a product of stabilization tendencies inherent in evolutionary pressures toward self-similarity and self-cognition of societies as wholes, or tribalisms. Steven Wolfram's *A new kind of science* on iterated simple algorithms from genetic unfolding, from which the concept of culture as an operating mechanism can be developed, and Richard Dawkins' *The Extended Phenotype* for discussion of genetic and memetic stability over time, through negative feedback mechanisms.

Cultures within a Society

Large societies often have subcultures, or groups of people with distinct sets of behavior and beliefs that differentiate them from a larger culture of which they are a part. The subculture may be distinctive because of the age of its members, or by their race, ethnicity, class or gender. The qualities that determine a subculture as distinct may be aesthetic, religious, occupational, political, sexual or a combination of these factors. In dealing with immigrant groups and their cultures, there are essentially four approaches:

- *Monoculturalism:* In Europe, culture is very closely linked to nationalism, thus government policy is to assimilate immigrants.
- *Leitkultur (core culture):* A model developed in Germany by Bassam Tibi. The idea is that minorities can have an identity of their own, but they should at least support the core concepts of the culture on which the society is based.
- *Melting Pot:* In the United States, the traditional view has been one of a melting pot where all the immigrant cultures are mixed and amalgamated without state intervention.

- *Multiculturalism:* A policy that immigrants and others should preserve their cultures with the different cultures interacting peacefully within one nation.

The way nation states treat immigrant cultures rarely falls neatly into one or another of the above approaches. The degree of difference with the host culture (*i.e.*, "foreignness"), the number of immigrants, attitudes of the resident population, the type of government policies that are enacted and the effectiveness of those policies all make it difficult to generalize about the effects.

Similarly with other subcultures within a society, attitudes of the mainstream population and communications between various cultural groups play a major role in determining outcomes. The study of cultures within a society is complex and research must take into account a myriad of variables.

Cultures by Region

Many regional cultures have been influenced by contact with others, such as by colonization, trade, migration, mass media and religion.

Africa: Though of many varied origins, African culture, especially Sub-Saharan African culture has been shaped by European colonialism, and is differentiated from North Africa from its lesser influence by Arab and Islamic culture.

Americas: The culture of the Americas has been strongly influenced by peoples that inhabitated the continents before Europeans arrived; people from Africa (the United States especially has a large African-American population, most of whom are descended from former slaves), and the immigration of Europeans, especially Spanish, English, French, Portuguese, German, and Dutch.

Asia: Despite the great cultural diversity of Asian nations, there are, nevertheless, several transnational cultural influences. Though Korea, Japan, and Vietnam are not Chinese-speaking countries, their languages have been heavily influenced by Chinese and Chinese writing. Thus, in East Asia, Chinese writing is generally agreed to exert a unifying influence. Religions, especially Buddhism and Taoism have had an impact on the cultural traditions of East Asian countries. There is also a shared social and moral philosophy that derives from Confucianism.

Hinduism and Islam have for hundreds of years exerted cultural influence on various peoples of South Asia. Similarly, Buddhism is pervasive in Southeast Asia.

Australia: Much of Australia's culture is derived from European and American roots, but distinctive Australian features have evolved from the environment and Aboriginal culture.

Europe: European culture also has a broad influence beyond the continent of Europe due to the legacy of colonialism. In this broader sense it is sometimes referred to as *Western culture*. This is most easily seen in the spread of the English language and to a lesser extent, a few other European languages. Dominant influences include ancient Greece, ancient Rome, and Christianity, although religion has declined in Europe.

Middle East and North Africa

Perhaps the defining characteristic of the Middle East and North Africa is Islam and variations of the Arab language, though this region is also home to Israel and Judaism, and significant Christian minorities. Further, several groups which are adherents to Islam do not consider themselves Arab.

Belief Systems

Religion and other belief systems are often integral to a culture. Religion, from the Latin *religare,* meaning "to bind fast", is a feature of cultures throughout human history. The *Dictionary of Philosophy and Religion* defines religion in the following way:

> *... an institution with a recognized body of communicants who gather together regularly for worship, and accept a set of doctrines offering some means of relating the individual to what is taken to be the ultimate nature of reality.*

Religion often codifies behavior, such as with the 10 Commandments of Christianity or the five precepts of Buddhism. Sometimes it is involved with government, as in a theocracy. It also influences arts.

Eurocentric custom to some extent divides humanity into Western and non-Western cultures, although this has some flaws.

Western culture spread from Europe most strongly to Australia, Canada, and the United States. It is influenced by ancient Greece, ancient Rome and the Christian church.

Western culture tends to be more individualistic than non-Western cultures. It also sees man, god, and nature or the universe more separately than non-Western cultures. It is marked by economic wealth, literacy, and technological advancement, although these traits are not exclusive to it.

Abrahamic Religions

Judaism is one of, if not the first, recorded monotheistic faiths and one of the oldest religious traditions still practiced today. The values and history of the Jewish people are a major part of the foundation of other Abrahamic religions such as Christianity, Islam, as well as Samaritanism and the Bahá'í Faith.

Christianity was the dominant feature in shaping European culture for at least the last 1700 years. Modern philosophical thought has very much been influenced by Christian philosophers such as St. Thomas Aquinas and Erasmus. European colonization and missionaries have spread it.

2

INDIAN CUSTOMS AND RITUALS

INTRODUCTION

The whole thrust is to help bring about greater awareness & love in the mind, and canalise the interest & energies into positive fields. The whole 'work' is on the mind alone, and is comparable to the work of a genetic engineer. The only difference is that while a genetic engineer plays & transforms with the basic structure, a teacher works to manifest the basic inherent beauty, freedom & potential which facilitates to carve out a dynamic, creative, intelligent & magnanimous personality. Interest is a very subjective thing, and has to come out from within. It can never be imposed.

The man Making is a science. Like a gardener, parents & teachers work on a person so that the best can flower out from him or her. Interests are created by impressions & knowledge. That is what ad agencies too do. They create impressions, and this 'works' on the mind of the person to bring about the interest in him in the desired field. Once the interest has been manifested we can just sit back and see the person work for his or her field of interest in a dynamic way.

While the experts of the advertisement world are generally seen to use this 'knowledge of impressing minds' for their selfish & commercial ends, the Vedic Masters used this knowledge to help bring out a positive & dynamic personality. While the former conditions the mind to the extent that the very thinking process of their target crowd is conditioned in their favour, but the Rishis saw to it that the very power to think & question daringly, independently & creatively grew.

Thus we have all our scriptures in the form of question & answers.

These deliberate & positive impressions which help create a deep & lasting impressions on the mind of a person—so as to generate interest in him about the Truth & Dharma, help bring out a positive personality and free the mind of its negativities are called 'Samskaras'. No one while living in the world remains free of the conditionings of his or her environs & teachings, so the question is not whether we can stop all conditionings but to see to it that a person is looked after like a plant and help his or her potentials bloom. To a question whether Samskaras are deliberate positive conditionings, well the answer is that, the objective of the entire exercise is to help a person awake to a state which is free from all conditionings, so while impressions are certainly put effectively & deliberately yet they are the very antithesis of what is implied by the word conditionings. This is one of the finest & blessed science, and has been perfected here as an art form too.

Samskaras are the turning points of life and need to be celebrated. Celebrations are very important ingredients of Samskaras. They directly or indirectly involve our respected elders, scholars, near & dear ones. Everyone gets together to convey their best wishes & blessings to the person concerned and thus there is social & religious sanction for the act & ceremony. Samskaras are great, time-tested tools in our traditional systems which help carve out a great personality. Apart from scriptural validation, history also proves to us the great effectiveness of these methods. When Vedic Masters had their way, India was on top of the world. The people of the far off land prayed that they will one day see this great land of plenty, prosperity & righteousness. In this section we shall present an introduction to these famous sixteen Samskaras of Hindus which cover the entire life span of a person and take him to the door steps to Truth.

1. *Garbhadan:* The first coming together of the husband & wife for bringing about conception.
2. *Pumsvan:* Ceremony performed when the first signs of conception are seen, and is to be performed when someone desires a male child.

3. *Seemantonayan:* A ceremony of parting of the hairs of the expectant mother to keep her spirits high & positive. Special music is arranged for her.
4. *Jatakarma:* After the birth of the child, the child is given a secret name, he is given taste of honey & ghee, mother starts the first breast-feeding after chanting of a mantra.
5. *Nama-karana:* In this ceremony the child is given a formal name. Performed on the 11th day.
6. *Nishkramana:* In this the formal darshan of sun & moon is done for the child.
7. *Annaprashana:* This ceremony is performed, when the child is given solid food (anna) for the first time.
8. *Chudakarana:* Cuda means the 'lock or tuft of hair' kept after the remaining part is shaved off.
9. *Karna-vedha:* Done in 7th or 8th month. Piercing of the ears.
10. *Upanayan and Vedarambha:* The thread ceremony. The child is thereafter authorized to perform all rituals. Studies of Vedas begins with the Guru.
11. *Keshanta:* Hairs are cut, guru dakshina is given
12. *Samavartan:* Returning to the house
13. *Vivaha:* Marriage ceremony
14. *Vanprastha:* As old age approaches, the person retires for a life of tapas & studies.
15. *Sanyas:* Before leaving the body a Hinddu sheds all sense of responsibility & relationships to awake & revel in the timeless truth.
16. *Antyeshthi:* The last rites done after the death.

The Stages of Life Systems

There are four stages of life, *viz.* Brahmachari (student), Grihasta (Householder) Vanaprasta (forest dweller or Hermit in semi retirement) Sannyasi (the renounced one in full retirement) and the Dharma of each is different. The four stages may be said to represent periods of Preparation, Production, Service and Retirement.

Brahmacharya (Celibate)

Brahmacharya means Student, usually between 12 and 24 years of age.The first stage is Brahmacharya. The duty of a student is to study. On initiation into Brahmacharya by means of the Upanayana rites, he becomes a 'Dvija' (a twice born). 'Upanayana' means 'bringing near'-the disciple is brought near the Guru for receiving the initiation of mantras. For the Brahmachari, celibacy is his forte, discipline is his norm, devotion to his Guru is his duty and concentration in studies is his vocation.

Grihastaashrama

Grihasta means House-holder usually between 24 and 48 years of age. The next stage is of the householder. After the 'Gurukula Vasa' he graduates himself into the mundane world, taking a wife to assist him in his performance of Dharmic duties. All Sastras proclaim the importance of the Grihastaasrama as the fulcrum of all other Ashramas. People in the other three Ashramas heavily lean on the Grihasta for support and sustenance required to carry out their respective duties. The Grihasta earns his livelihood by whatever a vocation befitting his being a member of his group, raising children, supporting his own family, kith and kin besides the persons performing their duties in the other three Ashramas. The life of a Grihasta is therefore, considered a 'Jivayagna'—a lifelong saga of self sacrifice for the benefit of others in society.

Vanaprasta Ashrama (The Anchorite)

Vanaprasta is the third stage of Elder Advisor usually between 48 and 72 years of age. A stage comes when business, family, secular life like the beauties and hopes of youth have exhausted themselves and need to be left behind. The person retires usually from worldly attachments to lead a life of contemplation and meditation alone or with his wife.

What life holds beyond middle age depends in the end not on fancy and imagination but on the realities of the values of life we regard as inviolable. Vanaprasta may be termed as the beginning of a person's real 'adult education' to evaluate his performance thus for as Grihasta and reorder his life in such a way as to discover who he is and what life is all about.

Sannyasa Ashrama (The Renounced): Sannyasi is the fourth stage of an Ascetic-Solitaire-usually beyond 72 years of age. This means 'Samyak Nyasa'—'Total detachment' from worldly pleasures including the bare necessities to subsist. This is the last 'Ashrama'. He does not aspire to be recognised as somebody who matters—he wish of the Sannyasi is just to be a 'persona non grata'—one who exists almost without giving any thought to his being-with no desire for name or fame or recognition.

Purusharthas

Purusha means human being and artha means object or objective. Purusharthas means objectives of man. According to Hindu way of life, a man should strive to achieve four chief objectives (Purusharthas) in his life. They are:

1. dharma (righteousness),
2. artha (material wealth),
3. kama (desire) and
4. moksha (salvation).

Every individual in a society is expected to achieve these four objectives and seek fulfillment in his life before departing from here. The concept of Purusharthas clearly establishes the fact that Hinduism does not advocate a life of self negation and hardship, but a life of balance, achievement and fulfillment.

Dharma: Dharma is a very complicated word, for which there is no equivalent word in any other language, including English. Dharma actually means that which upholds this entire creation. It is a Divine law that is inherent and invisible, but responsible for all existence.

Dharma exists in all planes, in all aspects and at all levels of creation. In the context of human life, dharma consists of all that an individual undertakes in harmony with Divine expectations and his own inner spiritual aspirations, actions that would ensure order and harmony with in himself and in the environment in which he lives. Since this world is deluded, a human being may not know what is right and what is wrong or what is dharma and what is adharma. Hence he should rely upon the scriptures and adhere to the injunctions contained there in. In short, dharma for a human being means developing divine virtues and performing actions that are in harmony with the divine laws.

Dharma is considered to be the first cardinal aim because it is at the root of everything and upholds everything. For example see what happens when a person amasses wealth without observing dharma or indulges in sexual passion against the social norms or established moral values. Any action performed without observing dharma is bound to bring misery and suffering and delay ones salvation. Hinduism therefore considers it rightly as the first cardinal aim of life. In ancient India dharmasastras (law books) provided guidance to people in their day to day lives and helped them to adhere to dharma. These law books were written for a particular time frame and are no more relevant to the modern world. The best way to know what is dharma and what is adharma, is to follow the religious scriptures such as the Bhagavad Gita and the Upanishads or any other scripture that contains the words of God.

Artha: Artha means wealth. Hinduism recognises the importance of material wealth for the overall happiness and well being of an individual. A house holder requires wealth, because he has to perform many duties to uphold dharma and ensure the welfare and progress of his family and society. A person may have the intention to uphold the dharma, but if he has no money he would not be able to perform his duties and fulfil his dharma.

Hinduism therefore rightly places material wealth as the second most important objective in human life. Lord Vishnu is the best example for any householder who wants to lead a life of luxury and still be on the side of God doing his duties. As the preserver of the universe, Lord Vishnu lives in Vaikunth amid pomp and glory, with the goddess of wealth herself by his side and yet helps the poor and the needy, protects the weak, upholds the dharma and sometimes leaving everything aside rushes to the earth as an incarnation to uphold dharma.

Hinduism advocates austerity, simplicity and detachment, but does not glorify poverty. Hinduism also emphasises the need to observe dharma while amassing the wealth. Poverty has become a grotesque reality in present day Hindu society. Hindus have become so poverty conscious that if a saint or a sage leads a comfortable life, they scoff at him, saying that he is not a true yogi. They have to remind themselves of the simple fact that none of the Hindu gods and goddesses are really poor.

Hinduism believes that both spiritualism and materialism are important for the salvation of human beings. It is unfortunate that Hinduism came to be associated more with spiritualism, probably because of the influence of Buddhism, where as in truth Hinduism does not exclude either of them. As Swami Vivekananda rightly said religion is not for the empty stomachs. Religion is not for those whose main concern from morning till evening is how to make both ends meet. Poverty crushes the spirit of man and renders him an easy prey to wicked forces. In ancient India Artha Sastras (scriptures on wealth) provided necessary guidance to people on the finer aspects of managing their wealth. Kautilya's Artha Sastra, which is probably a compilation of many independent works, gives us a glimpse of how money matters were handled in ancient India.

Kama: Kama in a wider sense means desire and in a narrow sense, sexual desire. Hinduism prescribes fulfilment of sexual passions for the householders and abstinence from it for the students and ascetics who are engaged in the study of the scriptures and in the pursuit of Brahman. The Bhagavad Gita informs us that desire is an aspect of delusion and one has to be wary of its various movements and manifestations. The best way to deal with desires is to develop detachment and perform desireless actions without seeking the fruit of ones actions and making an offering of all the actions to God. This way our actions would not bind us to the cycle of births and deaths.

Hinduism permits sexual freedom so long as it is not in conflict with the first aim, *i.e.* dharma. Hindu scriptures emphasise that the purpose of sex is procreation and perpetuation of family and society, while the purpose of dharma is to ensure order in the institution of family and society. A householder has the permission to indulge in sex, but also has the responsibility to pursue it in accordance with the laws of dharma. Marriage is a recognised social institution and marriage with wife for the purpose of producing children is legitimate and in line with the aims of dharma.

One of the important sects of Hinduism is Tantricism. It recognises the importance of sexual freedom in the liberation of soul. The Tantrics accept sex as an important means to experience the blissful nature of God and the best way to experience God in physical form. They also refer to the concept of Purusharthas to justify their doctrines. They believe that sexual energy is divine energy and it can be transformed into spiritual energy through controlled expression of sex. Just as the Dharmasastras were written for the sake of dharma, and Arthasastras for artha, Kamasastras were composed in ancient India for providing guidance in matters of sex. We have lost many of them because of the extreme secrecy and social disapproval associated with the subject.

Moksha: If dharma guides the life of a human being from below acting as the earth, showing him the way from above like a star studded mysterious sky is Moksha. Dharma constitutes the legs of a Purusha that walk upon the earth; both artha and kama constitute his two limbs active in the middle region; while Moksha constitutes the head that rests in the heaven. Human life is very precious because of all the beings in all the worlds, only human beings have the best opportunity to realise the Higher self. It is also precious because it is attained after many hundreds and thousands of lives. Rightly, salvation should be its ultimate aim.

Moksha actually means absence of moha or delusion. Delusion is caused by the inter play of the triple gunas. When a person overcomes these gunas, he attains liberation. The gunas can be overcome by detachment, self control, surrender to god and offering ones actions to God. If dharma is the centre of the wheel of human life, artha and kama are the two spokes and Moksha is its circumference. If dharma is at the centre of human life, beyond Moksha there is no human life, but only a life divine.

Ritual of Death

Many people believe that after death, they will continue to live on in new and different bodies. The theory of Karma and rebirth says that the mental qualities that we possess carry on from one birth to the next. But does this mean our memories are accurate? People believe they have memories of reincarnation. Some people, upon experiencing déjà vu, feel that the experience is a proof of existence of former lives. Some think the truth comes out under hypnosis while others believe just from their memory. But is this good evidence to back up the belief of life after death?

The doctrine of karma says that one experiences deja vu because of reincarnation. But how accurate is this statement? These people have the sense of having visited a place before. Many people argue that this sort of experience is vague in its nature. It might have many possible explanations. Since deja vu is a feeling, perhaps the feeling arose from something else. Something else in the environment could have caused one to feel like they've been here before. These explanations can be based on childhood memories that are "similar" but not identical. Maybe they saw a place that resembles the place they are claiming to have lived in before. It is also possible they saw a photograph of it.

They might feel it is dejavu when in fact they may have forgotten that they have been there before. Another explanation could be the possession of a disorder. Memories of former lives could be the result of an illness they might be suffering from. It can even be a memory disorder and the things they are claiming to be past memories might only be bits and pieces of former memories from their "present" life. Many people claim to have spontaneous or recovered memories of past births. But how do we know this isn't a mere hallucination? They might be seeing things or imagining them. Maybe this is a matter of wishful thinking. The person "wishes" they were reincarnated. Their obsession with it probably drove them to believe it. Fraud can also play a role in such cases. How do we know the person isn't lying?

Alleged memories of past lives are usually obtained by a procedure called hypnotic regression. Subjects are asked to recall experiences they had from present to past. They are then asked to recall events that happened before they were born. This produces memories of past reincarnations. But how do we know this is correct? The subjects could have invented such stories out of a natural desire to please the hypnotist or perhaps they don't know they are lying. People can also have false memories of past births/events because of the hypnotist himself. A hypnotist can instill false beliefs in easily affected subjects. It is possible that a hypnotist could induce the mind to generate a general type of fantasy that "feels" real. The hypnotist could make you believe you had a previous life. Thus, you can't fully believe that under hypnotic regression, the recalled memories are true.

But now, let us suppose the story of a past life seems to be accurate. How do we know it is really accurate? What proof do we have? The subject must have obtained the details either consciously or subconsciously. He may have obtained it from books, documents or other historical material. You need proof in order to say that an argument for life after death is based on memories of former lives. Critics might say that you don't need proof in order for something to exist.

But until there isn't proof that these memories are real, you can't say that life after death can be based on memories. Let's suppose the subject's account of experiences in a past life is demonstrated to be 100 per cent accurate, and they couldn't have obtained details and facts about them. Then how can we be sure that this person is the same person whose experiences have been recalled? They could be memories of someone else's former life.

This, then, shouldn't be used to prove the existence of life after death. Without proofs that what the subject believes is true from a former life, you don't have to believe it. One might believe that maybe it's possible that no one knows about this small detail which a subject has recalled as a past memory. But the subject still, could be making it all up. It is also possible that he might be making it all up for attention.

One might remember having no talents in a past life. And now that in this life they are born with extraordinary talents, they are sure they have been reincarnated. They believe they did good deeds in their former lives, and as a result, they have extraordinary talents in life. This can, though, be due to their environment, or maybe it just happened. It can be a matter of coincidence too. Maybe believers of the theory of life after death feel that if they meditate and think about their past lives, they will remember.

But these people usually focus their attention on one simple, repetitive thought. The more they think about it, the more they are likely to begin to hallucinate. Maybe one might remember speaking another language in the past. Upon hypnosis they recite some lines of that same language. They might be certain that they have learned this language in the past life. But maybe they just remember hearing it in their present life. You can't speak a language you never learned before. But just because you can speak another language doesn't mean that you know it.

The theory of karma and rebirth say that qualities from our mental character continue on from one birth to the next. These qualities include talents, likes and dislikes, ones emotions, and, etc. If this is true, then what about the people who claim to remember having certain qualities in their former life, but don't have these qualities in their present life? What about these subjects who claim to remember liking and disliking certain things, yet in this life, these likes and dislikes aren't the same?

If these qualities change, then what is the proof that the subject is the same person as who he claims to be? People may recall dying of an illness, accident or other diseases. Such things as accidents, drugs, surgery, shock treatments, strokes, tumors, and, etc., might have destroyed parts of their brains. If so, then how do we measure the accuracy of what they are presently saying? It is possible to lose memory, talents, likes and dislikes and many others because of head injuries. There is no need, then, to have faith on their memories if there are possibilities that parts of their brains might have been severely damaged.

Although people may claim to remember things from their past lives, people need not believe them. Without proof that the past even occurred, we don't have to believe it happened. If there is no way to distinguish the statements of memory from the statements from imagination, then there is no reason to believe that there is a life after death.

After Life

The Buddhism belief of death and after death is very different from any I have ever heard of. They consider the after death just as important as the person's time on earth. Buddhist believe that in your lifetime, nothing that you posses other then your "karma" follows you after death. In saying this, Buddhist people believe that if you live your life honestly and positive, then good thing will follow for you in your "resurrection" which may be the result of coming back to life as God, or something very beautiful. Contrary to that, if you cheat people out, and live a dishonest and negative life, you may resurrect into the "hells", or come back as a deformed and ugly person or animal.

The Jainism view life as an endless reincarnation, as the Buddha's do they are born, live their lives as long as they are given and then they are born again. Jains base their religion around karma, and if you have good karma then you will be given a good life and when you die you will receive a good fortune in your second life, or as they call it the Circle of Births. I think that if everyone based his or her life around having good karma we would be living in a pretty good world. I like this approach to life, what you practice in your life results in your outcome after to die.

Christianity again, is something again very different from the above afterlife beliefs. Within this religion, it is believed that when one person dies, depending on how honest and truthfully your life was lived, you will go to either "heaven" or "hell". Heaven is said to be "up in the clouds" where your soul raises, and where all bad becomes good. This is where you may "achieve your eternal happiness". Hell on the other hand, is stereotyped as a place where the "devil" is. It's a place where you will be "burned" in the devils fire.

Mourning Practices

Mourning practices for the Buddhism religion comes accrossed to me as being very extraordinary. They want to ensure that the persons after life is secure and they are ready to move on. They diseased body is cremated after eight days, following that, Buddhist people prayer for the diseased person for forty nine days after they day, in preparation for that person's death, and also to allow that person to seek the best possible after life that is possible. They spend several weeks after a person's death talking to them and reading from their holy scriptures. The way they take forty-nine days to make sure the person is ready for their new life is very difficult for me to understand.

Jainism look at life as their are two things: Soul & Matter, they say that soul is life, and how you value you life. If you value your life and other living creatures then you have good soul. They say that matter is lifeless and is not good. Matter is evil and is what results in a bad outcome in the circle of births. If a person has bad karma or bad matter it goes and affects the soul. Christianity follows the mourning system that many of us are probably used to. A person dies, and within a couple days their death is celebrated for family and friends by having a "wake" and a "funeral". At these ceremonies the diseased loved ones get their final chance to see them. After this, the person is either buried or cremated (depending on choice), and then put underground in a graveyard, with a gravestone. Many times loved ones will visit the gravestone to pray and leave flowers.

Traditions and Other Beliefs

There is a famous book that the people of the Buddhist culture study. The book is called Bardo Thodol, meaning the book of the dead. This book even dates back to having pre-Buddhist teachings in it. It preaches that the human soul abides for forty-nine days in a dream like state. This state is called Bardo. In this book they explain that this little device that is actually called a prayer wheel. This wheel is carried around by many Tibetan monks and is said to contain written prayers that are activated by movement.

Another interesting aspect of the Buddhist religion is that these teachings were carried into China soon after they became popular in India. I had no idea that this religion was carried to other countries. Our group would have never guessed that it would spread across several different countries. People of the Jainism religion can be "released from the circle of births", to do this which is considered a bad thing and will not receive any prayer or warship.It occurs from not believing in the religion or going against the religion such as bad karma, or killing innocent, or affecting others. The Jains are very pro life, they even will not harm a living creature, as they think it might go against their karma, they care so much about animals and will not eat meat if it has to be cooked.

Christianity began when communication was slow and authority was rather decentralised, they were looked upon for guidance and authority. Some of the beliefs that Christianity followed were as follows: "we believe in only one God, the Father Almighty, maker of all things visible and invisible. And in one Lord Jesus Christ, the son of God, begotten of the Father, the only-begotten; that is, of the essence of the Father, God of God, Light of Light, very God of very God, Begotten not made, being of one essence with the Father; by whom all things were made, both in heaven and on earth; who for us men, and for our salvation, came down and was incarnate and was made a man."

Some of the traditions of the Christian faith are that they celebrate the Eucharist on Sundays, and prey the word of the Lord. Take the body of Christ and reflect to your self-kneeling by your seat. You give a sign of peace through a handshake and rejoice with everyone around you.

When you walk into a Christian church you will become overwhelmed with great art work, and beautiful music and himms of rhythm. These are the visual components of attending mass combined with prayer. In my opinion I believe in this faith because that is the faith that I have been brought up to believe, therefore I will support all notions and practice all of their traditions.

Hindu Death Rituals and Beliefs

There is one thing that is certain in this lifetime: eventually we all must die. A belief in the cyclical reincarnation of the soul is one of the foundations of the Hindu religion. Death is viewed as a natural aspect of life, and there are numerous epic tales, sacred scriptures, and Vedic guidance that describe the reason for death's existence, the rituals that should be performed surrounding it, and the many possible destinations of the soul after departure from its earthly existence. While the ultimate goal is to transcend the need to return to life on earth, all Hindus believe they will be reborn into a future that is based primarily on their past thoughts and actions.

The first mortal to meet his fate with Death was named Yama. This dubious honour makes him uniquely qualified to lead the way for others after death. The sacred scriptures of the Rig Veda, which call him King Yama, promise that all who have been good will receive "admission to Yama's paradise and the everlasting enjoyment of all the heavenly pleasures, include the restoration of a sick body, the maintaining of family relations and the highly desired apotheosis". Yama is aided by two killer guide dogs that are described as the "four-eyed keepers of the path, who watch over men." These "two dark messengers of Yama with flaring nostrils wander among men, thirsting for the breath of life". Yet, once they have secured their prey, they lead them back to their heavenly realm, where Yama directs them to their destiny.

Cremation is a ritual designed to do much more than dispose of the body; it is intended to release the soul from its earthly existence. "Hindus believe that cremation (compared to burial or outside disintegration) is most spiritually beneficial to the departed soul." This is based on the belief that the "astral body" will linger "as long as the physical body remains visible." If the body is not cremated, "the soul remains nearby for days or months" The only bodies that are not generally burned are unnamed babies and the lowliest of castes, which are returned to the earth. The standard cremation ceremony begins with the ritual cleansing, dressing and adorning of the body. The body is then carried to the cremation ground as prayers are chanted to Yama, invoking his aid.

It is the chief mourner, usually the eldest son, who takes the twigs of holy kusha grass, flaming, from the Doms' (the untouchable caste who tend funeral pyres) eternal fire to the pyre upon which the dead has been laid. He circumambulates the pyre counterclockwise—for everything is backward at the time of death. As he walks round the pyre, his sacred thread, which usually hangs from the left shoulder, has been reversed to hang from the right. He lights the pyre. The dead, now, is an offering to Agni, the fire. Here, as in the most ancient Vedic times, the fire conveys the offering to heaven. After the corpse is almost completely burned, the chief mourner performs the rite called kapalakriya, the 'rite of the skull,' cracking the skull with a long bamboo stick, thus releasing the soul from entrapment in the body. After the cremation, the ashes are thrown into a river, ideally the Ganges river, and the mourners walk away without looking back.

The death ritual does not end with the elimination of the body. There is still the safety of the soul to look after. To ensure the passage during its voyage to the Otherworld, an eleven-day ritual called shraddha is performed. It "consist(s) of daily offerings of rice balls, called pindas, which provide a symbolic, transitional body for the dead. During these days, the dead person makes the journey to the heavens, or the world of the ancestors, or the 'far shore.'" "On the twelfth day, the departed soul is said to reach its destination and be joined with its ancestors, a fact expressed symbolically by joining a small pinda to a much larger one" Without these rites, the soul may never find it way to Yama's realm.

Those who have been "meritorious," but have not quite attained liberation through Self-knowledge, are sent to a heavenly realm to await their fate. "There the Gandharvas (demigods of fertility) sing to them and the bevies of celestial nymphs dance for them." Since there is no need for punishment, "they go forth immediately on very high divine carriages. And when they get down from those carriages, they are born in the families of kings and other noble people." There they "maintain and protect their good conduct" and live out their days before they are reborn enjoying "the very best of pleasures".

The fate for those who have participated in less honourable thoughts or actions is far less pleasant. The Arthasastra, a Hindu textbook from the second century BCE, offers a detailed description of some of the more frightening realms. Yet before reaching these dangerous destinations, one must first endure a miserable journey. "The hard-hearted men of Yama, terrifying, foul-smelling, with hammers and maces in their hands" come to get the deceased, who tremble and begin to scream. Filled with terror and pain, the soul leaves the body. "Preceded by his vital wind, he takes on another body of the same form, a body born of his own karma in order for him to be tortured."

The evil man becomes born as an animal, among the worms, insects, moths, beasts of prey, mosquitoes, and so forth. There he is born in elephants, trees, and so forth, and in cows and horses, and in other wombs that are evil and painful. When he finally becomes a human, he is a despicable hunchback or dwarf, or he is born in the womb of a woman of some tribe of Untouchables. When there is none of his evil left, and he is filled with merit, then he starts climbing up to higher castes, Sudra, Vaishya, Kshatriya, and so forth, sometimes eventually reaching the stage of Brahman or king of men. With so many unpleasant possibilities, it is easy to understand why reincarnation is not the only goal of every Hindu.

Those who lead a life of austerity, meditation and grace can look forward to the possibility of reaching Brahmaloka. This is the "highest among the heavenly planes" and the dwelling place of Brahma himself. "This is a place of intensely spiritual atmosphere, whose inhabitants live, free from disease, old age, and death, enjoying uninterrupted bliss in the companionship of the Deity." There is no need for them to return to earth because they have freed themselves "from all material desires." While they do experience a sense of individuality, they also experience a oneness with Brahma. This is the realm of immortality.

There is one other way to achieve liberation from samsara. This is to die within the city of Benaras, on the Ganges. "Death, which elsewhere is feared, here is welcomed as a long-expected guest." A city of many names, it was known in ancient time as Kashi, the city of light, and the Mahabharata refers to it as Varanasi. The funeral pyres, which are located on the river, burn nonstop. "Death, which elsewhere is polluting, is here holy and auspicious." People travel from around the country and the planet to spend their last days in Benaras because, "Death, the most natural, unavoidable, and certain of human realities, is here the sure gate to Moksha, the rarest, most precious, most difficult to achieve of spiritual goals".

For those who are unable to die in Benaras, cremation on the banks of the Ganges or the spreading of the ashes in her waters is the next best thing. Referred to as the "River of Heaven" or the "goddess and mother," she is considered to be sacred from her source in the Himalayas, all the way to the sea in the Bay of Bengal. Her power to destroy sins is so great that, people say, "even a droplet of Ganges water carried one's way by the breeze will erase the sins of many lifetimes in an instant".

Mourning, Burial at Sea: It must be understood that while this information was furnished by reliable sources, there are many different opinions between those of Hindu faith, and any Hindu contemplating cremation or burial at sea must seek the advice of a trusted priest. Hindu death rituals in all traditions follow a fairly uniform pattern drawn from the Vedas, with variations according to sect, region, caste and family tradition. Most rites are fulfilled by the family, all of whom participate, including the children, who need not be shielded from the death. Certain rites are traditionally performed by a priest but may also be performed by the family if no priest is available. Here is a simple outline of rites that can be performed by Hindus in any locality. Variations are noted and suggestions made for Hindus in Western countries.

As Death Approaches: Traditionally, a Hindu dies at home. Nowadays the dying are increasingly kept in hospitals, even when recovery is clearly not possible. Knowing the merits of dying at home among loved ones, Hindus bring the ill home. When death is imminent, kindred are notified. The person is placed in his room or in the entryway of the house, with the head facing east. A lamp is lit near his head and he is urged to concentrate on his mantra. Kindred keep vigil until the great departure, singing hymns, praying and reading scripture. If he cannot come home, this happens at the hospital, regardless of institutional objections.

The Moment of Death: If the dying person is unconscious at departure, a family member chants the mantra softly in the right ear. If none is known, "Aum Namo Narayana" or "Aum Nama Sivaya" is intoned. (This is also done for sudden-death victims, such as on a battlefield or in a car accident.) Holy ash or sandal paste is applied to the forehead, Vedic verses are chanted, and a few drops of milk, Ganga or other holy water are trickled into the mouth. After death, the body is laid in the home's entryway, with the head facing south, on a cot or the ground—reflecting a return to the lap of Mother Earth. The lamp is kept lit near the head and incense burned. A cloth is tied under the chin and over the top of the head. The thumbs are tied together, as are the big toes. In a hospital, the family has the death certificate signed immediately and transports the body home. Under no circumstances should the body be embalmed or organs removed for use by others. Religious pictures are turned to the wall, and in some traditions mirrors are covered. Relatives are beckoned to bid farewell and sing sacred songs at the side of the body.

The Homa Fire Ritual: If available, a special funeral priest is called. In a shelter built by the family, a fire ritual (homa) is performed to bless nine brass kumbhas (water pots) and one clay pot. Lacking the shelter, an appropriate fire is made in the home. The "chief mourner" leads the rites. He is the eldest son in the case of the father's death and the youngest son in the case of the mother's. In some traditions, the eldest son serves for both, or the wife, son-in-law or nearest male relative.

Preparing the Body: The chief mourner now performs Aarti, passing an oil lamp over the remains, then offering flowers. The male (or female, depending on the gender of the deceased) relatives carry the body to the back porch, remove the clothes and drape it with a white cloth. (If there is no porch, the body can be sponge bathed and prepared where it is.) Each applies sesame oil to the head, and the body is bathed with water from the nine kumbhas, dressed, placed in a coffin (or on a palanquin) and carried to the homa shelter. The young children, holding small lighted sticks, encircle the body, singing hymns. The women then walk around the body and offer puffed rice into the mouth to nourish the deceased for the journey ahead. A widow will place her tali (wedding pendant) around her husband's neck, signifying her enduring tie to him. The coffin is then closed. If unable to bring the body home, the family arranges to clean and dress it at the mortuary rather than leave these duties to strangers. The ritual homa-fire can be made at home or kindled at the crematorium.

Cremation: Only men go to the cremation site, led by the chief mourner. Two pots are carried: the clay kumbha and another containing burning embers from the homa. The body is carried three times counterclockwise around the pyre, then placed upon it. All circumambulating, and some Aarti, in the rites is counterclockwise. If a coffin is used, the cover is now removed. The men offer puffed rice as the women did earlier, cover the body with wood and offer incense and ghee. With the clay pot on his left shoulder, the chief mourner circles the pyre while holding a fire brand behind his back. At each turn around the pyre, a relative knocks a hole in the pot with a knife, letting water out, signifying life's leaving its vessel. At the end of three turns, the chief mourner drops the pot. Then, without turning to face the body, he lights the pyre and leaves the cremation grounds. The others follow. At a gas-fueled crematorium, sacred wood and ghee are placed inside the coffin with the body. Where permitted, the body is carried around the chamber, and a small fire is lit in the coffin before it is consigned to the flames. The cremation switch then is engaged by the chief mourner.

Return Home; Ritual Impurity: Returning home, all bathe and share in cleaning the house. A lamp and water pot are set where the body lay in state. The water is changed daily, and pictures remain turned to the wall. The shrine room is closed, with white cloth draping all icons. During these days of ritual impurity, family and close relatives do not visit others' homes, though neighbours and relatives bring daily meals to relieve the burdens during mourning. Neither do they attend festivals and temples, visit swamis, nor take part in marriage arrangements. Some observe this period up to one year. For the death of friends, teachers or students, observances are optional. While mourning is never suppressed or denied, scriptures admonish against excessive lamentation and encourage joyous release. The departed soul is acutely conscious of emotional forces directed at him. Prolonged grieving can hold him in earthly consciousness, inhibiting full transition to the heaven worlds. In Hindu Bali, it is shameful to cry for the dead.

Bone-Gathering Ceremony: About 12 hours after cremation, family men return to collect the remains. Water is sprinkled on the ash; the remains are collected on a large tray.

At crematoriums the family can arrange to personally gather the remains: ashes and small pieces of white bone called "flowers." In crematoriums these are ground to dust, and arrangements must be made to preserve them. Ashes are carried or sent to India for deposition in the Ganges or placed them in an auspicious river or the ocean, along with garlands and flowers.

First Memorial: On the 3rd, 5th, 7th or 9th day, relatives gather for a meal of the deceased's favorite foods. A portion is offered before his photo and later ceremonially left at an abandoned place, along with some lit camphor. Customs for this period are varied. Some offer pinda (rice balls) daily for nine days. Others combine all these offerings with the following sapindikarana rituals for a few days or one day of ceremonies.

31st-Day Memorial: On the 31st day, a memorial service is held. In some traditions it is a repetition of the funeral rites. At home, all thoroughly clean the house. A priest purifies the home, and performs the sapindikarana, making one large pinda (representing the deceased) and three small, representing the father, grandfather and greatgrandfather. The large ball is cut in three pieces and joined with the small pindas to ritually unite the soul with the ancestors in the next world.

The pindas are fed to the crows, to a cow or thrown in a river for the fish. Some perform this rite on the 11th day after cremation. Others perform it twice: on the 31st day or (11th, 15th, etc.) and after one year. Once the first sapindikarana is completed, the ritual impurity ends. Monthly repetition is also common for one year.

One-Year Memorial: At the yearly anniversary of the death (according to the moon calendar), a priest conducts the shraddha rites in the home, offering pinda to the ancestors. This ceremony is done yearly as long as the sons of the deceased are alive (or for a specified period). It is now common in India to observe shraddha for ancestors just prior to the yearly Navaratri festival. This time is also appropriate for cases where the day of death is unknown.

Hindu funeral rites can be simple or exceedingly complex. These ten steps, devotedly completed according to the customs, means, and ability of the family, will properly conclude one earthly sojourn of any Hindu soul. Religions such as Hinduism offer our own immortal souls satisfying answers to questions of life and death. Their ancient mythic texts provide real reasons for our existence here on earth. They also demonstrate that death is something that can be prepared for instead of being feared. In addition, they offer the possibility of something to look forward to, so we need not dread our last days on this planet. A true hindu shall love death as he loves this life.

Customs and Rituals in Other Indigenous Religions

India is the birthplace of many religions, Hinduism, Buddhism, Jainism and Sikhism are all progeny of this part of our globe. But they are not the only religions that exist here. Adherents of Christianity, Islam, Zoroastrianism and Judaism also to be found in India. Over countless generations there has been significant exchange of customs,, traditions, beliefs, rituals, etc., between these different religions Such an exchange is not peculiar to India and has been occurring the world over throughout the past. In India though, the existence of many religions in the same social environment created a situation favourable for such an interchange of customs and rituals.

The other fact that some religions existing in India are offspring of the amalgam of beliefs that coexisted under the heading Hinduism. This has also led to the presence of many features of the parent religion in the offspring religions. At times this has blurred the line dividing Hinduism from the offspring religions leading occasionally to tension of the offspring religions with their parent.

One instance of this is the ire against the constitution of India wherein the term 'Hindu' includes Buddhists, Jains and Sikhs.

But interchange of customs and rituals has taken place even between religions originating in India and those brought into India from other parts of our globe. This interchange has also been a massive one for the reason that apart from the fusion of customs as a result of coexistence of different forms of worship, the adherents of religions originating in other parts of the globe like Christianity and Islam are largely converts from Hinduism. This does not apply in the case of Zoroastrianism and Judaism as these two religions have tended to be insular and have jealously guarded against the entry of members of other faiths by way of conversion. But even then they display many traits which they have absorbed from other religions especially Hinduism.

Although this interchange has been quite substantial, it has not succeeded in bringing about identity in many important respects. Communal riots are still not a thing of the past, sectarian feelings are still very much with as and there normally run counter to the spirit of nationalism and secularism. The result of this is perhaps India's having the dubious distinction of being a Secular society without a common civil code. For an appraisal of contemporary Indian society to be complete we ought to examine the nature and genesis of the different religions that exist around us, and also the extent to which they have influenced each other. To obtain an insight into every religion, we shall briefly state the history of every religion since its inception, what it has borrowed from other faiths and what it has lent to it.

We start with the religion which is not only professed by a vast majority in India, but has also been the birthplace for many customs found in other religious communities in India.

Jain Rituals

Birth—Priyodhbhav Sanskar: This ritual takes place after the birth of a child. Ten days of cleansing or ***Sutak*** are observed after delivery. During this period no rituals are performed. But in the temple the priest recites mantras and receives offerings on behalf of the new-born.

Namkaran Sanskar: This is the naming ceremony. It is done on the eleventh, thirteenth or twenty-ninth day after the birth of a child. For Namkaran the name is selected from the 1008 Jinasahasranam for the boys and names of the girls are selected from famous women of the Puranas. The priest, chanting mantras declares the name and thenthe child is blessed.

Death: The Jains cremate the dead as soon as possible. First the body is rubbed with a wet cloth. The corpse is then clothed and placed in a *bier* and covered with a *kafan*. The body is tied to the bier and taken to the crematorium. A suitable place without any living organisms like grass or insects is selected so as not to harm them. There a platform of wood is erected. The body is taken from the bier and placed on the platform with logs of wood over it. Ghee, camphor and sandalwood powder are sprinkled all over the body and the eldest son of the deceased does the last rites.

The son goes round the pyre three times sprinkling water allover the body. Chanting the *Namokar Mantra*, he lights up the pyre. Then after sometime they pour milk over the place. The remains are collected in bags and the place is thoroughly cleansed. The remains are not immersed in rivers as they can pollute the water. Instead they dig a hole in the earth and put the remains and sprinkle salt all over, so that it dissolves easily.

The Jains believe that the dead soul would be reborn immediately. So for them death is a festival or Mahotsav. Loud wailing and observing anniversaries are not part of the Jain Tradition.

Jainism and the Puja Ritual

The central objects of veneration in a Jain temple are statues of human figures in marble, stone, or metal. These austere and rigid figures, always sharply sculpted and finely polished, sit with their hands folded on their lap or stand bolt upright in meditation. They are the Jinas or Tirthankars, the twenty-four divine ascetic renouncers who have founded and re-founded the Jain religion.

Although there are many other idols and sacred representations in Jain temples, it is essentially to the Tirthankars that the *puja* is addressed. Each temple is named after its one main Tirthankar, but statues of others gleam from every wall and dark corner, and it is as though, going into the temple, one enters a space which is already peopled by a crowd of silent identical predecessors.

In this chapter we shall introduce the Jinas and explain the general outlines of the Jain religion. Our exposition is brief because excellent studies of Jainism by Jaini (1979), Dundas (1992), and others, are available to interested readers. However, we do make a detailed description of the daily morning *puja* as it is actually practised (this not being provided elsewhere), and we indicate its place among other Jain religious rituals.

Throughout the book we shall make most of our points about ritual in general through the example of the Jain *puja* and this is why a certain minimum of information about the religion is provided here, but readers interested mainly in the theory of ritual as a mode of action could proceed directly to Chapter 3. The latter part of this chapter will show that even one religion (Jainism) may react to ritual through various understandings.

In the case of the *puja* these responses range from devoted participation to outright rejection. Since such reactions emerge in specific historical and social contexts, we describe the present socio-economic position of the Jains, and we also provide a short history of the reforms and debates about ritual in the Khartar Gacch, the Jain tradition to which most of our friends in Jaipur belong.

Jain Wedding: Jainism advocates the peaceful coexistence and interaction of two different living organisms in mutual beneficence or mutual dependence. Life is regarded as a gift to be shared together, helping each other to exist and grow. Jains have this wonderful prayer in their hearts always for forgiveness for all living beings also seeking and receiving the forgiveness of all beings. Also prayer craving for the friendship of all beings. Jains regard marriage as more or less a worldly affair. Marriage and family raising are recommended to all the Jain Shravakas. Because children born of the wed-lock would follow the Jain dharma only.

Marriage through the Ages

The Jain marriage custom is governed by the traditional practices which of course vary from community to community. Some rituals are of course common to all Jain marriages. For the Jains, marriage means a public declaration of a man and a woman's intention to be together for the entire life. The community gives support to the couple by being a part of it. The Jain community assemblies on various occasions have condemned the practice of negotiating a dowry before marriage. Jains believe that there should be no waste of money or time.

Nevertheless, marriage is an once-in-lifetime occasion that has to be celebrated properly and grandly. Jain marriages are mostly conducted by the Jain pundits only

Match Making: Jains believe in marrying within the community only. They feel that the children thus born would also become Jains only. They mostly find partners for their eligible boy or girl by word of mouth. They intimate their willingness to get their children married to the other known people in their community. Modern day advertising through newspapers and engaging marriage bureaus are also in vogue these days.

Costumes

Bridal Wear: The Jain brides wear sarees only. The preferred color is red or any other bright color.

Groom's Attire: The Jain grooms wear the traditional Kurta Pyajama or the Dhoti Kurta.

Rituals before Marriage: In Laghana Lekhan, the marriage is fixed. On this occasion, pooja is held at the girl's house and relatives are invited. The lagna, also known as the mahurat is determined by the priest. At the end of the rituals, the lagna patrika or a letter telling you about the time of marriage, is sent to the boy's house. It is also customary to send ¾ kg of sweets, especially laddoos at the time of engagement or sagai. The sweets could also be sent in an auspicious time.

Lagna Patrika Vachan: The Lagna Patrika Vachan is read out in the boy's house. This is done either on the engagement day or any other auspicious moment. After this the priest reads the letter after the groom has performed the Vinayakyantra Pooja.

Sagai: Engagement or sagai ceremony is held at the groom's house. The groom would wear the traditional Jain headgear, wash his hands and do the Vinayakyantra. After the Vinayakyantra pooja, the bride's brother applies tilak on the groom's forehead and gifts him a gold chain, a ring, clothes, coconut, sweets and money. The groom is then presented the lagna patrika. The priest reads out the patrika and the groom seeks the blessings of the elders.

Mada-mandap: After Sagai, the next most important ceremony is Mada-mandap, which is held a day or two before marriage. This ceremony is celebrated both at the groom's as well as the bride's places. The hour for the occasion is a predetermined auspicious hour. The priest would perform all the rituals.

Barati: The barati is a ritual that takes place at the girl's place. It is upon arrival of the barat or the groom's procession that the bride's brother receives the groom and applies tika on his forehead. He is also presented with coconut, money, sweet and clothes. In return, the groom also apply tika on the forehead of the bride's brother and presents him a coconut.

Aarti: After receiving the groom with all honour, it's time when the married women do an aarti of the groom They also sing the Mangala Geet.

Phere: Phere is perhaps the most important ceremony in Indian marriages. For the Phere also an auspicious time is being decided. For this the groom and the bride would be taken to the mandap and made them seated. The girl sits to the right of the groom, the groom and the bride changing position after taking the seven vows.

Kanyavaran: Also known as the kanyapradan ceremony, it has the parents or the uncle of the bride keeping one rupee and twenty-five paise and rice on the right hand of the bride. And then the presentation of the bride to the groom takes place. The father would publicly proclaim this formal presentation of the bride in front all the assembled guests. The groom thus receives the bride. This occasion is marked with the priest pouring water on the hands of the bride and groom chanting the mantra three times.

Havan: The havan starts after the Phere. During the havan, a series of mantras are chanted those of the Peethika, Atha Gathu, Atha Nistarak, Atha Surendra, Atha Parmarajadi and Atha Paramesthi are recited and offerings are made. At the end of these mantras, the Shanti mantra is chanted nine times.

Granthi Bandhan: Granthi Bandhan takes place after the havan. In this a married woman takes the corner of the pallu of the bride's sari and then ties it to the shawl of the groom. A mantra is also recited in this occasion. Following which the couple takes four rounds of the fire. In this the bride leads while taking the first round. Then they exchange positions and take another three parikramas around the havankund. There takes place the recitation of Mahaveerakshak stoot in the background.

The women also start singing the mangal geet at this time. A muhurta (auspicious moment) has been already decided previously. After the phere, the groom and the bride exchange the seven vows separately. When both of them have accepted the seven vows, the priest makes the bride sit on to the left of the groom. After this the bride will be called vamangi, which means she is the left half of the body. This follows with the couple exchanging garlands. Ultimately, the havan ends with the Shantipath and Visarjan.

Rituals after Marriage: Once the marriage is over, parents and relatives bless the couple. Alongwith the priest also blesses the newly weds and chants a mantra. As in all marriages, a wedding feast for the assembled guests follow this. Now the remaining ritual is left and that of sending the bride to the groom's house. The Jains believe in giving away alms in Jain temples as a thanksgiving to the god.

Celebrations

Music & Dance: When the women receive the groom at the reception, they do the Aarti and also sing the Mangala Geet.

Cuisine: Jains are strictly vegetarians. The usual wedding menu consists of the specialities of the localities. The Gujaratis would arrange traditional vegetarian dishes and other may go for the Marwari vegetarian fare. Still others may go for the vegetarian Punjabi dishes.

Some Strange Customs: Ghudhchadi is a ritual that takes place before on the marriage day before the barat or the groom's procession leaves for the bride's place. The Ghudhchadi ritual has the groom given his headgear and his mother and all the relatives apply tika on his forehead. After this the groom rides the horse and then he goes visiting a temple.

Sikh Rituals

The religion of the Sikhs called Sikhism is not an ethnic religion and anyone can join its fold. The Sikhs believe in the omnipotence, omniscience, omnipresence and formlessness of one God called Wahe Guru. They believe that community worship and community service are related to Godliness. The Sikh symbols are called *Panch Piyara* and they include the five K's: *Kanga* or Comb, *Kaccha* or shorts, *Kada* or bangle, *Kesha* or hair and *Kirpan* or dagger. Every Sikh is supposed to carry these five symbols on his self all the time.

Birth: There are no particular rituals connected with the birth of a child in the Sikh community. Some sections of the Sikhs recite the five verses of the Morning Prayer, Japji Sahib into the ears of the newborn child.

Gurthi: A respected, intelligent and favorite member of the family gives a drop of honey to the new born child so as to give his characters later in life, to the newborn child. This is not a ritual and it mostly takes place in the hospital itself.

Shushak: When a child is born into the Sikh fold, the maternal grandparents gift him a package called *Shushak*, which consists of clothes for the child and his family, a spoon, glass, and a bowl for the child, money and gold ornaments for the child according to their financial status.

Death: In the Sikh community after the death of a person, the *Kirtan Solah* is read. Loud lamenting and breast-beating are strictly forbidden among the Sikhs. People gather around the body and recite the morning prayers. The corpse is bathed and dressed along with the fives K's. The Sikhs cremate their dead like the Hindus and they do it before sunset. The eldest son of the deceased lights the funeral pyre. The priest sings the holy hymns. After the cremation, people go to the Gurudwara where some texts from the Granth Sahib are read. *Prasad*, is which is cooked with coarsely ground atta, water, sugar and Desi ghee is served to the people.

On the third day after the cremation, the relatives go to the cremation ground, take the bones of the dead and wash them in unboiled milk. Then they collect the bones and the ashes in a bag and immerse it in the Beas River or in the river flowing near their Gurudwara. They don't observe *Shraddh* or Anniversary for their dead. The period of mourning for the dead can go up to 10 days, until which the holy texts from the Granth Sahib are read daily in the house.

Zoroastrian Rituals

Birth: After the birth of a child in a Zoroastrian family, the new mother is normally confined to the house for 40 days. This is to prevent her and her child from any diseases. A lamp is lit on the day of birth and is kept in the room for about 40 days to ward off any evil elements. Some families observe the *Pachori* on the fifth day while some observe *Dasori* on the tenth day of the child. On the fortieth day, the new mother is given a ceremonial bath with consecrated water being administered by the head priest. This is done to cleanse her so that she can interact with other people.

Para Haoma: The event of giving the first drink to the newborn is called Para Haoma. It is consecrated Haoma juice and it is supposed to make the child healthy. But these days a sweet drink made of molasses or sugar is also administered.

Navjote: The formal admission of a child into the Zoroastrian fold is called Navjote. It is done between the seventh and the eleventh year of the child. First the child takes a special bath called *Nahn* and then he is given a purifying drink. Then the child stands in a raised platform and his mother performs the *Achoo Michoo* ceremony where certain items are rotated over the head of the child seven times. This is done to invoke the blessings of the seven *Amesha Spentas* on the child.

Then certain prescribed texts are read and the Kushti is worn round the waist of the child. Then a long prayer is held when the child declares that he will be a true Zoroastrian and follow the rules and regulations. Both the Parsi boys and girls are given this privilege. Finally the priest recites the *Doa Tandorosoti Prayer*, which calls for the well being of the child, his parents and the community in particular.

Marriage: The marriage involves the groom going to the bride's house along with his relatives and friends. The priest heads the assembly and women carry the *Varni*—the gifts meant for the bride. Music bands accompany them.

The bride's house is usually decorated with strings of flowers. When the groom arrives the bride's mother welcomes him by applying *Kumkum* on his forehead and sprays rice grains over him.

During the ceremony the couple shower rice over each other and the priest also throws rice grains over them as a mark of blessing. A coconut is taken round the head of the groom three times, then it is broken and the water is applied at the feet of the groom. The bridegroom is made to sit on the hand of the bride. Both of them face the eastern direction. One person with a burning flame is allowed to stand near the couple as a reverence to their God of fire. A candle is also placed on both the sides and it burns for the whole ceremony.

The priest gets the consent of the couple and then joins their hands and showers rice grains over them. Then the couple is seated facing each other, with a curtain between them. The couple is made to hold each other's right hand and a piece of cloth is passed round the chairs so as to enclose them. The ends of the cloth are tied symbolizing the marriage knot. Then the writings of the *Yatha Ahuvairyo* are read. Finally the curtain is dropped and the couple shower rice grains on each other. The relatives and friends then clap approving the marriage. Then a grand feast is given.

Death: According to the Zoroastrians, if the soul has left the body then it should be disposed off with minimum harm to those living. The Zoroastrians have strict ideals of sanitation, segregation, purification and cleanliness. The part of the house where the body was kept before the funeral will be washed and cleansed thoroughly.

When death of a person is imminent, two head priests are called. They recite the ***Patet***—the prayer for repentance. A few drops of the Haoma juice are administered to the dying person. Nowadays pomegranate juice is also given.

Buddhist Rituals

The essence of Buddhism lies in the four Noble truths: (Sanketas) *e.g.* suffering; its cause; its cessation and the path leading to the cessation of suffering. The eight fold path leading to the removal of suffering consists of right conduct, right motive, right resolve, right speech, right livelihood, right attention, right effort and right meditation. Following this path one can conquer his cravings for worldly things. The Buddha held that, the 'mind' is the nerve centre of every human activity. In Buddhism, therefore, Vipasana, (meditation) is more important than the prayer and various abstinences which border upon asceticism. By controlling his mind and conquering his cravings, one can hope to attain 'Nirvana'; the state of complete peace.

The three characteristics of Buddhism are: Anicca (transiency), Dukkha (sorrow) and Anatta (soul-lessness). In other words, life is constantly changing and all conditioned things are transient. Whatever is transient, is painful, and where change and sorrow prevail, the question of a permanent immortal soul does not arise. He did not accept that there was an immortal entity which survived the death of the body and was born in other forms through a series of incarnation. Nevertheless the principle of Sansara wandering (rebirth) was accepted by the Buddha.

A Buddhist is a person who reveres the Buddha, as the highest spiritual guide and strives to live according to his teachings. A person taking refuge in the Triple-Gem (Tri-Ratana) not only reveres the Buddha but also undertake to practice Dhamma in his daily life and to support the Bhikkhu-Sangha. Three refuges are followed by the five Moral precepts (Pancha Sila) which form the bed rock of the Buddhist way of life.

They are, to abstain from killing, stealing, adultery, lying and intoxications. The refuge-cum-precepts formula is recited in Pali by the devout Buddhists daily in the morning as well as in the evening and at all religious ceremonies and social functions.

The Buddhist are divided into two classes *i.e.* the Upasakas and the monks. The term Upasaka is a lay devotee, or a lay follower who has taken refuge in the Buddha, Dhamma and the Sangha. Those who renounce the life of a recluse by joining the Sangha are known as monks (bhikkhus). In Buddhism, there are four classes on the basis of the observance of the ethical precepts they are: Upasakas observing five precepts;

Upasakas observing eight precepts, Sremners observing ten precept and Bhikkhus observing 227 precepts.

The Buddhists have four sacred days in a month which are observed as days of fasting. These days are the new moon, full moon and the two quarter moon days, they are called Uposatha (Roya in Sri Lanka) *i.e.* fast day. On the uposatha days, the devout Buddhist follow the eight precepts (Atthanga Sila) and abstain from worldly pleasures. They visit viharas and offer Dana to the Bhikkhus.

The most sacred and the most important festival for all the Buddhist is Vaisaka Purnima, known in India as Buddha Purnima or Buddha Jayanti. It is fixed by the full-moon day of Vaisakha which falls in May. This day is the Thrice Blessed day as Lord Buddha was born, attained enlightenment and entered into Mahaparinirvana on this day.

Buddhist Marriage Ceremony: Although wedding ceremonies have always been regarded as secular affairs in Buddhist countries, the parties concerned have nevertheless obtained the blessing from monks at the local temple after the civil registration formalities have been completed.

In view of the traditional importance that the marriage ceremony has in the West, moreover, local, and especially isolated Buddhists without access to a temple or a monk might well adopt the following service that could be performed by relatives and friends of the bride and groom:

Tribal Customs and Rituals

Adivasi (Tribes) Contributions to Indian Culture and Civilization: Adivasi traditions and practices pervade all aspects of Indian culture and civilization, yet this awareness is often lacking in popular consciousness, and the extent and import of Adivasi contributions to Indian philosophy, language and custom have often gone unrecognized, or been underrated by historians and social scientists.

Although popular myths about Buddhism have obscured the original source and inspiration for it's humanist doctrine, it is to India's ancient tribal (or Adivasi) societies that Gautam Buddha looked for a model for the kind of society he wished to advocate. Repulsed by how greed for private property was instrumental in causing poverty, social exploitation and unending warfare—he saw hope for human society in the tribal republics that had not yet come under the sway of authoritarian rule and caste discrimination. The early Buddhist *Sanghas* were modelled on the tribal pattern of social interaction that stressed gender equality, and respect for all members. Members of the *Sanghas* sought to emulate their egalitarian outlook and democratic functioning

At that time, the tribal republics retained many aspects of social equality that can still be found in some Adivasi societies that have somehow escaped the ill-effects of commercial plunder and exploitation. Adivasi society was built on a foundation of equality with respect for all life forms including plants and trees. There was a deep recognition of mutual dependence in nature and human society. People were given respect and status according to their contribution to social needs but only while they were performing that particular function. A priest could be treated with great respect during a religious ceremony or a doctor revered during a medical consultation, but once such duties had been performed, the priest or doctor became equal to everyone else. The possession of highly valued skills or knowledge did not lead to a permanent rise in status. This meant that no individual or small group could engage in overlordship of any kind, or enjoy hereditary rights.

Such a value-system was sustainable as long as the Adivasi community was non-acquisitive and all the products of society were shared. Although division of labor did take place, the work of society was performed on a cooperative and co-equal basis—without prejudice or disrespect for any form of work.

It was the simplicity, the love of nature, the absence of coveting the goods and wealth of others, and the social harmony of tribal society that attracted Gautam Buddha, and had a profound impact on the ethical core of his teachings.

To this day, sharing is a vital and integral part of the philosophy of the Mullakurumba Adivasis of South India. When the Mullakurumbas go hunting a share is given to every family in the village, even those who may be absent, sick or cannot participate for any other reason. An extra portion is added for any guest in the village and even a non-tribal passersby will be offered a share. Not sharing is something they find difficult to comprehend.

Nevertheless, tribal societies were under constant pressure as the money economy grew and made traditional forms of barter less difficult to sustain. In matters of trade, the Adivasis followed a highly evolved system of honour. All agreements that they entered into were honoured, often the entire tribe chipping in to honor an agreement made by an individual member of the tribe. Individual dishonesty or deceit were punished severely by the tribe. An individual who acted in a manner that violated the honor of the tribe faced potential banishment and family members lost the right to participate in community events during the period of punishment. But often, tribal integrity was undermined because the non-tribals who traded with the Adivasis reneged on their promises and took advantage of the sincerity and honesty of most members of the tribe.

Tribal societies came under stress due to several factors. The extension of commerce, military incursions on tribal land, and the resettling of Brahmins amidst tribal populations had an impact, as did ideological coercion or persuasion to attract key members of the tribe into "mainstream" Hindu society. This led to many tribal communities becoming integrated into Hindu society as *jatis* (or castes) while others who resisted were pushed into the hilly or forested areas, or remote tracks that had not yet been settled. In the worst case, defeated Adivasi tribes were pushed to the margins of settled society and became discriminated as outcastes and "untouchables".

But spontaneous differentiation within tribal societies also took place over time, which propelled these now unequal tribal communities into integrating into Hindu society without external violence or coercion. In Central India, ruling dynasties emerged from within the ranks of tribal society.

In any case, the end result was that throughout India, tribal deities and customs, creation myths and a variety of religious rites and ceremonies came to absorbed into the broad stream of "Hindu" society. In the Adivasi traditions, ancestor worship, worship of fertility gods and goddesses (as well as male and female fertility symbols), totemic worship—all played a role. And they all found their way into the practice of what is now considered Hinduism. The widespread Indian practice of keeping '*vratas*', *i.e.* fasting for wish-fulfillment or moral cleansing also has Adivasi origins

Mahashweta Devi has shown that both Shiva and Kali have tribal origins as do Krishna and Ganesh. In the 8th century, the tribal forest goddess or harvest goddess was absorbed and adapted as Siva's wife. Ganesh owes it's origins to a powerful tribe of elephant trainers whose incorporation into Hindu society was achieved through the deification of their elephant totem. In his study of Brahmin lineages in Maharashtra, Kosambi points to how many Brahmin gotras (such as *Kashyapa)* arose from tribal totems such as *Kachhapa* (tortoise). In Rajasthan, Rajput rulers recognised the Adivasi *Bhil* chiefs as allies and *Bhils* acquired a central role in some Rajput coronation ceremonies.

India's regional languages such as Oriya, Marathi or Bengali developed as a result of the fusion of tribal languages with Sanskrit or Pali and virtually all the Indian languages have incorporated words from the vocabulary of Adivasi languages.

Adivasis who developed an intimate knowledge of various plants and their medicinal uses played an invaluable role in the development of Ayurvedic medicines. In a recent study, the All India Coordinated Research Project credits Adivasi communities with the knowledge of 9000 plant species—7500 used for human healing and veterinary health care. Dental care products like *datun,* roots and condiments like *turmeric* used in cooking and ointments are also Adivasi discoveries, as are many fruit trees and vines. Ayurvedic cures for arthritis and night blindness owe their origin to Adivasi knowledge.

Adivasis also played an important role in the development of agricultural practices—such as rotational cropping, fertility maintenance through alternating the cultivation of grains with leaving land fallow or using it for pasture. Adivasis of Orissa were instrumental in developing a variety of strains of rice.

Adivasi musical instruments such as the *bansuri* (flute) and *dhol* (drum), folk-tales, dances and seasonal celebrations also found their way into Indian traditions as did their art and metallurgical skills.

In India's central belt, Adivasi communities rose to considerable prominence and developed their own ruling clans. The earliest Gond kingdom appears to date from the 10th C and the Gond Rajas were able to maintain a relatively independent existence until the 18th C., although they were compelled to offer nominal allegiance to the Mughal empire. The Garha-Mandla kingdom in the north extended control over most of the upper Narmada valley and the adjacent forest areas. The Deogarh-Nagpur kingdom dominated much of the upper Wainganga valley, while Chanda-Sirpur in the south consisted of territory around Wardha and the confluences of the Wainganga with the Penganga.

Jabalpur was one of the major centers of the Garha-Mandla kingdom and like other major dynastic capitals had a large fort and palace. Temples and palaces with extremely fine carvings and erotic sculptures came up throughout the Gond kingdoms. The Gond ruling clans enjoyed close ties with the Chandella ruling clans and both dynasties attempted to maintain their independence from Mughal rule through tactical alliances. Rani Durgavati of Jabalpur (of Chandella-Gond heritage) acquired a reputation of legendary proportions when she died in battle defending against Mughal incursions. The city of Nagpur was founded by a Gond Raja in the early 18th century.

Marriage System of Tribals

Among the social institutions, marriage appears to be the most important one. It is practiced almost universally by the tribal people, the only exception being the has of Kolhan. The extreme cupidity of fathers of kolhan brides and their high sense of family dignity have made them to demand an unusually high price for the hands of their daughter in marriage. Maiden aged 40 to 50 are a common-sight in Kolhan villages. However, recently young man and women began to arrange for their own unions without the knowledge of their parents and went through the operations of mock capture of the bride. The father of the bride in such cases demanded a higher price but not with the hope receiving any payment.

The tribals of India have more advanced views regarding the age of marriage of the young people than their advanced neighbours. The practice have come under the influence of Hindu culture. Among the Gonds, Kulis and Bhumias in Orissa, child marriage was said to be common, because of the influence of Hindu culture. This practice has yielded place to marriage of adults. The Souras, Koyas, Kondhs, Gadabas and Bondas of Koraput district marry at a fair age and infant marriages are unknown among them. The groom is generally older than the bride in the tribal area.

There is enough opportunity for the satisfaction of sex impulses outside marriage among the tribes of India. Pre-marital sexual chastity is not very rigidly insisted upon in a large number of tribes. Among the Murias of Madhya Pradesh, for instance, it is a custom on certain days of the week, for those boys and girls of dormitories who are prefects to spend the nights with each other and have sexual relations.

Half a century ago each oraon bachelor had a sweet heart in the spinsters house. If the girl refused to accept a lover, she was cut of by the older girls who refused to dance with her till she accepted a paramour. Before marriage love affairs and even intimate relationships are permitted and widely practiced among the Bondas, Koyas, Gadabas and Soura women in Koraput region.

Even after marriage on some festive post-marital laxity is also found among Hos and Oranos, during important festivals, when men and women freely indulge in sex relations. However, sex activity is not the only objective of marriage. Economic cooperation as found in the division of labour between husband and wife seems to be another important consideration for marital union among tribals.

The selection of mateis an important affair even in primitive tribal society. The rules of endogamy, exogamy, hypergamy, preferential mating and prohibited degrees operative simultaneously and there by considerably restrict the freedom of choice. Among the koyas and kondhs marriage with the maternal uncles daughter is prevent and is preferred to marriage with others. However, among Bondas this custom is absent. Marriage within the clan and certain brother clan is strictly prohibited among the tribes in Orissa. Generally marriage also does not occur with in the same village. The ways and means of acquiring a mate in tribal society are varied and interesting Eight important ways of acquiring a mate maybe listed for Indian tribes. They are:

1. Probationary Marriage
2. Marriage by captures
3. Marriage by trial
4. Marriage by Service
5. Marriage by Purchase
6. Marriage by exchange
7. Marriage by mutual consent and elopement
8. Marriage by intrusion.

Marriage by purchase and marriage by service are accepted way of finding a bride. The amount of bride price varies according to the economic conditions of tribe. The Bhumias, Oraons, Saharas, Juangs, Santals, Hos, Nagas, Bhils and many other tribes pay for their brides as a general rule. A Kondha of Koraput who is not able to pay the bride price is asked to workunder the father-in-law's house till his final payment.

Probationary marriage Marriages by trial and intrusion marriage are found in limited cases of tribes in India.

Marriages among the Bonda tribe are arranged in an extra ordinary manner. About two months before Dashara festival each village Naikdig a hole of about 8 square and nine feet deep and roofed with logs and mud so arranged as to leave one small opening. In this all unmarried girls of the village have to sleep. Any youth desirous of matrimony joins them there a night and next morning leaves his brass bracelet with the girl of his choice.

The pair after wards goes together to the girl's people and explain matters. Ultimately with relatives on both the side, they repair to jungles, where a fire is lit and the girl applies it to the boys buttocks. If he cries out in pain the girlre fuses him, but if he makes no sound the couple are considered to be man and wife. The system has the advantages of giving both parties a choice in the matter.

The marriage customs and rituals among the tribles are elaborate and vary from tribe to tribe. It effects the economics life of aper son, who gets a wife, to a great extent. It is necessary to discuss in brief the marriage customs and rituals, which is generally found among the tribes.

The parents of the bridegroom initiate marriages amongst the Soura. They visit the girls parents bearing with them a present of apot containing palm wine. The reason for their visit is not immediately made plain. However, sooner or later, the name of the girl is mentioned and she is informed by her parent of the proposal. If she consents, they accept the pot of wine and ceremonially drink it before several witness. After several such visits the bride price is finalized. The presentation of an arrow and its acceptance by the bride's family is equivalent of an engagement. About a year after the engagement the bride is brought to the bridegrooms house and made to the ancestors by a shahman.

Each tribal marriage is accompanied by a lot off easting and dancing. These are done at Bridegroom's house at his cost. Marriage of a tribal boy becomes very expensive as it becomes a source of exploration by the money lenders and land grabbers, who are ready to advance money to the tribles at the time of marriage and charge very high rate of interest.

MORTUARY CUSTOMS

Among the Bauris the dead are either burnt or buried. The corpse is borne in the hands, or on a bier, by four men. Soon after the village boundary is crossed, the widow of the deceased throws rice over the eyes of corpse, and also a little fire, after taking it three times round.

Among the Bhumias the dead are burnt and pollution lasts for nine days. On the tenth day a ceremonial bath is taken and a feast with copious supplies of liquor is held.

The Bhottadas burn their dead and observe pollution for ten days during which no agricultural work is done and no food is cooked in the Vasma if the deceased which is fed by some relatives. On the tenth day on which bath is taken some fried rice and new pot are carried to the burning ground and left there.

Among Chitra-Ghasis the dead are burnt and death pollution is observed for three days during which the caste occupation is not carried on. On the third day the ashes are collected together and a fowl is killed. The ashes are then buried or thrown into running water.

When a Koya dies, a cow or bullock is slaughtered, and the tail is cut off and put in the dead man's hand. The liver is said to be put in his mouth. It is customary among the more prosperous families to put a few rupees into the mouth of a corpse before the funeral pyre is lighted. The money is made to represent the value of the animal sacrificed.

Among the Gadava males, as a rule are burnt but if aper son dies in the night or on a rainy day, the corpse is sometimes buried. Women and children are usually buried presumably because they are not thought worth the fuel necessary for cremation. Only relations are permitted touch acorpse. Death pollution is observed for three days, during which the caste occupations must not be engaged in. Stone slabs are erected to the memory of the dead, and sacrifices are offered to them now and again.

Saora death is an embarrassment, as every death in a family adds a new danger from the other world. But it is not a separation. After death the corpse is laid on its back across the mortar in the central room of the house and is covered with a cloth. Women carry the corpse out of the house and lay in on a plank of wood in the street outside. They remove most of the ornaments, bathe the body and comb the hair.

RITUALS OF WEDDING

India is known for its rich cultural heritage and diverse customs and rituals of different religions. Each religion has its own traditions be it Hindu, Muslim, Sikh, Parsi or Christian everybody has their own wedding customs. Indian wedding is mainly associated with the Hindu marriage ceremony, which is quite an elabourate celebration lasting for several days. And every region has its own unique way of celebrating their wedding functions.

Most of the weddings rituals are based on their regional traditions but the common tie among the weddings of all the religions is the fun and excitement part. It involves a large gathering of friends and relatives.

The Hindu marriage is held in a big marquee, either in the bride's home yard or in a rented wedding hall. Rituals are traditional in a Hindu wedding ceremony, but they may vary from one community to another. Different rituals are held pre-marriage, on the main day and post-marriage. Customs like Ganesh puja, which is done before the ceremony for his blessings. Than there are rituals like Tilak, the sacred mark on forehead, mehendi (henna), sangeet (song and dance), barat (procession), jai mala (garland exchange), vivah, (the main wedding ceremony), kanya daan and vidaii, which are the most important Hindu wedding rituals.

Marriage in Hindu

In Hindu dharma, marriage is viewed as a sacrament and not a contract. Hindu marriage is a life-long commitment of one wife and one husband, and is the strongest social bond that takes place between a man and a woman. Grahastha Ashram (the householder stage), the second of the four stages of life begins when a man and a woman marry and start a household.

Now let us consider the elabourate process of the marriage according to the Veda, and its scientific significance. A day before the wedding the palm and feet of the bride are decorated with "Mahendi". A canopy or mandapa decorated with flowers is erected at the place of wedding.

On the wedding morning, various ablutionary rituals are performed on both the bride and the groom in their own homes. Their bodies are anointed with turmeric, sandalwood paste and oils, which cleanse the body, soften the skin, and make it aromatic. They are then bathed to the chanting of Vedic mantras

One important point to be noted is that in the Vedic Age the school going is both for the boy and the girl. And the Upanayana is to be performed for both of them. At the time of the marriage the women starts wearing the ornaments and the man is tied with the sacred thread.

The points like why women wear ornaments and keep bindi are beyond the purview of this discourse.

So when both complete the Education (comprehensive education for the development of the individual and the society) the parents used to find the match by comparing the Horoscopes of the probable matches and in confirming the alliance by Horoscopes matching, Yoni matching is one of the matching that is mainly looked into. Yoni matching signifies the classification of the genetal organs of bride and groom as per sastra and it ensures a happy congress between the couple. Gana matching signifies a particular set of mental traits, and for any marriage at least 24 ganas should match, *i.e.*, should of the same count for the boy and girl.

Kanya Danam—offering of the daughter for the marriage.

Kanya means virgin girl (namely the bride). 'Daan' means giving away.

There are so many Daans or Dhanas advocated by the Hindu scriptures and of these Kanya Daan is stated to be the supreme daan. Hindu Dharma says one who is bestowed with the act of Kanya Daan or One who has the opportunity of making a Kanya Daan in his life is the beloved child of the Lord and he will never have rebirth.

Kanya Daan is an important part of the marriage ceremony in which the bride's parents give her away to the groom by entrusting her to the bridegroom. The officiating priest chants appropriate verses in Sanskrit.

The people in the audience (the public) is now notified that the parents have willingly expressed their wish and consent by requesting the groom to accept their daughter as his bride. As soon as the groom indicates his acceptance the marriage ceremony begins. The parents now bestow their blessings on both the bride and the groom and pray to the Lord to shower His choicest blessings on them.

From then the Veekshana is the right time for the bride and the groom to see each other. The parents of the bride now hands over their daughter to the parents of the groom by stating that "I have nurtured this child till this age and am handing over to you for the progeny and prosperity of your family. Consider her as your daughter and be the guide and philosopher for her till she lives with you".

The Grasping of the Hand. The process of the first physical contact between the bride and the groom starts.

The bride facing the East while the groom faces the West, the bridegroom takes the bride's hand...and says

"O Sarasvati, gracious one, rich in offspring, you whom we hymn first of all the Gods, may you prosper this marriage." "I seize your hand."

The Circumambulation of the Fire: All solemn rites and ceremonies commence with the performance of Homa (sacred fire ceremony) among the followers of Vedic religion. The idea is to begin all auspicious undertakings in an atmosphere of purity and spirituality. This atmosphere is created by the burning of fragrant herbs and ghee and by the recitation of suitable Mantras.

Now comes the Mangala Sutra Dharana that is the tying of the thread containing the marks of the Vishnu or Shiva in the neck of the bride by the groom. The Mangala Vadya is played at this time with vigour and bliss. Holy akhsatha, the unbroken rice mixed with turmeric powder, is poured on the heads of the groom and bride by all the visitors gathered at the marriage as a mark of their blessings and well wishes for the bride and groom to begin their new married life.

Asmarohana [The Treading on the Stone]: The bridegroom says the words while she stands up: "Come, beautiful one." And he lets her put the tip of the right foot on the stone, saying: "Come, step on the stone; be strong like a stone. Resist the enemies; overcome those who attack you."

Saptapadi [The Seven Steps]: The Sapthapadi or the walking of seven steps around the Agni signifies that the bride and groom go together in all the seven planes of consciousness in performing the dharma. The seven planes of the Consciousness are signified by the seven Vyahrithis of the Gayatri Mantra. Actually the union of bride and groom takes place only at the stage of Saptapadi and the process of the bride and groom becoming as the wife and husband is immediately begun from that time.

Then they walk around the fire, the bridegroom repeating:

"First now they bring to you in bridal procession this Surya, guiding her steps in circular motion. Return her now, O Agni, to her husband as rightful wife, with hope of children to come."

While the bride takes the seven steps to the northeast, the bridegroom sings the following verses:

"One step for Vigour, Two steps for Vitality, Three steps for Prosperity, Four steps for Happiness, Five steps for Cattle(Wealth), Six steps for Seasons, Seven steps for Friendship. To me be devoted."

After the seventh step he makes her remain where she is and says:

"With seven steps we become friends. Let me reach your friendship. Let me not be severed from your friendship. Let your friendship not be severed from me."

Then the entire rite is repeated twice more, beginning with the rite of the fried grain. At the fourth round she pours into the fire all the fried grain from the mouth of the winnowing basket saying: "To Bhaga swaha!"

Dhruvadarsana [Looking at the Polestar]: Dhruvadarsana or Arundhathi Darshanam is the showing of the Saptha Rishi Mandala and the star Arundhathi underneath the star of Vashistha.The significance is to remind the pair about their cosmic responsibilities they have to perform in the coming walks of life. These seven sages and their families are the originators of the Vedic Lore of the Hindus. In memoriam of these great sages we named the seven stars in the Great Bear constellation after their names. It is the Darshan of these Great Sages will remind the couple the heritage they have to carry and the Debt of the sages to be performed.

The groom shows her the polar star to the bride. The bride says that:

"You are firm and I see you. Be firm with me, O flourishing one! Brhaspati has given you to me, so live with me a hundred years bearing children by me, your husband."

Grihapravesam is the taking of the bride and the groom to the house of the groom. Sobhanamu is the Nuptials arranged by the parents of the bride in their residence first and in the residence of the groom next. This is the starting of the enjoyment of the joy of the sex as learned in the Gurukula by reading the Kama Sastra and implementing it in a socially acceptable way for the joy and the bliss and for the progeny of the race.

Gharbhadanamu is the act of sex for the progeny. This is set on the day that is neutral from the cosmic influences like the moons gravity and the suns gravity or other disturbances to create the foetus for the Jiva to enter in to the Womb of the mother to take the birth to perform his cycle of karma and to make the parents to fulfil the cycle of the karma.

Scientific Observations from the Ceremony: The dress pattern on all the Vedic Marriages is in conformity with the modern day scientific non infection dressing. The decoration with mango leaves or the performance of the home is in a way more advanced systems of the pollution control at a group level. The wearing of the ornaments at the ceremony of the marriage is in conformity with the Advanced Magnetic Resonance Preventive Medicine of the Present day Medical world.

This is the wisdom taught by Hindu dharmas and is dedicated to the lotus feet of all Sages who found the Dharma and this science of the marriage.

Muslim Wedding

Muslim wedding are celebrated on a grand scale in India. The wedding custom and rituals has come down from the Mughal rulers in the medieval India. Muslim families in India follow the traditional way of wedding. Indian Muslims mostly follow the same customs and rituals in Nikah, as followed by the Middle Eastern Muslims. Just like Hindu religion Muslim wedding is also divided into three parts the pre wedding celebration, main day celebration and post wedding celebration. And each celebration has its own significance and importance.

Pre-wedding Ceremonies

Mehndi Ceremony: The Mehndi ceremony is mainly held at the bride's place on the eve of the wedding ceremony or a few days before the wedding. It is mainly a ladies function where female friends, family members and relatives of the bride come together to apply turmeric paste to the bride to bring out the glow in her complexion. A mehndiwali or a relative applies mehndi on the hands and feet of the bride. While she applies mehndi to the bride the woman folk sings traditional song and dance to the tune of those songs. The event gives a festive touch to the celebration.

On this occasion the bride wears light colour clothes and dresses soberly. According to the custom the bride should not step out of the house for the next few days till her marriage. On mehendi function the bride's cousins applies a dot of mehndi on the palm of the groom. Other than the mehendi celebration there are some other ceremonies in both the bride and groom's house.

Main Day Ceremony: The wedding is normally held in the bride's place if not than it is celebrated at a common venue. On the main day the groom arrives with his family and friends at the wedding venue. This ritual is known as welcoming the baraat. And his guests are called baraati. A band of musicians also accompanies the baraati and the groom. The groom shares a drink of sherbet with the bride's brother. The bride's sisters play pranks and slap the guests playfully with batons made of flowers.

Nikah: The main wedding ceremony is called Nikah in Muslim religion. The wedding ceremony is normally conducted at the bride's place or at any common venue. A Maulvi or priest in the presence of close family members, friends and relatives, conducts the wedding rituals. In orthodox families the men and women are seated separately. The 'Walis' (the father of the bride and of the bridegroom) play a vital role in the wedding ceremony. The Maulvi reads selected verses from the Quran and the Nikah is complete after the Ijab-e-Qubul (proposal and acceptance).

The groom's side proposes and the bride's side conveys her consent. The mutual consent of the bride and groom is of very importance for the marriage to be legal. The Mehar is a compulsory amount of money given by the groom's family to the bride on the day of the wedding. It is a custom according to the rules laid down in Islam. The Nikahnaama is a document in which the marriage contract is registered. It contains a set of terms and conditions that must be followed by both the families, it also gives the bride the right to divorce her husband. The contract is legal only when the bridegroom, the bride, the Walis, and the Maulvi duly sign it. After the wedding ceremony is over the newly wedded bride and groom receives blessings from the elders and older women of the family and the guests pray for their happy married life.

Dinner, Prayers and Aarsimashaf: After the wedding a dinner party is organised for the guests and relatives. After the dinner, the newly wedded couple sits together for the first time. The Quran is placed between the couple and they are allowed to see each other only through mirrors.

Post-wedding Ceremonies

In the post wedding rituals there are the function of Rukshat where the bride's family bids farewell to her as she leaves her father's home and goes to her husband's house. It is a very emotional moment for the bride's family. The bride's father gives her hand to her husband and tells him to take care of her.

Welcoming the Bride: After the bride reaches her husband's house her mother-in-law welcomes her. The groom's mother holds the Quran above the head of her new daughter-in-law as she enters her new home for the first time after the wedding.

Chauthi: On Chauthi the bride visits her parent's home. It is the fourth day after the wedding, when she visits the home of her parents. She receives a grand welcome from her family members.

Valimah or Reception Ceremony: It is the reception given by the groom's family. The Valimah is a grand reception hosted by the groom's family after the Nikah. It is a fun and joyous occasion that brings together the two families. It is the good time to meet the friends and relatives of both the families. It builds a new bond and relation between the two families.

Christian Wedding

Normally all Christian wedding are celebrated in a Church. The friends and family members of the bride and the bridegroom attain the wedding celebration. Just like any other wedding in other religion Christian wedding is also celebrated over a couple of days. As there are pre wedding, wedding and post wedding rituals. An Anglo-Indian Christian bride traditionally wears a white gown in western style and the groom wears a suit. The wedding rituals are conducted along with the holy mass. Like in all Indian matrimonial rituals, this community too, has an interesting lecture with an emphasis on the sanctity of marriage given by the priest. Christian wedding rituals and customs are simple and easy to follow.

Among the main pre-wedding rituals there are functions like bridal shower, which is an informal hen-party hosted by the bride's female friends. It is mainly a female get together to celebrate the occasion. It is a fun filled function where games are played, they sing and dance the whole night. The friends and relatives shower gifts upon the bride. The bride serves a pink cake with a thimble hidden inside. According to tradition, the girl who gets the slice of cake with the thimble in it will be the next to marry.

Just like the bridal shower, which is an all girl's party a bachelor's party is also celebrated by the groom and his male friends. It s from the Bible. The priest then delivers the homily, with an emphasis on the sanctity of marriage. The next ritual is the blessing and the exchange of the wedding rings. The ceremony comes to an end with the final blessing of the priest. The guests, towards the end, shower their blessings on the newly-wedded couple. The last formality is the couple then signs the register and walk down aisle, arm in arm.

In the post wedding rituals like weddings in all Indian community Catholic weddings is followed by a reception for celebration the reception party is a grand affair where the newly-weds enter the venue and are welcomed by all with a shower of confetti.

They cut the wedding cake and feed each a bite of the first slice. The Toastmaster proposes a toast in honour of the couple. The reception is mostly celebrated with dance and dinner party. In many function a live band performs and everybody dances to the tune of the band. This is how most Christian weddings are celebrated.

Parsi Wedding

Pre-Wedding Rituals: Just like wedding rituals and customs of different communities, Parsi wedding traditions are spread over a couple of days. In Parsi wedding also the wedding celebration is divided into three parts pre wedding rituals, wedding day rituals and post wedding rituals. Among the pre wedding rituals or customs we have Madhavsaro, which is celebrated four days before the lagan, the families of the bride and groom each plant a young tree in a pot, amidst recitation of prayers by the family priest, and place this at the entrance of their homes. This is generally a mango plant and is treated as a symbol of fertility. The plant is watered every morning till the eighth day after the wedding and then transplanted elsewhere.

Adarni is the third day before the lagan, and it is celebrated as a day for gift exchanging. On this day the groom's family visits the bride's home to present her with all kinds of gifts like clothes, jewelry, etc. This is ritual of gifting the bride is known as Adarni. The relatives, neighbours and friends are invited for a traditional meal of sev and dahi, boiled eggs and bananas. The day before the wedding is called Supra nu Murat it is more like the mehendi and haldi ceremony of the Hindus.

In this ritual four married women are given a supra each, containing paan, supari, haldi, dates and a piece of coconut. While singing traditional songs, these supras are exchanged seven times among the women cross-wise, length-wise and breadth-wise. A fifth lady sits in the middle with a khalbatto and dry turmeric. Then a paste of it is applied by all to the groom and bride along with a showering of blessings.

Wedding Day Rituals: Nahan is the day of the lagan, on this day the staircase, doorway and gate is decorated with beautiful decorative designs of Rangoli. According to the Zorastrians the time immediately after sunset or very early in the morning is considered auspicious for marriage. For the marriage ceremony the bride dresses in her madhavate the white, ornate wedding saree given by her parents, while the groom wears the traditional Parsi dagli and feta a white kurta like garment and a black cap.

The Parsi lagan is called Achumichu, which takes place either at a baug or at an agiary (the fire temple). A stage is build up for the couple and before they step on it, the groom first, a ritual called achumichu is performed. The bride's mother takes a tray with a raw egg, supari, rice, coconut, dates and water and begins the ceremony with her son-in-law to be. In Ara antar ceremony the couple is made to sit facing each other with a cloth held between them, so they cannot see the other. Among the other main day rituals are chero bandhvanu, haath borvanu, etc.

Post-Wedding Rituals: In the post-wedding rituals the reception is held in a grand manner with varied menu of food, drink and music. The party is a whole night affair where all the guests have a lovely time. The menu mainly comprises of traditional Parsi dishes like Parsi bhonu like sarya (crisps), achaar-rotli (pickle and rotis), patra ni macchi (steamed fish), salli margi (chicken with potato crisps), lagan nu custard, pulao-dal and ice cream. The wedding ceremony ends with the couple being accompanied home by the bride's family and the achumichu being performed once again by the groom's mother for the well being of the couple.

Sikh Wedding

In a Sikh Indian wedding, the wedding ambiance is set a week before the wedding. There are various rituals, which are followed before and after the wedding. Shagun or engagement is the first ceremony to mark the beginning of the wedding celebration. On this occasion the two families exchange gifts to conform the engagement. Among the pre wedding rituals engagement is the occasion where both the families meet and the bride's father takes care of all the ceremonial activities on this day. Various auspicious items are required on this day that includes coconut, dry dates, sugar and money and these are sent to the groom's family.

It is also called the Tilak ceremony, which is performed by a bhaiji or preacher from the Gurudwara who first reads the hymn, offers a date to the groom and applies tilak on his forehead, marking the engagement. After the tilak ceremony, the groom's father sends gifts of clothes, sugar, coconut, rice, jewellery and henna to the bride. Similarly the bride's father also offers gifts to the groom and his family members. Another important pre-wedding ritual involves the bangle ceremony or the choora ceremony, which is held at the bride's place where the maternal uncle and aunt of the bride put white and red bangles on the bride's wrists. Light ornaments of beaten silver and gold called kalira are tied to the bangles.

Maiya is a pre wedding Sikh custom followed by the bride and the groom where both are not allowed to leave their house for few days before the wedding. Gana is another such ritual where an auspicious red thread is tied to the right wrist of the groom and the left wrist of the bride. It is regarded as a good omen for the bride and the groom and it protects them from ill omen. Vatna is a ritual celebrated a few days before the wedding ceremony where vatna a scented powder consisting of barley flour, turmeric and mustard oil is applied to their bodies to be followed by a ritual bath.

On the eve of the wedding, mehndi ceremony is celebrated when henna is applied on the hands and feet of the bride. Gharoli is another such pre wedding ritual, which is celebrated in the morning of the wedding day at groom's place in which the groom's sister-in law accompanied by other female relatives go to a nearby well or Gurudwara to fill an earthen pitcher or gharoli with water which is later used to bath the bridegroom.

The main day wedding ritual or ceremony includes Milni ceremony, which is celebrated at the groom's place where his sisters tie a sehera or floral veil to the boy's forehead and a garland of currency notes adorn his neck. On reaching the bride's house the milni ceremony is held with the elders of both families embracing and wishing each other. Shabads are sung and the ardaas recited as the procession enters the Gurudwara breakfast is served to the guests.

On the main wedding function the bride and the groom sit together to attend the Guru Granth Sahib Kirtan. The groom drapes a chunni draped by the bride's father one end held by groom, which is usually red, pink and orange in colour around his neck, the other end of which is held by the bride throughout the ceremony. The bhaiji of the Gurudwara recites the hymns from the Guru Granth Sahib, which are then sung and the bride and groom circle the Guru Granth Sahib. The bridegroom walks ahead of the bride with a sword in his hand. Relatives and friends garland the newly wedded couple and the marriage ceremony concludes with a grand feast.

Among the post-wedding rituals the vidaai or doli ceremony marks the end of the wedding celebration. It is a very emotional affair for the bride's family as she departs from her parent's house she throws back handful of rice over her shoulder, thereby wishing prosperity for her parents and family she leaves behind to start a new life with new dreams and aspirations.

INDIAN SOCIETY

People of India: India is a fascinating country where people of different communities and religions live together in unity. Indian Population is polygenetic and is an amazing amalgamation of various races and cultures. It is impossible to find out the exact origin of Indian People. The species known as Ramapithecus was found in the Siwalik foothills of north western Himalayas.

The species believed to be the first in the line of hominids (Human Family) lived some 14 million years ago. Researchers have found that a species resembling the Austrapithecus lived in India some 2 million years ago. Even this discovery leaves an evolutionary gap of as much as 12 million years since Ramapithecus.

There are diverse ethnic groups among the people of India. The 6 main ethnic groups are as follows.

1. Negrito
2. Proto-Australoids or Austrics
3. Mongoloids
4. Mediterranean or Dravidian
5. Western Brachycephals
6. Nordic Aryans

Negroids: The Negritos or the Brachycephalic (broad headed) from Africa were the earliest people to have come to India. They have survived in their original habitat in Andaman and Nicobar Islands. The Jarawas, Onges, Sentinelese and the Great Andamanese are some of the examples. Some hill tribes like Irulas, Kodars, Paniyans and Kurumbas are found in some patches in southern part of mainland India.

Pro-Australoids or Austrics: These groups were the next to come to India after the Negritos. They are people with wavy hair lavishly distributed all over their brown bodies, long headed with low foreheads and prominent eye ridges, noses with low and broad roots, thick jaws, large palates and teeth and small chins. The Austrics of India represent a race of medium height, dark complexion with long heads and rather flat noses but otherwise of regular features. Miscegenation with the earlier Negroids may be the reason for the dark or black pigmentation of the skin and flat noses.

The Austrics laid the foundation of Indian civilization. They cultivated rice and vegetables and made sugar from sugarcane. Now these people are found in some parts of India, Myanmar and the islands of South East Asia. Their languages have survived in the Central and Eastern India.

Mongoloids: These people are found in the northeastern part of India in the states of Assam, Nagaland, Mizoram, Meghalaya, Arunachal Pradesh, Manipur, and Tripura. They are also found in northern parts of West Bengal, Sikkim, and Laddakh. Generally they are people with yellow complexion, oblique eyes, high cheekbones, sparse hair and medium height.

Dravidians: These are the people of South India. They have been believed to come before the Aryans. They have different subgroups like the Paleo-Mediterranean, the true Mediterranean, and the Oriental Mediterranean. They appear to be people of the same stock as the peoples of Asia Minor and Crete and pre-Hellenic Aegean's of Greece. They are reputed to have built up the city civilization of the Indus Valley, whose remains have been found at Mohenjodaro and Harappa and other Indus cities.

Western Bracycephals: These include the Alpinoids, Dinarics and Armenoids. The Parsis and Kodavas also fall in this category. They are the broad-headed people living mainly on the western side of the country such as the Ganga Valley and the delta, parts of Kashmir, Kathiawar, Gujarat, Maharashtra, Karnataka and Tamil Nadu.

Nordics or the Indo-Aryans: This group was the last one to immigrate to India. They came to India somewhere between 2000 and 1500 B.C. They are now mainly found in the northern and central part of India.

FOOD HABIT

Indian food is different from rest of the world not only in taste but also in cooking methods. It reflects a perfect blend of various cultures and ages. Just like Indian culture, food in India has also been influenced by various civilizations, which have contributed their share in its overall development and the present form.

Foods of India are better known for its spiciness. Throughout India, be it North India or South India, spices are used generously in food. But one must not forget that every single spice used in Indian dishes carries some or the other nutritional as well as medicinal properties.

North Indian Food: Food in the North India, to begin with, Kashmiri cuisines reflect strong Central Asian influences. In Kashmir, mostly all the dishes are prepared around the main course of rice found abundantly in the beautiful valley. Another delicious item cooked here is the 'Saag' that is prepared with a green leafy vegetable known as the 'Hak'.

But on the other hand states like the Punjab, Haryana and Uttar Pradesh show high consumption of chapatis as staple food. Again, these chapatis are prepared with a variety of flours such as wheat, rice, maida, besan, etc. Besides chapatis other closely related breads baked in these regions include Tandoori, Rumaali and Naan, etc. However in the northern region impact of Mughlai food is quite obvious.

West Indian Food: In western India, the desert cuisine is famous for its unique taste and varieties of food. Rajasthan and Gujarat are the states that represent the dessert flavour of Indian food. Here an immense variety of dals and achars (pickles/preserves) is used that simply substitutes the relative lack of fresh vegetables in these areas.

In the states like Maharashtra, the food is usually a mix of both north as well as south cooking styles. Here people use both the rice and the wheat with same interest. Along the coastline of Mumbai a wide variety of fishes is available. Some of the delicious preparations include dishes like the Bombay Prawn and Pomfret.

In Goa, that is further down towards south, one can notice Portuguese influence in the cooking style as well as in the dishes. Some of the major dishes of this regiun are the sweet and sour Vindaloo, duck baffad, sorpotel and egg molie, etc.

East Indian Food: In the eastern India, the Bengali and Assamese styles of cooking are noticeable. The staple food of Bengalis is the yummy combination of rice and fish. Usually the Bengalis love eating varieties of fishes. A special way of preparing the delicacy known as 'Hilsa' is by wrapping it in the pumpkin leaf and then cooking it. Another unusual ingredient that is commonly used in the Bengali cooking is the 'Bamboo Shoot'. Various sweets prepared in this region, by using milk include the 'Roshogollas', 'Sandesh', 'Cham-cham' and many more.

South Indian Food: In the southern India, the states make great use of spices, fishes and coconuts, as most of them have coastal kitchens. In the foods of Tamil Nadu use of tamarind is frequently made in order to impart sourness to the dishes. It simply distinguishes the Tamil Food from other cuisines.

The cooking style of Andhra Pradesh is supposed to make excessive use of chilies, which is obviously to improve the taste of the dishes.

In Kerala, some of the delicious dishes are the lamb stew and appams, Malabar fried prawns, Idlis, Dosas, fish molie and rice puttu. Another famous item of this region is the sweetened coconut milk. Yet another dish is Puttu, which is glutinous rice powder steamed like a pudding in a bamboo shoot.

Indian food is as varied as anything else in that country; there is no easy definition of an "Indian meal". Indian food is often thought of as very spicy, but there are some simple breads, sweet deserts, and milder 'one-pot dishes' that defy the norm.

Many Indians are vegetarian, but then, some are not. There are regional specialities, different ways to serve the meal, and staple ingredients in each state. This combines to create a diverse cuisine that never becomes boring.

Breakfast

Chappathi/Roti: Measure and sieve whole wheat flour and salt into a vessel. Slowly add three-fourths cup of water. Mix well. Knead into medium soft dough. Add more water if required. Cover the vessel and leave it for fifteen minutes. Divide into 14 equal portions. Make them into balls. Roll them out into six-inch rounds on a board by adding flour occasionally (So that they do not stick to the board). Cook on a griddle or a non-stick pan for about half a minute. Turn and cook on the other side for fifteen seconds. Cook till puffed and cooked on both sides. Turn over and press gently with a spatula or a cloth to puff up the chappathi/roti. Serve hot, topped with cooking oil or ghee (optional).

Dosa: On a flat frying pan/skillet, the batter has to be poured and spread as a thin round. Add a teaspoon of cooking oil/ghee/butter to both the sides of the Dosa. When it turns golden brown, its ready to be taken off the frying pan and ready to serve too. Different types of Dosas can be made. The thinner and crispier the dosa, the better it tastes! Masala Dosa is another option.

Idli: Grind the ingredients separately into a fine paste by adding sufficient water. Add salt to taste and blend the dough well and keep it overnight for fermentation. Next morning once again, mix the dough with a spoon and pour in scoops on the Idli tray and steam it for five minutes.

Poori: Divide into small balls about golf-ball size, and roll out into 6" rounds with a roller, on an oiled board. Heat vegetable oil in a work or saucepan. Add a little salt to the oil to keep it from smoking. Fry the puri one at a time, holding them under the oil on the first side until they puff. Turn and fry till light brown; drain.

Eating Styles: Indian food is often eaten with the hands, however, this custom is guided by some basic rules. For instance, it is considered impolite to allow the food to pass the first joint of the fingers. The fingers should never touch the mouth directly. In addition, only the right hand may be used in eating. Since most Indian meals include a kind of flatbread that is traditionally used to scoop or roll vegetables or rice. A spoon is provided for soup, but the bread may even be used to eat that! Meat, if served, may be eaten with a knife and fork, but it will more often be served pre-cut, so it may be easily managed by the fingers. Indians usually eat their largest meal at mid-day, preferring to end with a light evening meal. People either bring their mid-day meal to work or use a lunch packing service called "tiffin" that delivers traditional hot meals to their workplace. If possible, many Indians like to come home for the mid-day meal.

Regional Food

Punjabi: Possibly the most famous Punjabi contribution to Indian food is the tandoori style of cooking. This method uses large earthen ovens that are heated to high temperatures using coal fires. Once hot, many types of meat, breads, or vegetable dishes may be cooked inside. This method gives food a distinctive flavour and seals in the aroma of the item. Many people in Punjab eat some meat. Thus, the state has developed many chicken and lamb dishes that are coated in spicy onion and mustard or sweet cream sauces. This is thought to be an influence of the Mughals during their time in India. Milk products such as yoghurt lassis and fresh cheeses are also an important part of the Punjabi diet, as are pulses and wheat.

Gujarati: Gujarati food is mainly vegetarian. The staple grain of the area is millet, with wheat as a secondary grain. Other products include peanuts, sesame, and many types of vegetables. Pulses are very important in this region as a source of protein, whether as a side dish or made into soups called dahls, as the majority of the population does not eat meat.

Gujarati food is usually served as a "thali" meal, meaning that all items are served at once on a large plate. A traditional thali includes two vegetables cooked with spices, dahl, a flatbread, rice, pulses, and a sweet. There are also simple meals of mild rice and lentils known as "khichdi", served with a lightly spiced buttermilk or yoghurt soup called "kadhi".

Maharashtrian: In contrast to the mainly vegetarian Gujarati food, Maharashtrians enjoy eating meat and fish with their meals. Fish may be stuffed or lightly fried, and meat is braised and spiced with sweet and sour ingredients. Peanuts and cashew nuts are widely used, as is the distinctive kokum berry, a sweet deep purple item with a slightly tangy taste. On the coast, people eat crab, prawns, and shellfish. Maharashtrians also popularised fried rice-flour balls called "vada" (now eaten throughout the country) and a type of thin pancake called amboli made of semolina, urad dal, and fermented rice. A common sweet dish is puran poli, a flatbread stuffed with gram flour, brown sugar, and honey.

Bengali: Bengal is known for its fish and its sweets. Located on the eastern coast of India, fish has become a staple of the Bengali diet. It may be sauted in yoghurt or marinated in Bengal's famous spice mixture. This region uses five basic spices, known collectively as "pachphoron". They are: aniseed, cumin seed, black cumin seed, mustard, and fenugreek. Even the oil that is used is mustard oil.

Many sweets eaten all over India originated in Bengal. Most are milk or cottage cheese based, including rasgolla, gulab jamun, and sundesh. Bengali sweets are often served with a sticky sweet syrup, and may even be found ending a traditional Gujarati or Goan meal.

Kerela, Karnataka, and the South: Kerela food, from southern India, is traditionally served on a large banana leaf. The method is still used for feasts today. The staple food of southern India is rice. Different preparations of the grain may even be eaten for breakfast. The other staple is the coconut. Coconut is made into chutney, served as a refreshing desert, and incorporated into vegetable or fish dishes as a flavoring. This often gives Kerela food a surprising flavour that mixes sweetness with spices.

One can see the uses of these ingredients in many of the famous dishes of the south. For example, rice flour and urad flour are made into a batter and steamed to form rice cakes called "idli", eaten with a type of stew made of pulses and vegetables called "sambhar". Another dish, "appam", is a thin crepe made with rice flour and the sap of the cocomut palm. It is eaten with the "sambhar" mentioned above.

Snack Food: Indian snacks may be salty, spicy, or sweet. Street vendors sell many different kinds, including warm dishes.

Sometimes, they are substantial enough to serve as a light meal. The "pav bhaji" is a patty made of mixed vegetables that have been mashed and shallow fried and then served on a slice of bread. Another popular snack throughout the country is "bhel", a mixture of puffed rice, crunchy chickpea flour chips, onions, tomato, green peppers, and tamarind chutney.

"Pani puri" is small, hollow breads stuffed with a bit of potato, onion, or chickpea and topped with a "pani" of seasoned water. Nuts are another common choice, but they are roasted with a hot spice blend of turmeric, paparika, and cumin powder. Often a little lemon juice is squeezed on top.

Drinks: The most common drink in India is tea. This is prepared with milk, sugar, and a blend of ginger, nutmeg, cinnamon, cloves, and cardamom. Most people will drink this tea, called "chai" with breakfast and in the late afternoon. In fact, it may be served at any time and is a popular refreshment for guests.

An example of a common cold Indian drink is "lassi", which is a yoghurt or buttermilk drink that is sweetened and flavored with rose, mango, or served plain.

Tea and Coffee: It is one of the favorites of Indians across the country. Be it Railway Station, Airports, Small Restaurants, you will always find people having Tea and Coffee. Tea is relatively more popular in North whereas Coffee is more popular in South.

Water: Water is safe and chlorinated in large cities but it is always suggest carrying one bottle of mineral water with you. Mineral Water is normally safe to drink & is easily available throughout India.

Soft Drinks: There is also good number of options for Soft Drinks in India. Majors like Coke and Pepsi offer various brands and tastes.

Juices and Other Drinks: Popular juices like Apple and Orange juices are easily available & a safe alternate to normal water. Coconut Milk is also a popular drink in India.

Alcoholic Drinks: Alcohol is normally expensive in India. Indian Beers are also very popular as alcoholic drinks and normally being sold for Rs. 25 to 160 depending upon the Restaurant and its facilities. Indian imitations of popular brands are also available but it is advisable to stick to your brand.

INDIAN COSTUMES

India is a land of colour and diverse cultures, so obvious in the varied dresses that adorn its people. Indian dressing styles are marked by many variations, both religious and regional with a wide choice of textures and styles. The many hued saris draped gracefully in different styles, brightly mirrored cholis, colorful lehangas and the traditional salwar-kameez have all fascinated the traveller to India.

The sari, simple, understated yet supremely elegant is increasingly becoming a fashion statement in urban India.

One of the most commonly worn traditional dresses, it is essentially a rectangular cloth measuring about 6 yards, though in Maharashtra, women wear the nine yard sari which is passed through the legs and tucked in at the back. The sari comes in a profusion of colours, textures and designs, determined largely by the region. There are several ways of draping a sari, which is first wound around the waist, before being pleated seven or eight times at the centre and tucked into the waistband. These pleats are called the patli. The remaining sari, called the pallu is then pleated again and draped across the left shoulder to fall gracefully behind. There are regional variations, like in Gujarat, the pallu comes from the back, and drapes across the front over the right shoulder. The sari is worn with a tight-fitting choli or blouse. The style and length of the choli varies according to fashion trends and from region to region.

The traditional dress for women in Rajasthan and Gujarat is the lehenga choli or ghagra choli. These cholis are brightly embroidered, waist-length bare-backed blouses. Ghagras or lehengas are gathered ankle-length skirts secured around the waist. The attire is completed by a veil-cloth called odhni or dupatta draped across the neck or over the head. The lehenga-choli or ghagra choli is extremely colourful, adding verve and colour to the surrounding landscapes. Tribal women in theses area bedeck themselves from head to toe with chunky silver jewellery. Young girls in south India wear a half saree, somewhat similar to a lehenga choli. The only difference is that the dupatta is wound across the waist and draped across the left shoulder like the saree pallu.

A popular, comfortable and convenient dress is the salwar kameez or churidar kurta. This was traditonally the dress worn in Punjab, but is now worn almost everywhere, particularly among the younger generations. The kameez or the kurta is a knee-length flowing tunic worn over a salwar or churidar. A salwar is a pyjama-like trouser which tapers slightly towards the ankles, while the churidar is a tight-fitting trouser which gathers at the ankles. These gathers at the ankles look like bangles (churis) and hence the name. A dupatta generally completes the ensemble.

Western dressing styles are increasingly gaining popularity among the urban youth of both sexes, but women largely restrict themselves to fashion trends within Indian dressing mores. Young girls wear skirts and dresses, particularly to schools. After adolescence, and almost certainly after marriage, women are expected to wear traditional Indian clothing. This trend is changing with more women entering the urban work force, but this is confined to sections of society that are highly exposed to international lifestyles. Men are considerably less traditional when it comes to dressing.

In India, as elsewhere, accessories are an integral part of the ritual of dressing. The world over, Indian women are associated with the 'dot' in the middle of their forehead, called Kum Kum or bindi. Traditionally round, the bindi is now available in various colours, shapes and sizes. A bindi was traditionally a sign of marriage, or in some states, was worn as soon a s a girl reached young adulthood. Today it is for the most part an adornment. Vermilion or sindoor applied at the parting of the hair indicates a married woman.

A traditional Indian woman is rarely seen without jewellery. A mangal-sutra, a necklace made with black and gold beads is considered sacred, and in many areas is always worn by a married woman. Many women, particularly in the rural areas of Rajasthan, Maharashtra and Gujarat wear ornately crafted nose-rings. Gold, silver or colourful glass bangles are another favourite, dating from the tradition of never having your hands bare. Women in Rajasthan wear bangles that go all the way to their shoulders. Indian women generally have their ears pierced, and commonly sport ear-rings.

Men are considerably less traditional when it comes to dressing. In urban areas, they have adapted to a western style of dressing. In villages men generally wear kurtas, a knee length shirt-styled tunic, with lungis, dhotis or pyjamas. The lungi originated in the south but is now worn all over india. It is a piece of cloth wrapped around the waist. A dhoti is longer than a lungi, has sari style pleats and is draped through the legs.

In states like Rajasthan, Gujarat, Punjab and Maharashtra men wear a safa or turban on their heads. Elsewhere too, various kinds of topis are it is a long scarf which is wound round the head in different ways. The Pathani suit is very similar to the salwar-kameez and is generally worn by men in north India. The Achkan is a long collarless jacket worn over a churidar for formal occasions.

THE FAMILY CUSTOMS

Family is important in India, and is what their life is centred around. It is common for several generations to live in the same house as an extended family. When a woman marries, she leaves her birth family, many times without seeing them again, and goes to her husband's village and becomes part of his family.

There is significant discrimination toward girls and women. While young girls are expected to help with the women's work (which consists of fetching water, preparing meals, cleaning, and caring for animals) as well as care for their younger siblings; boys have it much easier. They may be required to herd goats and other animals to and from the fields, but in general have it much easier than their female counterparts and this discrimination doesn't end with adulthood.

A simple draped cloth is still the basic attire for many Indians. The women wear a sari, which is worn with a blouse underneath, with the material ranging from cotton to silk. Men generally wear a dhoti, which can be worn full length or as "pants" depending on the region. In northern India, western clothing has replaced that of the traditional for men, while women still wear saris or other Indian styles of dress. In rare cases women will wear slacks and blouses, but that is generally among the elite.

Clothing: To the foreign traveler, one of the powerful attractions in India is the colourful and diversified attire of its people. The silk saris, brightly mirrored cholis, colourful lehangas and the traditional salwar-kameez have fascinated many a traveler over the centuries.

Attire for Women: For a single length of material, the sari must be the most versatile garment in existence. It is only one of the many traditional garments worn by women, yet it has somehow become the national dress of Indian women. A sari is a rectangular piece of cloth which is five to six yards in length. The style, colour and texture of this cloth vary and it might be made from cotton, silk or one of the several man-made materials. The sari has an ageless charm since it is not cut or tailored for a particular size. This garment can fit any size and if worn properly can accentuate or conceal. This supremely graceful attire can also be worn in several ways and its manner of wearing as well as its colour and texture are indicative of the status, age, occupation, region and religion of a woman.

The tightly fitted, short blouse worn under a sari is a choli. The choli evolved as a form of clothing in 10th century AD and the first cholis were only front covering; the back was always bare. Bodices of this type are still common in the state of Rajasthan.

Apart from the choli, women in Rajasthan wear a form of pleated skirt known as the ghagra or lehanga. This skirt is secured at the waist and leaves the back and midriff bare. The heads are however covered by a length of fine cotton known as orhni or dupatta.

Another popular attire of women in India is the salwar-kameez. This dress evolved as a comfortable and respectable garment for women in Kashmir and Punjab, but is now immensely popular in all regions of India. Salwars are pajama-like trousers drawn tightly in at the waist and the ankles. Over the salwars, women wear a long and loose tunic known as a kameez. One might occasionally come across women wearing a churidar instead of a salwar. A churidar is similar to the salwar but is tighter fitting at the hips, thighs and ankles. Over this, one might wear a collarless or mandarin-collar tunic called a kurta.

Attire for Men: Though the majority of Indian women wear traditional costumes, the men in India can be found in more conventional western clothing. Shirts and trousers are worn by men from all regions in India. However, men in villages are still more comfortable in traditional attire like kurtas, lungis, dhotis and pyjamas.

The traditional lungi originated in the south and today it is worn by men and women alike. It is simply a short length of material worn around the thighs rather like a sarong. A dhoti is a longer lungi but with an additional length of material pulled up between the legs. Pyjama-like trousers worn by the villagers are known as the lenga.

Indian dressing styles are marked by many variations, both religious and regional and one is likely to witness a plethora of colours, textures and styles in garments worn by the Indians.

VARNA SYSTEM IN HINDU RELIGION

The Hindus have Varna System. It is not at all caste-equivalent. It simply indicates a social division based on Gunas There exists all over the world one sort of division or the other in a society, which is so inevitable for social growth and prosperity. Each individual is possessed of a particular ability by nature.

One may well perform a physical labour, another may be more of a thinker and some may be artistic some inclined to technology, music. Medicine, trade, industry or any other material or spiritual activity. The Lord speaking on action and inaction in Geeta (IV-13) says,'the four Varnas have been created by Him according to differentiation of Gunas and Karmas.' These Varnas are 1-Brahman; 2-Kshatriya; 3-Vaishya; and 4-Sudra.

Varna means different shades of texture or colour. They represent mental temper. There are three Gunas—Sattva, Rajas and Tamas. Sattva is white, Rajas red and Tamas black. These in combination of various proportions constitute the group or class of people all over the world with temperamental differences.

The above classification is based on this assumption. In continuation, Veda Vyasa says in the same couplet, 'by the differentiation of the mental quality and physical action of the people.' It is clear that the type of ones action, the quality of ego, the colour of knowledge, the texture of ones understanding, the temper of fortitude and the brilliance of ones happiness defines ones Varna. Not by birth a man becomes Brahman but by cultivating noble thoughts and good intentions of service alone, one can ever aspire to Brahman hood.

The Brahman is generally Sattvik. Sama and Dama are his valuable assets. He is serene and self-controlled and is possessed of the quality of austerity. (Tapas) He has purity, uprightness and forbearance. He has a will to acquire knowledge (Jnan), Vigyan (Wisdom) and faith.

The Kshatriya is a warrior class, powerful of physique and might. They are possessed of more of Rajas Guna with base of Sattva. They have a duty to protect the Dharma and the people. They are bold, alert and full of fortitude, generosity. discipline and modesty along with masterly behaviour mingled with Ishvar Bhava (Love of God).

The Vaishya class is a trader class and prefers business of all kinds. It is possessed of Raj Guna mixed with Tamas. They deal with wealth and gold and strive for material prosperity of the self as well as of the people in general. The Sudras are working class people, artisans and craftsmen. They are physically strong and hard working. They are possessed of Tamas with a base of Rajas. Really speaking, Sudra class is indispensable to society as they are like a spiral chord on which rests the social structure.

Thus it is clear that the whole Varna System stood on the basis of Gunas and karmas of the individual. It has nothing to do with birth. To quote Mahabharata, the serpent god asked Yudhisthir to tell him the virtues of the caste. He says that those Brahmans who were fond of personal pleasures, prone to violence, had forsaken their duties and were red limbo, fell into the category of Kshatriya. Those Brahmans who derived their livelihood from kine, who were yellow and sub-divided by agriculture and who neglected to practice their duties, fell into the category of Vaishyas. Those Brahmans who were addicted to mischief and falsehood and were covetous, lived by all kinds of works and fell from purity and were black went to the condition of Sudra. As a conclusion, the serpent god says that the man in which the marks of a Sudra are not found is no Sudra, whereas while a Brahman who acts so is not a Brahman and may be called a Sudra. It is clear that the world being the projection of Brahma is therefore Brahma-roopa and these castes came up later as a creation of man in society. Therefore it stands for modification and change according to times.

The Intent of Varna System

The various stratification of Varna system was meant to settle the Hindu life and regulate the society for a united action. Every society in the world has some form of groups that works for the common cause of social progress and general prosperity. In the various spheres of life, cultural, spiritual, religious, economic, political and social, medical, science and technology and even unskilled workers, there are groups united differently to work for the social cause of all the people.

In Hinduism, this division is called Varna System. Each Varna has its social purpose, its own code, norms of behaviour and keeps its independent identity. Still each part remains an integral part of the whole. The whole is always present in the part and the part is ever a part of the whole.

This is the spirit behind the creation of Varna System. The four Varnas represented the people of wisdom, of action, of compassion and loving feelings, and of service to people. It was not intended to be hereditary and connected with birth. and therefore free interchange and intermixing was liberally permitted.

It is indeed unfortunate that the Varna System came to be connected with the Caste System. We can not know how and why and when it so happened. It grew up with a sort of spiritual monopoly of a certain group bent upon its material prosperity. It established the class of Brahman by birth to safeguard their posterity. It is they who created and developed the ideas of inferiority and superiority among the people.

This led to discrimination and distinction between various groups of occupations and the degradation of society began and reached so low as there came out people such as untouchables and pariahs. Thus the Varna turned Caste System brought about social degradation and downfall dividing people as low and high and the lowest. The Varna System, so sound and healthy and perfect came to such a pitiable state. It needs a reconstitution at this stage.

Conclusion: India is a developing nation. It has a responsibility to safeguard the rights of people as enshrined in the Constitution, irrespective of considerations of caste, creed, colour or sex. It is the need of the day that the Hindu scriptures be thrown open to all people of caste and sex so that they may have right understanding of their faith It may lead to the fall of the man-made Caste System like a sand hill. When the boundaries of the world are vanishing and there is open mixing of people and ideas, there has to be a ready flow of crossovers among the people as in the past. The watertight compartments only stink. The Hindu society has to be wellknit for the good of the world.

It is a fact that the Buddhists discarded the Vedas to preach against Caste System; Kabir followed the same path of denouncing the Hindu scriptures while opposing the Casts System. A proper understanding of scriptures can remove the ignorance and illusion. Gandhi and Aurobindo favoured Varna System though opposed Caste System. Swami Dayananda with authority on Vedas declared that Vedas do not mention about Caste System and opposed caste system tooth and nail while defending the scriptures. There is nothing in the scriptures to justify the caste division, only the Varna System exists as an integral part of the whole society. It is not the Caste System at all.

There are people in large majority who realise that the most oppressed people today called as Sudra were really a great adherent of Hinduism. In the Buddhist dominated era, they did not change their religion though the call was in their favour. During the terror rule of Islam for conversion, they did not convert and suffered from the rulers as well as from their own people who called them by many abusive names such as Sudra, Chamar. Bhangi. Harijan. Achuta or untouchables and even today remain bracketed in schedule caste and schedule tribes. They had opportunity to convert and be saved from humiliations and insults but they preferred to stay as Hindus and suffer as Hindus.

It is high time we get rid of such abuses and grant same and equal rights to these religious heroes as are enjoyed by the others in the Hindu society. Are they not a part of the whole and is the whole an invalid one? No, we have to restore their dignity as in the Vedic days. We have to treat them as a part of either Brahman class or as Kshatriya class to which they really belong. The ancestors of Raiyadas were Chanvar Kshatriyas and so are others. Restore them to their past glory and while doing so do not forget to undo what we have done by granting them the prevalent privileges intact for their growth without any restriction. We have to do it. No one else can do it. Do it now and here for unity of Hindu life and religion as we have a duty to rescue the present world from terror, chaos. disbelief and confusion. It is only the Hindu philosophy of unity in Diversity that can bring relief to the confused masses of humanity today.

Indian Caste System

A Graver intellectual confusion than that caused by the non-translation of the word Caste there has seldom been. The assumed impossibility of finding an equivalent for the idea in English has led to the belief that there is something mysterious and unprecedented in the institution. People become bewildered as to whether it is a religious or a social obligation. Every one demands of the reformer a conflict with it. The whole question grows obscure and irritating.

Yet all this time we have had an exact synonym for the word, and the parallel is the closer since our word connotes the same debatable borderland between morals and good taste. Caste ought to stand translated as honour. With Oriental quaintness, it is true, India has given a certain rigidity to this idea, but her analysis of the thing itself is as profound as it is acute

Our conduct is commonly governed far more by social habit than by considerations of right and wrong. When the tide of the ethical struggle has once set in over some matter, we may regard ourselves as already half-lost. Why are my friend's open letters absolutely safe in my presence, though I am longing for the information they convey? Why can money given for one purpose not be used for another, when all the canons of common sense and expediency urge that it should? Who will confess to an effort in speaking the truth at any cost whatever? Why, when I am annoyed, do I not express myself in the language of Billingsgate? To each of which questions one would reply, somewhat haughtily, that the point was one of honour, or, that such happened to be the custom of one's class.

Yet if we examine into the sanction which honour can invoke there is nothing beyond a rare exercise of the power of ostracism. The Church excommunicates, the law imprisons, but society merely "cuts" the offender in the street. Yet which of these three inflicts the deepest wound? It is as true of London as of Benaras that caste-law is the last and finest that controls a man. For it comes into operation at that precise point where tribunals fail. It takes cognisance of offences for which no judge could inflict penalties.

It raises standards and demands virtues that every man will interpret according to the stringency of his pride, and yet that no one can feel himself to have wholly fulfilled. And it does all this without once permitting the sensation of merit. Having done all, one remains an unprofitable servant. For no one would count the punctual discharge of debts (all debts are debts of honour), the hauteur that brooks no stain upon the name, and the self-respect that builds the whole ethical code upon itself, as religious observances. These things were due, we say, to our birth or blood, or position before men.

It is true that their non-fulfillment would leave a stain upon the conscience, and it is also true that the attempt to work out the obligations of honour must be the immediate test of the sincerity of one who proposes to lead a life of greater devotion and earnestness than common. Still, caste is not the same thing as personal piety and perhaps for this reason complete renunciation of its claims and benefits is essential in India to the monastic life.

There is another point about our Western conception of noblesse oblige. Few as the persons may be who could formulate their sentiment; the fact pervades the whole of the social area. Each class has its own honour. If honourable employers feel compelled to think of the comfort of their workers, honourable servants feel equally compelled to keep their lips shut on their masters' affairs, and either responds to an appeal in the name of his ideal. The priest may find the honour of his profession in conflict with that of the detective, but all the world will uphold the faithfulness of both.

The efficient realisation of his ideals by the schoolmaster will involve an occasional pardon, even of a grave offence, if he conceives forgiveness to be the best formative influence which at the moment he can command. The very same effort in the merchant will require a distribution of punishment that is rigorous and just, since order, integrity, and unfailing promptitude—not the development of human character—are his ends. Thus every man, in every critical act of his life, calls silently for the judgment of his peers and refuses all other.

The weaknesses of caste everywhere are manifold. For society, like the individual, is always apt to insist upon the tithing of mint and rue, and to neglect the weightier matters of the law. But it is not usually the martyr who marks its worst failure. He is the white dove cast forth by crows, that is, a member of a higher tried by consensus of the lower castes. We have here a case of government usurping the functions of society, much as if the headmaster should exercise authority in a dispute among boys. For it is essential to the very idea of honour that every caste should be autonomous.

The true failure of caste occurs whenever it establishes such an ascendancy of social opinion over the individual's conscience that his power of advance is impeded and he becomes less of a man, or less really beneficent socially, by remaining more of a gentleman—a state of things which is not uncommon among ourselves. For we may postulate that all ideals are helpful only in so far as they subserve a man's manhood and freedom, and destructive the instant they render him less able to express his own inmost will. It is he; therefore, who ought to have been a martyr and chose ease who is the true caste victim, not the hero of an auto-da-fe.

That this is a real danger we all know. What Protestant has never exalted the creed of his sect over freedom of thought? What Catholic has never put comfort above spirituality? What politician has not preferred party above principle? What student of science has never been prejudiced against new truth? And if we look without, where do we not see the mere breaker of conventionality treated as outside brotherhood? Where do we not find persons conforming to usages that displease them, merely because they would be inconvenient to dispute?

A certain sweeping justification of such facts may be urged, inasmuch as there are circumstances under which the cohesion of the group is well worth the sacrifice of the liberty of a few individuals. And the habitual outrage of custom without reason is perhaps rightly held to be as anti-social as any felony. In the last resort, however, social pressure must be held in bounds, for nothing should interfere with a man's right to try himself, or sap the roots of his independence. And society is a vague and irresponsible magistrate, with so little illumination as to his own purposes and tendencies that he frequently mistakes the pioneers of his march for deserters and orders the stoning of prophets, whose sepulchers and monuments will be erected by his children.

The question of the inner trend or intention of the social movement must form the law in whose name all doubtful cases are tried. And, while it is never easy to determine the point accurately for one's own people, in the case of the Hindu race the supreme purpose of their past evolution is quite apparent. Even a cursory reading of the Laws of Manu displays Indian society as united in a great cooperation for the preservation of the ancient race-treasure of Sanskrit literature. The feeling must have grown up when the Vedas alone required conserving, and the families entrusted with various portions were encouraged to become in all ways dependent on the community, that every energy might be devoted to the task in hand. This is the real meaning of prostration at the feet of Brahmans, of the great merit acquired by feeding them, and of the terror of the crime of killing one. It is not the man; it is race-culture that is destroyed by such an act.

As ages went on and the Upanishads and other things were added to the store, that which was hitherto memorised became entrusted to writing. The Vedas became Scriptures—and now the method, of psychology, of astronomy, of mathematics, made themselves felt as integral parts of the Aryan treasure, in common with Sanskrit literature. This widened the conception of culture without liberalising the social bearings of the question, and the Brahman caste continued to be recognised as the natural guardians of all learning, the old religious compositions being still regarded as the type. If we ask how it happened that the Aryan folk became so early conscious of their responsibility in the matter of Sanskrit letters, there can be only one answer. They found themselves in the presence of other and unlearned races. This point brings us to the question of the origin of strongly differentiated castes in general. In its nature caste is, as we have seen, honour; that is to say, an ideal sentiment by whose means society spontaneously protects itself from some danger against which it is otherwise defenceless.

For instance, life in Texas having been for many years dependent on the possession of horses, and safeguards against the horse-thief being few and difficult, he came to be the object of unprecedented social abhorrence. Horse-stealing was the last crime a lost soul would stoop to. In a similar way, as some think, may have grown up the Indian feeling about cow-killing. If the cattle, in time of stress, were killed for food, agriculture would be unable to take a new start, and so a people accustomed to eat beef grasped the situation perhaps, and renounced the practice. But since these two sentiments pervade whole nations, they are not exactly what we are accustomed to think of as caste, inasmuch as in the latter there is a distinct gradation of rank connected with the sentiment.

In the term "blackleg" applied by trade unionists to competing forms of labour, we have an instance of the kind we want. Here we have an occupational group giving birth immediately to the ideal which is necessary to its safety. Throughout the worlds of love, of war, and of work, indeed, honour is an instinct of the very greatest potency. How few men, after all, desert to an enemy as spies! How strong is the feeling of class-obligation amongst servants and working men! This element is very evident in the Indian industrial castes, which are often simply hereditary trade-unions. No Englishman is so powerful, nor is any Hindu so hungry, that one man could be bribed to take up the trade of another. Nothing would induce the dairyman, for instance, to take charge of a horse, or a laundryman to assist the household.

But the very strongest, and perhaps also ugliest, of all possible roots of caste is the sense of race, the caste of blood. We have an instance of this in the animosity that divides white men from negroes in the United States, and we have other instances, less talked of, all up and down our vast British possessions. There is probably no other emotion so inhuman which receives such universal sympathy as this. For it is fundamentally the physical instinct of a vigorous type to protect itself from fusion. And both sides participate in the revulsion. Here we have the secret of rigid caste, for the only rigid caste is hereditary, and of hereditary caste the essential characteristic is the refusal of intermarriage.

Granting, then, what could not well be denied, that the Aryan forefathers found themselves in India face to face with inferior and aboriginal races, what may we gather, from the nature of the caste system today, to have been the elements of the problem, as they more or less clearly perceived it?

Those elements we may infer to have been four in number:

1. They desired above all things to preserve the honour of their daughters from marriage with lower and savage peoples. Exclusion from marriage with any but one's own caste became the rigorous rule, the penalty fell on the father and the family that permitted a woman to go unguarded on this head. To this day, if a son marry beneath caste he degrades himself; but if a daughter be wrongly given, the whole family becomes out-casted.
2. They seem to have desired to preserve the aboriginal races, on the one hand from extermination, and on the other from slavery of the person two solutions which seemed later the only alternatives to Aryan persons in

a similar position! Those aborigines, therefore, who became dependent on the Aryan population, had their definite place assigned them in the scale of labour, and their occupations were secured to them by the contempt of the superior race.

We must not forget, in the apparent harshness of this convention, its large factor of hygienic caution. The aborigines were often carrion-eaters, and always uncleanly in comparison with their neighbours. It was natural enough, therefore, that there should be a refusal to drink the same water, and so on.

On the other hand, it is one of the mistakes of caste everywhere, that it institutionalises and perpetuates an inequality which might have been minimised. But we must not forget, in the case of the Indian system, the two greater evils which were avoided altogether.

3. The Aryans realised very clearly that it was not only their race but also their civilization that must be maintained in its purity. The word Aryan implies one acquainted with the processes of agriculture, an earer of the ground, to use an Elizabethan word—accustomed therefore to a fixed and industrialised mode of living, evidently in contrast to others who were not.

Fire and the processes of cooking and eating food are easily distinguished as the core of the Personal life and establishment in a climate where habits can at any time be made so simple as in India. It is these that can never be dispensed with, though they may be arranged for to-night in a palace, and tomorrow in the jungle under a tree.

In view, then, of the necessity of safeguarding the system of manners grew up the restrictions against eating with those of lower caste, or allowing them to touch the food and wants of their betters. The fact that the Aryan could eat food cooked by Aryan hands alone implied that the strictest preliminaries of bathing had been complied with.

By a continuous crystallisation, all caste laws—from being the enunciation of broad canons of refinement as between Aryan and non-Aryan—came to be the regular caste-barriers between one class and another of the same race. In this way they lost their invidious character. It is undeniable that this caste of the kitchen, so wittily named "don't touchism" by a modern Hindu leader, lends itself to abuse and becomes an instrument of petty persecution more readily than the intermarriage laws. Some of the saddest instances of caste-failure have occurred here. Nevertheless, the original intention remains clear and true, and is by no means completely obscured, even with the lapse of ages.

4. It was, however, in their perception of the fourth element of the problem that the early Aryans triumphantly solved the riddle of Humanity. They seem to have seen clearly that amongst the aborigines of India themselves were many degrees of social development already existent, and that these must be preserved and encouraged to progress.

From such a comprehension of the situation sprang the long and still growing graduation of non-Aryan castes, some of which have established themselves in the course of ages within the Aryan pale. Marriage, for instance, is an elabourate and expensive social function in the highest classes. But as we descend it becomes easier, till amongst the Baghdis, Bauris, and other aboriginal castes, almost any connection is ratified by the recognition of women and children. This is a point in which Eastern scores over Western development; for in Europe the Church has caused to be reckoned as immoral what might, with more philosophy, have been treated as the lingering customs of sub-organised race-strata.

As is the nature of caste, mere social prestige constitutes a perpetual stimulus and invitation to rise, which means in this case to increase the number of daily baths and the cleanliness of cooking, and to restrict to purer and finer kinds the materials used for food, approximating continually toward the Brahman standard. For is it not true that noblesse oblige? This fact it is that makes Hinduism always the vigorous living banyan, driving civilization deeper and wider as it grows, and not the fossilised antiquity superficial observers have supposed.

Such, then, is the historic picture of the rise of caste. The society thus originated fell into four main groups:

(1) Priests and learned men—the Brahmans;

(2) The royal and military caste;

(3) Professional men and merchants—the middle-class or bourgeoisie, as we say in Europe; and

(4) The working people, or sudras, in all their divisions.

(Of the second group only the Rajput branch remains now stable. For the military caste, finding itself leaderless under the Maurya dynasty, is said to have become literary, and is certainly now absorbed in the bourgeoisie.)

This functional grouping, however, is traversed in all directions nowadays by the lines of caste. In the mountains it is no uncommon thing to find the Brahman acting as a labourer, impressed as a coolie, or working as a farmer, and in the cities he belongs largely to the professional ranks. Many of India's most learned and active sons, on the other hand, belong to the third and even fourth divisions. And the new castes, which are of constant growth, are less easy than the old to classify.

Every new community means a new caste in India. Thus we have the Mohammedan, the Christian, and the modern reform castes—of all of which one peculiarity is non-belief in the caste principle!—as well as others. And who shall determine, for instance, to which of the four main grades Islamism, with its inclusion of peasant, citizen, and prince, belongs?

The fact is, if a man's mode of life be acceptable to his own caste-fellows, the rest of Indian society has no quarrel with it. And this autonomy of castes it is which is the real essential for social flexibility and fundamental equality. As bearing on this point, few utterances have ever been so misquoted as the great dictum of Buddha, that "he who attains to God is the true Brahman." For this is misquoted whenever it is made to imply that the Brahman holds in any sense a monopoly in religion. No possible statement could be more foreign to the genius of Hinduism. When we read that shortest and greatest of India's gospels, the "Bhagavad Gita" (a poem composed by Brahmans, preserved by Brahmans, and distributed through the length and breadth of the country, always by Brahmans), we find ourselves in the presence of the most comprehensive mind that ever contemplated Hindu life.

The compassion of Buddha, perhaps, looms greater across the centuries, but in dealing with social problems his very tenderness and spiritual fire make him second to Krishna, who was always calm, broad, and consistently national in his outlook. We must accept the Gita as an authoritative pronouncement on Hindu society. And the Gita rings with the constantly reiterated implication that "he who attains to God is the true man," while it interprets all life and responsibility as a means to this end.

Thus, "Better one's own duty, though imperfect, than the duty of another well discharged. Better death in one's own duty; the duty of another brings on danger." We have to remember, too, that the Gita is made up of the very best of the Vedas and Upanishads, and was specially written for the benefit of women and the working classes, who, as destitute of classical learning, had little chance of studying these great scriptures.

But its contents were to depend upon Brahman effort for promulgation. Another witness to the fact that spirituality has always been regarded in India as the common human possession lies in the Hindu word for religion itself—dharma, or the man-ness of man. This is very striking. The whole weight, of the conception is shifted away from creed, much more from caste or race, to that which is universal and permanent in each and every human being. And, last of all, we may remember that the greatest historical teachers of Hinduism—Rama, Krishna, and Buddha, besides many of the Upanishadic period—were men of the second, or military, caste.

No, the Brahman was never in any sense the privileged monopolist of religion: he was a common channel of religious lore, because his actual function was Sanskrit culture, and Sanskrit happens to be the vehicle of the most perfect religious thought that the world ever produced, but "realisation" itself has always been recognised as a very different matter from this, and, Brahman or non-Brahman, has been accepted wherever it appeared. The advantage that the priestly caste did undoubtedly enjoy, however, lay in the fact that in their case the etiquette of rank led directly to the highest inspiration, as the scholar's life, even in its routine, will be nearest to that of the saint.

One peculiarity of the place of the religious life in the Indian system is that it is an inclusive term for all forms of higher individuation. Theoretically, to the Hindu mind, all genius is inspiration, the perception of unity; and the mathematics of Euclid or the sculpture of Michael Angelo would be as authentic an expression of the religious consciousness as the sainthood of Francis. Only the result of this method of interpretation is that sainthood takes precedence of all others as the commonest form of greatness. Scientific research, as in the astronomy of Bhashkar Acharya and the psychology of Patanjali, has not had sufficient opportunity of securing defined and independent scope. And literature has been yoked to the car of mythology as much as the art of medieval Italy.

Nevertheless, India is too well acquainted with genius to forget that the caste of the spirit is beyond human limitation, often beyond recognition. It is held that the best lower men can do for that brotherhood which asserts itself in the consciousness of greatness is to give it freedom. Hence a man can always be released from social obligations if he desire to live the life of ideas, of the soul. Only, it is held that if he will not fulfil the law, neither shall he add to the burdens of the community. So he who claims to be one of the great spiritual beyond-castes must renounce family and property, relying upon the charity of men for his daily bread, and knowing well that for any work of scholarship—such as the observatories at Benaras and Jeypore—a Hindu government at least would provide him ample means. It is only as long as one avails oneself of the benefits of the social structure that it is held not unreasonable to require conformity to its usages.

This renunciation is Sannyas, the Indian form of monasticism, and Sannyas, theories to the contrary notwithstanding, has always been open to all castes. Indeed, it is held that when the responsibilities of life are over, a man's duty is to leave the world and spend the remainder of his days in that state; and in some parts of Northern India one meets with "Tyagi Mehtars," or monastics who were by birth the lowest of the low.

Theoretically, the monk is caste-fellow of the whole world, prepared to eat with any one; and where, by sheer dint of spirituality and self-discipline, such a feeling is realised; every Hindu in India considers the broken bread of this lover of mankind as sacramental food. It is usual, too, to eat from the hands of holy men without inquiry as to their standing when in the world. One of the most interesting points in all this to a Western mind is the difference implied and established between the caste of priests or chaplains on the one hand, and the fact of spiritual realisation, outside all caste, on the other. Nothing in the Indian thought about life can be more striking than this. The family chaplain in Bengal may be the official teacher, but every man and woman discards his authority silently the instant they find some soul (in the world or out of it; it may be husband or child, or the holy man living in his garden; usually it is an ascetic), with a quickening spiritual touch upon their own. He or she then becomes the guru, or teacher, and this relationship is made the central fact of life.

The appearance of this new teacher, when he is powerful enough to be an important social phenomenon, is the historic origin of almost all new castes. The Sikh nation was formed in this way by a succession of gurus. Chaitanya welcomed all castes to Vaishnavism and made it possible for them to rise thereby. The scavengers, too low to venture to claim either Hinduism or Islamism as their own, were raised in consideration and self-respect by Guru Nanak and Lal Begi Mehtar—the last a saint of their own degree.

The preacher arises and proclaims the new idea. He gathers about him men of all classes: the educated won to the service of his thought, the ignorant swept in by the radiance of his personality. Amongst his disciples distinctions of caste break down. The whole group is stamped with his character and prestige. Eventually, if it contain a preponderance of Brahman elements, it may take rank with the best, carrying certain individuals up with it. But if it be composed chiefly of the scum of society, it will remain little considered; and yet, in the strength of its religious and intellectual significance may certainly claim to have progressed beyond its original point. Such is likely to be the fate of the present Christian converts. Those who are recruited from the lowest pariahs may acquire a certain prestige from their new faith and take a better place in the social scale, consequently, in centuries to come. At the same time we must not forget that forty or fifty years ago, conversions were made that undoubtedly involved great sacrifices, and the descendants of these Christians may lose rather than gain in the long run.

Taking the history of Hinduism as a whole, we observe a great systole and diastole of caste, the Buddhist and the present Christian periods ranking as well-marked eras of fusion, while the intervening centuries are characterised by progressive definition, broken every now and then by a wave of reform which thought itself a movement towards caste abolition, but ended simply in the formation of a new group. For this is the fact in which all would-be reformations in India find at once their opportunity and their limit. It may now be taken as proved that in order to affect caste widely the agitator would need to aim deeper than the external phenomena, at underlying spiritual impulses.

If this theory of caste be valid, then, we find that the word signifies not so much mere rank in society as the standard of honour which is associated with rank. And as the private's conduct may be governed as much as his officer's by enlightened self-respect, we have seen that honour is something which applies to the whole of society equally. Even Tennyson, it will be remembered, pictures the country youth as outvaunting Lady Clara Vere de Vere in her pride of birth. The word caste, therefore, is by no means that antithesis of democracy which has been so commonly assumed.

Neither, amongst a people familiar with the process of self-organisation, would it prove any barrier to efficient cooperation. For the one essential to this power is an established habit of ignoring all points of mutual difference not germane to the matter in hand. What we call good-breeding, or what India calls caste, ought to make this easier. For any group of men met together for a common purpose find their individual rights secured to them in this way, and are free, by age-long acceptance, from any suspicion of another's desire to interfere with them. This is a basis of strength and not of weakness; so that it seems, if Indian men and women are not at present capable of combined action to any great degree, it is a matter of their own neglect of the habit, and not a necessary consequence of their institutions. We need not too readily accept the statement of such weakness, either, as infallible. My own observation has been that the Hindu people are capable enough of vigorous cooperation along the lines natural to them, those of the undivided family, the village community, and others. That inability which Europeans would show to face these tests, they may be expected to display before ours

To be absolutely just, however, we must admit that the observance of caste law has entailed many foolish and irritating losses upon society during the last fifty years. We have seen that there are definite reasons, not wanting in cogency, why a man of good birth should not eat in all companies, or of food cooked by hands supposed less cleanly. Such rules, however, cannot be kept by those who, for any reason, cross the seas to Europe. This fact, more than any other detail, makes it a matter of out-casting to take the journey and persecutions have sometimes ensued which are shocking to contemplate. A man may care little about the loss of station for his own sake, but the shoe pinches when he finds himself unable to make worthy marriages for his daughters; hence he will often submit to a heavy fine in order to buy back his position.

This rouses the cupidity of ignorant and conventional persons who happen to have authority with the stay-at-home community., and such are apt to be unscrupulous in bringing about the ruin or recantation of any who resist their power. This is a series of events which does occur occasionally; but it need not be supposed that every Europe-returning Hindu who is kept at arm's length is a martyr. There is an element of distrust for the moral results of a visit to the West in the situation; and this is not altogether unreasonable. It is chiefly with regard to possibilities of political, practical, or technical education that caste deterrence is to be regretted, and it is obvious that as communities progress in the power of estimating modern conditions, they must recognise the suicidal nature of such an attitude.

Yet it is curious to note here how caste may become thus a very real instrument of equality, for the power of the individual to advance is by this means kept strictly in ratio to the thinking of the society in which he lives. This fact is characteristic. The good of caste, of race, of family stands first and only second that of the individual man or woman in India. To take another plane. Let a man of the lower castes become wealthy, and he is compelled to educate men of his own rank to marry his daughters. Thus the group to which he owes birth, vigour, and development receives from him again the benefits of his life's work. This is the exact opposite of the European device, where the upper class absorbs money, talent, and beauty from the lower, while that is continually recruited by the failures from above.

The fact that every human force is polar in its moral activity needs little demonstration in the case of social pride. Every day we see this working on the one hand for the highest idealism, on the other for revolting egotism. Social exclusiveness may be condoned, it may even robbed of its sting but, especially when coupled with personal exultation, it can never be made anything but vulgar-looking to the disinterested outsider. It is not to be supposed that Indian caste forms any exception to this rule of double effect. Nevertheless, it is well to understand the conditions of the sentiment, perceiving how inevitably this very thing repeats itself wherever two physically-distinguishable races are found side by side.

And it cannot be denied that great benefits as well as great evils have accrued from caste. It is an institution that makes Hindu society the most eclectic with regard to ideas in the world. In India all religions have taken refuge the Parsi before the tide of Muslim conquest; the Christians of Syria; the Jews. And they have received more than shelter—they have had the hospitality of a world that had nothing to fear from the foreigner who came in the name of freedom of conscience. Caste made this possible, for in one sense it is the social formulation of defence minus all elements of aggression. Again, surely it is something that in a country conquered for a thousand years the doorkeeper of a viceroy's palace would feel his race too good to share a cup of water with the ruler of all India.

We do not easily measure the moral strength that is here involved, for the habit of guarding the treasure of his birth for an unborn posterity feeds a deep, undying faith in destiny in the Hindu heart. "Today here, tomorrow gone," says the most ignorant sotto voce as he looks at the foreigner, and the unspoken refrain of his thought is, "I and mine abide for ever." Caste is race-continuity; it is the historic sense; it is the dignity of tradition and of purpose for the future. It is even more: it is the familiarity of a whole people in all its grades with the one supreme human motive—the notion of noblesse oblige. For though it is true that all men are influenced by this principle, it is also probably true that only the privileged are very conscious of the fact. Is caste, then, simply a burden, to be thrown off lightly, as a thing irksome and of little moment?

And yet, if India is ever to regain national efficiency, this old device of the forefathers must be modified in the process,—exactly how, the Indian people themselves can alone determine. For India today has lost national efficiency. This fact there is no gainsaying. Her needs now are not what they were yesterday. The Brahmans lose distinctiveness in these days of cheap printing and widespread literacy. But this only means that the country requires multiplied methods of self-expression as the goal and summit of her national endeavour.

She wants a greater flexibility, perhaps, a readier power of self-adjustment than she has ever had. But it ought to come in an influx of consciousness of those great spiritual tides on whose surface all questions of caste and non-caste can be lifted into new and higher inter-relations. Chief among all her needs is that of a passionate drawing together amongst her people themselves. The cry of home, of country, of place is yet to be heard by the soul of every Indian man and woman in Hindustan and following hard upon it must sound the overtones of labour and of race.

Then the question of whether to walk or not in the ways of the forefathers will be lost in the knowledge of the abundant power to hew out new roads, as those fathers did before them. Has India the possibilities still left in her own nature which can bring to her such an epoch?

There are some who believe that there is no task beyond the ultimate power of the Hindu peoples to perform. The nation that has stood so persistently for righteousness through untold ages has conserved such vast springs of vigour in itself, as must ultimately enable her to command Destiny. The farseeing wisdom and gentleness of her old constitution may unfit her for the modern world, but they are a sure proof, nevertheless, of her possession of sufficient sense of affairs to guide her to a full development once more.

For, after all, who were these old forefathers, with their marvelous cunning? What inspired them so to construct the social framework that every act of rebellion and invasion should end henceforth only in contributing a new morsel of colour to fit into the old mosaic? Ah, who were they indeed?

We may well ask, for have we not all this time been calling by their name one far greater than they, one infinitely more deserving of our reverence—the Communal Consciousness, namely, of a mighty patient people, toiling on and on through the ages up the paths of knowledge, destroying never, assimilating always, what they gain of truth and science, and hesitating only a little before fresh developments, because they are so preoccupied with the problems of the past that they do not realise that stage is done, and that the sun is risen today on a new landscape, confronting them with fresh perils and unthought-of difficulties?

3

HISTORY OF INDIAN DANCES

The fascination for Indian dance all over the world is indicative of the deep-felt needs to use the human body to express and celebrate the great universal truths. Indian dance does just that in a heightened, reverential form. Also, since dance is physical and visual, it illuminates India's culture in a direct manner, playing on the sensibilities of the onlooker. Thus, those who are attracted to India will find the idiom of dance the best introduction to India's rich ethos and traditions.

Indian Dances illuminate & express India's culture in a direct manner, playing on the sensibilities of the onlooker. India offers a number of classical dance forms, each of which can be traced to different parts of the country. Each form represents the culture and ethos of a particular region or a group of people. It is said that the gods created dance as a device for entertainment. Later, in order to please the gods, human beings enacted the tale and glory of the gods. Thus began a cycle of celebration manifested in the joyous abandon of movement and music. Over a period of two millennia, dance in India acquired a set grammar, which led to a certain codification of technique.

Thus were sown the seeds for Bharata Muni's celebrated treatise on dance, the *Natya Shastra*. Bharata's Natya Shastra (believed to be penned between second century B.C. and second century A.D.) is the earliest available treatise on dramaturgy. All forms of Indian classical dances owe allegiance to Natya Shastra, regarded as the *fifth Veda.* There are many types of dance in India, from those which are deeply religious in content to those which are danced on more trivial happy occasions.

Classical Indian Dances are usually always spiritual in content, although this is often true also of Folk dances. The most popular classical styles seen on the Indian dance stage are Bharata Natyam of Tamil Nadu, Kathakali and Mohiniattam of Kerala, Odissi of Orissa, Kathak of Uttar Pradesh, Kuchipudi of Andhra Pradesh and Manipuri of Manipur. Indian mythology, legends and classical literature provide the themes of the Indian dance, both of the classical and folk variety. The classical dance is based on rigid rules and dance discipline.

Its forms include Bharata Natyam, Kuchipudi, Odissi and Kathak as also a tradition of dance-dramas—Kathakali, Kutiyattam, Mohiniattam, etc. Indian dance is divided into nritta—the rhythmic elements, nritya—the combination of rhythm with expression and natya—the dramatic element. Nritya is usually expressed through the eyes, hands and facial movements.

Nritya combined with nritta makes up the usual dance programmes. Indian classical dance is the embodiment of a whole range of expressions, which include fantasy and yogic discipline. The different forms represent the meeting point of three arts: music, drama and dance. Though highly defined and codified, they are perceived primarily as a form of worship, as homage to the almighty. Their classicism lies in the continuity of an unbroken history of over five thousand millennia, one which overwhelms yet inspires. Using the body as a medium of communication, the dance programmes.

Nritya comprises abhinaya, depicting rasa (sentiment) and bhava (mood). To appreciate natya or dance drama, one has to understand and appreciate Indian legends. Most Indian dances take their themes from India's rich mythology and folk legends. Hindu gods and goddesses like Vishnu and Lakshmi, Rama and Sita, Krishna and Radha are all depicted in classical Indian dances. Each dance form also draws inspiration from stories depicting the life, ethics and beliefs of the Indian people.

It is said that Brahma-the Creator, created Natya, taking literature from the Rig Veda, song from the Sama Veda, abhinaya or expression from the Yajur Veda and rasa or aesthetic experience from the Atharvana Veda.

It also contains deliberations on the different kind of postures, the mudras or hand formations and their meanings, the kind of emotions and their categorisation, the kind of attire, the stage, the ornaments and even the audience. All dance forms are thus structured around the nine Rasas or emotions, Hasya (happiness), Krodha (anger), Bhibasta (disgust), Bhaya (fear), Shoka (sorrow), Viram (courage), Karuna (compassion), Adbhuta (wonder) and Shanta (serenity). All dance forms follow the same hand gestures or Hasta Mudras for each of these rasas. The dances differ where the local genius has adapted it to local demands and needs.

THE ORIGINS OF INDIAN DANCE

The Natya Shastra was created in the beginning of Treta Yug by Brahma on the request of Indra and other devas as an object of diversion (Kridaniyaka). As the lower castes (Sudras) were not entitled to listen to the four Vedas (Sama, Yajur, Rig and Atharava), Brahma created the Natya Shastra as the fifth Veda which was open to all, irrespective of caste and creed.

Prior to the creation of the Natya Veda, Brahma entered a yogic trance in which he recalled the four Vedas. He drew the recitative (Paathya) from the Rig, songs (Geeta) from the Sama, histronic representation (Abhinaya) from the Yajur and sentiments (Rasa) from the Atharva. These aspects are the four main constituents of the Natya Veda. When the Natya Veda was ready, the Gods expressed their inability to practise it, and Brahma passed it to Bharata Muni and his one hundred sons who were asked to practise it. The dance was first seen at the Flag Festival of Indra to celebrate the victory of the Devas against the Daahavas. Shiva learnt the Tandava (masculine) form of the dance, whereas Parvati, his consort learnt the Lasya (feminine) form.

Nataraja

One of the most enduring symbols of India is the figure of Nataraja-Shiva (The King of Dancers). Shiva's cosmic dance is believed to encompass creation, preservation, and destruction and this idea has been embedded in Hindu thought and ritual since the dawn of civilization. He holds a small drum (Damaru) in his upper right hand. His lower right hand shows the fear-negating gesture (Abhaya), his upper left hand is in half-moon pose (Ardhachandramudra) which holds a tongue of flame which is the fire (Agni) that finally destroys the world and is then quenched in cosmic waters.

Thus the hand holding the drum and the one holding fire balance the forces of creation and destruction. The second left arm is held gracefully across the chest (Gajahastamudra) with the hand pointing to the uplifted foot, denoting favour or grace for the devotee.

Elements of Indian Dance

Abhinaya: Abhinaya is common to all Classical Indian dances. Abhinaya is the expressional aspect of dance, or nritya. In contrast to this, Nritta is composed of only pure dance and will feature striking and aesthetic poses, but will have no expressional meaning and symbolism. Abhinaya has been analysed in the Natya Shastra and has been categorised into four types:

- Angika or physical, using movements of every part of the body to convey meaning, with hastamudras (hand gestures), mandis (postures) and even the walk of the dancer.
- Vachikabhinaya or vocal/verbal, used formally today by members of the orchestra or supporting, non-dancing cast.
- Aharyabhinaya or external, expression, mood and background as conveyed by costume, makeup, accessories and sets.
- Satvikabhinaya or psychological, shown by the eyes in particular and as a whole by the entire being of the performer, who feels the mood, the character and the emotion as emanating from the self, not as an act or practical presentation.

The Navrasas: In addition, the navrasas, or nine emotions, give all dance a completeness that allows the dancer and the rasikas (audience) to experience the full beauty and meaning of the lyrics and the movements they are portrayed by.

KUCHIPUDI

Kuchipudi is a classical dance form from Andhra Pradesh, a state of South India. Kuchipudi is the name of a small village in the Divi Taluq of Krishna district that borders the Bay of Bengal and with resident Brahmans practising this traditional dance form, it acquired the present name.

With the dance form attaining perfection by the time of Golconda king Abdul Hassan Tanesha, Kuchipudi Brahmans are said to have received 600 acres (2.4 km^2) of land as an endowment from Tanesha for the great presentation before him. Siddhendra Yogi is said to be the first scholar to give it the current form of dance drama. *Bhamakalapam* is one of his celebrated compositions. He also reserved the art to males by teaching it to young Brahman boys of the village. However, in modern times, the art has been dominated by women.

The performance usually begins with some stage rites, after which each of the character comes on to the stage and introduces him/herself with a daru (a small composition of both song and dance) to introduce the identity, set the mood, of the character in the drama. The drama then begins. The dance is accompanied by song which is typically Karnatic music. The singer is accompanied by mridangam (a classical South Indian percussion instrument), violin, flute and the tambura (a drone instrument with strings which are plucked). Ornaments worn by the artists are generally made of a light weight wood called *Boorugu*.

Some of the well-known people in this tradition are Dr. Vempati Chinna Satyam, Vedantam Lakshminarayana, Tadepalli Perayya, Chinta Krishna Murthy, Padma Sri Vedantam Sathya Narayana Sarma, Pasumarthi Venu Gopala Krishna Sarma, Raja Reddy and Radha Reddy, Mrinalini Sadananda, Nilimma Devi, Anuradha Nehru and "Hamsa Awardee" Sarala Kumari Ghanta.

The Kuchipudi Arts Academy, was established in Chennai by Dr. Vempati Chinna Satyam specifically for kuchipudi training. Many of Dr. Vempati Chinna Satyam's students became famous names themselves; Some of his illustrious disciples include Shobha Naidu and Manju Bhargavi.

There are now a number of Kuchipudi teachers, choreographers and dancers in North America; Most of them have trained under the master teacher Dr. Vempati Chinna Satyam. Some of the well known teachers in North America are Sasikala in Atlanta, Kamala Reddy in Pittsburg, Ratna Papa in Texas, Himabindu Challa in the San Francisco Bay Area and Sandhya Atmakuri in Detroit.

The name Kuchipudi denotes both the dance style that has come to prominence since the 50s and the tiny, remote village where it was born. Kuchipudi, little known outside a few villages skirting it, has no come to occupy a very significant place on the dance map of India, though it has yet to acquire the prestige and acceptability it fully deserves. Situated in the Krishna district of Andhra Pradesh, it is 32 miles from Vijayawada.

Its particular location proved very fortunate for its people and its art. Kuchipudi has a great history. Six miles away from it lies Srikakulam, the ancient capital of the Satavahana Empire (2nd century BC). The rulers of the Satavahana dynasty were great patrons of art. From the inscriptions found here, on the temples of Andhra Vishnu, which was the most sacred shrine of those days, it is evident that no fewer than 300 devadasis consecrated to the deity, received royal patronage. The sculptures excavated in this area have crystallised into stone the effulgent grace of those women whose dance was an act of worship.

As any other art form, dance also enjoyed the patronage of rulers prior to the advent of Kuchipudi style in its present accent, because of the prevalence of the devadasi system. In course of time, unfortunately devadasis became the victims feudal abuse.

In later years, Buddhism flourished at two particularly prominent centres. Nagarjuna, the great exponent of Mahayana school, liver near Kuchipudi during his early years. Ghantasala, another place five miles away, was a great Buddhist pilgrim centre from the 2nd century AD to the 14th century. It was prosperous port too; tempting traders from far away countries till the Krishna River changed her course.

Movva, the birthplace of Kshetrajana, the great composer of devotional Padams, is about two miles away from Kuchipudi.

From all this can be surmised that the location of the Kuchipudi village has been, over a long period spanning twenty centuries, historically as well as culturally most important with a halo around it. The whole vicinity of Kuchipudi was filled with flavours of art.

As empires rose and fell in the Andhra territory, religions also shared their fate. The Satavahana Empire declined and with it the Vedic religion that the rulers practised received a setback. Buddhism rose to greater importance and held way till about the 4th century AD. That is till it was replaced by Jainism under the Easter Chalukyas. In order to propagate their religion, these Jain rulers exploited all the available dance forms patronising liberally both the classical and Margi style of devadasis-some of the whom by then had degenerated into Rajanartakis or court-dancer and folk or Desi style rooted in the soil.

The Chalukyas gave away to the Kakatiyas of Waranagal by about the 12th century. Originally Jains, the Kakaitya rulers took to the Pasupata Virasaiv cult under the influence of Basava. In 1230 AD a powerful ruler of the Kakatiyas, Kakati Ganapati Deva, invaded divi and subjugate the ruler, Jayappa of the Ayya dynasty and later appointed him commander of his own elephant corps. An ardent lover of dance in all its many slandered forms, Jayappa wrote and excellent treaties on the subject, entitled Nritta Ratnavali. The Kakatiya rulers, being followers of the Virsaiva cult, used the local dance forms to spread their own religion. Palkuriki Somanatha an eminent poet of the Kakatiya court listed all these dance forms in his book, Panditaradhyacharitra, in Telugu.

The Muslim ruler Mohammed bin Tughlak, invaded Warangal and humbled the Kakatiyas. In course of time, Viranarasimha III, ruler of neighbouring kingdom of Kalinga, annexed the region around Srikakulam and renovated the Andhra Vishnu temple. Being a devotee of Lord Vishnu and having renovated the temple of Lord Jagannatha at Puri, he decided to propagate vaishatvism in the Srikakulam region once again. With the raise of Vaishnavism, the prevalent cult of Virasaivism declined. He was also great lover of art and patron of dance.

Anand Tirtha, the great devotee of Lord Kirshna preached his Vaishnava cult through out his region, even persuading two ministers of kalinga court, Sobhana Bhatta and Syama Sadtry, to become his disciples. They came to be known as Padmanabha Tirtha and Narahari Tirhta respectively. Narayana Tirtha became regent after the demise of the Kalinga ruler, Bhanu deva, in 1227 AD. In this capacity, he visited Srikakulam, which was then part of Kalínga Empire.

He stayed there for 11 years propagating the Krishna cult. Jayadeva's Getthagovindam enriched the local devadasis and Rajannartakis.

One of the disciples of Narahari Bhatta, Gopalakrishna Saraswathi, lived in this region. He composed many songs on the Leela of Lord Krishna as did Lilasuka, composer of Sri Krishna Karnamrita. At this time about the 14th century AD, the worship of Krishna held complete away from the minds of local people and the dancer reelected this feeling of total devotion to the Blue God. Into this prevailing atmosphere of Krishna-Intoxication was born a boy name Siddhappa. He was an orphan.

But the villagers knew him to be a Brahman. A kind landlord performed his Upanayam (sacred thread ceremony). Later Siddhappa married but hardly remembered his infant Instead of her young handsome bridegroom, she saw an ascetic, dressed in the ochre robes of hermit. Siddhappa now remembered his promise and rose above all temptations of sensuality. Now before his eyes, appeared Lord Krishna and Sathyabhama. From that movement on, he saw in all women, including his wife, the image of Sathyabhama who lover her Lord passionately and possessively claiming him exclusively for herself and refusing him to share him even with his Pattamahisihi Rukmini. "Satya" in the "Truth" for the realisation of whichever seer and saint had been meditation, from time immemorial.

Thus Siddhappa, released from his family ties, came to be known as Siddhappa or Siddhendra Yogi. He began to propagate the Bhama cult, also known as Madhura Bhakti, like Satyabhama, every devotee imagines Lord Krishna to be the Supreme Lover, the Lokabharata, and himself to be cast in the image of Satyabhama, longing to unite with Sri Krishna and keep him entirely to herself. Song after song poured out of the heart, at the separation from her divine lover, into these inspired works.

The songs compiled together became the vehicle of a dance drama of unsurpassed beauty and came to be called Bhamakalapam. The Bhamakalapam songs were so enchanting and so full of rich imager that the temple dancers and court dancers residing at Srikakulam and Ghantasala were eager to learn them and dance to their tunes and lines. But Siddhendra Yogi feared that, since the theme centred to the romantic love between Sri krishna and Satyabhama and since the dancers already excelled in the art of portraying the Sringara rasa or romantic love, they may exaggerate the sentiments and destroy its lofty spiritual ethos.

Naturally he decided to initiate only young and good-looking Brahman boys into the art. He taught them the Bhamakalapam Song. He overcame the objections of their families to this unprecedented step by assuring them of salvation—an assurance that was further strengthened by a letter from the head of the math of Udipi offering them his patronage. He made these few families take a vow that at least one male child born into each one of them would devote the entire life time to singing and dancing the glory of the lord. Bell tied around the waist of the new-born boy symbolises this vow.

- Asthana Vidwan by Sri Venkateswara Temple (Pittsburgh)
- T.T.K.Memorial Award by the Madras Music Academy
- Kalidas Puraskar by Government of Madhya Pradesh
- Kalai mamani by Govt. of Tamil Nadu.
- The Mayor of Miami presented the Golden Key award to him in 1984
- The Mayor of Dayton, Ohio declared September 25,1994 as Vempati Chinna Satyam Day
- The Mayor of Ghana, Ohio declared April 27,1984 as classical Indian Kuchipudi Ballet dance Drama and The Mayor of Atlanta declared 3rd November 1994 as Kuchipudi Dance Drama Day.

- The Mayor of Cleveland conferred honorary citizenship on Dr. Vempati.
- The Mayor of Memphis declared September 24, 1994 as 'Ramayana Day' and the Key to the city was awarded to him.
- Gold medal was presented to him by the President of Tunisia at the Cartage Festival. Citations and Honors conferred at the Avignon Festival, France in 1995.

Invocation

A dance in praise of Rabindranath Tagore's Chandalika, Kuchipudi art, and the members of the orchestra Chandalika awakens early in the morning and tends to her chores. She hears the call of flower sellers in the market and goes in search of them. When Chandalika approaches them, high cast women intervene and forbid the flower sellers to sell to her, an Untouchable girl, Similarly, Chandalika is shunned while trying to buy milk from the milkmaids and bangles from the bangle sellers. Chandalika is at first bewildered and hurt, Then becomes filled with fury and rages at the injustice and oppression committed by society. Hurt and angered by this encounters, Chandalika becomes depressed.

Her mother, Maya, Finds her daughter's listlessness difficult to understand. She scolds Chandalika, urging her to tend to her daily chores and work. Chandalika expresses her frustration to her mother, asking why she had ever been born an untouchable, blaming god and her mother for her plight. "Why was I born in to this life of isolation?" She asks. Unable to understand her daughter, Maya leaves, perplexed. A weary Buddhist monk, Ananda, enters and sks Chandalika for some water to quench his thirst. Legend has it that the monk was Ananda, The principal disciple of the great Buddha himself, the Enlightened One. Chandalika refuses initially to serve Ananda, saying her low Chandala Caste forbids her from serving someone as fortunate and blessed as he.

To her surprise, he rejects this explanation, saying that all human beings are created equal in the eyes of the God. He calmly asks her to judge herself by her own standards rather than the artificial standards of an unjust society. These were revolutionary wards to Chandalika, yet they articulated the same feelings churning within her heart. Entranced by these words, she serves him water from the well. Ananda proceeds on his journey, and Chandalika is at first unwilling to accept that her encounter with the monk was real. Seeing the water bucket placed in a different location, near where thought she had seen the monk, convinces her that the conversation with Ananda had been real. Chandalika filled with a sense of renewed life, freedom, and joy, dances in ecstasy. The encounter with Ananda has transformed Chandalika. She is brimming with gratitude and love for him. He has become her world, her only focus, and her reason for living.

BHARATA NATYAM

Bharata Natyam is one of the oldest dance forms of India. It was nurtured in the temples and courts of southern India since ancient times. Later it was codified and documented as a performing art in the 19th century by four brothers known as the Tanjore Quartet whose musical compositions for dance form the bulk of the Bharata Natyam repertoire even today. The art was handed down as a living tradition from generation to generation under the Devadasi system under which women were dedicated to temples to serve the deity as dancers and musicians forming part of the elaborate rituals.

These highly talented artists and the male gurus (nattuvanars) were the sole repository of the art until the early 20th century when a renewal of interest in India's cultural heritage prompted the educated elite to discover its beauty. By this time the Devadasis had fallen upon evil days due to lack of state patronage and changed social mores. The revival of Bharata Natyam by pioneers such as E. Krishna Iyer and Rukmini Devi Arundale brought the dance out of the temple precincts and onto the proscenium stage though it retained its essentially devotional character.

Today Bharata Natyam is one of the most popular and widely performed dance styles and is practised by male and female dancers all over India. Due to its wide range of movements and postures and the balanced melange of the rhythmic and mimetic aspects lends itself well to experimental and fusion choreography. Degree and Post-Graduate courses covering the practice and theory of Bharata Natyam as well as the languages associated with its development are available at major universities of India.

It has been aptly said that Bharata Natyam is a symbol of beauty and aesthetic perfection. As a philosophy, it is a search of human soul for ideal. As a religion, it is the man's quest for the Supreme and the desire to unite with the Ultimate. As a science, it is to attain the perfection of body technique and corporal movement and as poetry, it is the symbol of rhythmic lyricism.

Bharata Natyam, has been one of the oldest and the richest classical dance of India. It's antiquity lies about 3000 years ago with a mythological as well as a historical origin. It was initially known as Sadir-attam (court dance) and also Dasiattam (performed by the daasis-the servants of God).

In its popular connotation, the name Bharata Natyam is understood in two ways:

- It is the dance (natyam), that beautifully blends the three elements-'Bha'-Bhava (from expressions), 'Ra'-Raga (from musical melody) and 'Ta'-Tala (from rythm).
- The name 'Bharata' is after the great author of the treaties, "Natya Shastra" (an encyclopedia on Dance, Drama and Music).

As in any classical dance form, Bharata Natyam requires total dedication, vigorous practice and full concentration. A basic training of minimum 6 years is required to present a full recital on stage. It requires a mastery over the technique of movements to achieve grace, balance, suppleness, physical endurance and a faultless sense of rhythm.

Dance as a form of Worship

The intimate association of dance with religion and as a ritual, a form of worship in the temples is well established. The institution of the Devadasis, servants of the God, contributed in perpetuating and preserving the art. In ancient times, the system of dedicating young dancers to the temples as devadasis seems to have prevailed. Dance has special mention in two important Tamil works Silappa Dikaram and Manimekhalai of the Sangam age (500 B.C-500 A.D).

The sacred texts of the Shaivagamas prescribed the mode of worship and referred to the consecration of dancing girls in the service of the gods. The temples were not only places of communication between man and God, but also strongholds of the Arts.

In the beautiful Nata-Mandapas (dance-halls) of the magnificent temples, the devadasis used to perform ritual dances as votive offerings to the presiding Deities.

Various Steps

As in any Indian Classical Dance, Bharata Natyam too requires vigorous practice, hard work and full dedication. In order to achieve the balance, grace and mastery over the technique, one has put in her/his best effort, dedication, faith and interest. The Bharata Natyam Training begins with a *Namaskar*. Then some exercises are done to warm before learning the basic steps *(Adavus, Korvais)*. The Bharatnayam dancer uses the hand gestures as her language of expression *(Abhinaya)*. Gradually, the student is taught the various items beginning from simple to complex *(Margam)*. And when the Guru thinks that the student is ready, her first public performance is done *(Arangetram)*.

Namaskar: The training begins with the learning of a prayer and a Namaskar. The disciple first pays her salutation by saying a prayer to Nataraj/Mother Earth and then performs the traditional Namaskar to Mother Earth, the God, the Guru and the audience. She bows to Mother Earth when she touches the floor and prays to God when she keeps her hand in 'Anjali' hasta (that is, joined as in doing Namaste in Indian tradition) a little above her head. She prays to the Guru when her 'Anjali' hasta is on her forehead and to the audience when her 'Anjali' hasta is on chest. Namaskar is done to ask permission and forgiveness from Mother Earth for stamping her. This salutation is done before and after every dance session, be it a recital or a class.

Adavus: Then the disciple is taught the basic steps called the '*Adavus*'. But before that it is always a good practice to do some Exercises to warm up and help the body in achieving flexibility, balance and poise in the basic positions and movements. While carrying out the Adavus, special importance is paid to the 'Angashuddha', that is, correct posture of the limbs which includes the 'Nritta hastas'; the 'Paadabhedaas'; 'Taalashuddha', that is, accurate rhythm; then the 'Taandava' (strong movements) and the 'Laasya' (graceful movements). The style of these Adavus vary with each Guru and Sampradaya (tradition).

There are about hundred variations of Adavus which are practised before the main items are taught. Then these Adavus are combined to form the *Korvais* or Jethis, that is a group of Adavus in varied permutation and combination. The Korvais are in turn combined to form the *Teermanams* (sequence of Korvais) and *Aridis* (endings with the repetition of particular adavus for three times on special rhythmic syllables).

There are varieties of Adavus like Tattadavu, Natadavu, Tatta Mettadavu, Kattadavu, Kudittamettadavu, Maiadavu, Mandiadavu, Jati, Nadai and many more....The posture is always half sit that is 'Ayata' or 'Aramandi' except in cases where mentioned otherwise. After the teachings of Adavus, the main items (Margam) are taught beginning with Alarippu, Jatiswaram and so on.

Margam: Margam means a path or a course followed. It is one full definite course where in dance items are performed in a traditional order. The items that are included are Alarippu, Jatiswaram, Shabdam, Varnam, Padam, Tillana and Sloka or Verse. According to some scholars, it does not mean that these are the only items that can be performed but any traditional dance item or any song which can give scope for the exposition of Nritta and Nritya at their best can be included. Therefore, Pushpanjali, Kauthukam (Kauvutvam), Mallari, Javalis and others are also found in the repertory of certain schools of Bharata Natyam.

In early 19th century, the four famous and great musicians, nattuvanars, dancers, poets of Tanjore, namely, Chinnaiya, Ponnaiya, Shivanandam and Vadivelu (1777-1832) have created and propagated the present format of a Bharata Natyam recital from the traditional Sadir Natya or Dasiattam. According to the great legendary dancer T.S. Balasaraswati, "The traditional order of the Bharata Natyam—alarippu, jatiswaram, shabdam, varnam, padam, tillana and sloka or verse, is the correct sequence for revealing the spiritual through the corporeal."

She has compared the Bharata Natyam Recital to a grandly structured Temple: *"We enter through the Gopuram (outer hall) of Alarippu, cross the Ardhamandapam (half way hall) of Jatiswaram, then the Mandapam (great hall) of Shabdam and enter the holy precinct of the deity in the Varnam. In dancing to the Padams, one experiences the contentment, cool and quiet of entering the sanctum from its external precinct. It is akin to the juncture when the cascading lights of worship are withdrawn and the drum beats die down to the simple and solemn chanting of sacred verses in the closeness of God. Then the Tillana breaks into movement like the final burning of camphor accompanied by a measure of din and bustle."*

Arangetram: A minimum of 6-7 years is required to know the technique and learn the Margam. That is when the dancer is ready to give her first performance in public. This is called as the 'Arangetram'. Arangetram is a Tamil word, 'Aranga' meaning a raised floor and 'Etram' meaning climbing or entering. After taking the training from her Guru, the dancer is sort of qualified and is introduced in the field of Performing Arts. In real sense this is just the beginning of a dancer's life and there is a along way to go. It is a great and a prestigious event for the Guru as well as the shishya the student. It is the test of the Gurus teachings as well as the test of talent and virtuosity of the student dancer.

Language of Gestures

The language of dance is conveyed through the gestures. In the abhinaya items which mostly consists of lyrics, poetry or a narrative set to music and rhythm, the sahitya (lyrics) is interpreted by the dancer through a series of *Angika abhinaya*.

That is, through hand gestures and movements of eyes, eyebrows, eyeballs, etc. and through the expression on the face. Through the feet, the tempo (laya) is followed. Thus we see that the whole of body acts as a vehicle to express and reach out to the audience. These parts are categorised as Anga, Upaanga and Pratyanga. The hand gestures are the focal point of language.

Hence the student dancer is taught all hand gestures, Drishtibhedaas (movements of eyes), Grivaabhedaa (movement of neck), Shirobhedaa (movement of head), Padabhedaa (various movements and positions of leg and feet) and so on, in the form of slokaas which are in Sanskrit. The movements of hand gestures have been grouped under those of single (asamyukta hasta) hand gestures and those of double (samyukta hasta) hand gestures. These primary hand gestures can be used to as they are or suggestively to represent things, places, rivers, animals, human beings, relationships or to convey ideas and emotions or they can be used as symbols.

The movement of head, eyes, eyebrows, etc., especially help in conveying the bhaava and rasa, that is the mood and the inner emotions. Thus in words of Dr. Kapila Vatsayan, "through hand gesticulation, the universe can be comprehended". Today most of the Bharata Natyam dancers follows more or less the 'Abhinaya Darpanam' as a reference for 'Angika Abhinaya'

Costume and Jewellery

Costume: The costume of Bharata Natyam has been developed from time to time. The costume that were prevalent earlier have been improvised and designed according to the needs and aesthetics. But the most commonly used styles include the Skirt/Sarree style and the Pyjama Style. Some also use the normal sarree and stitch it temporarily for the dance purpose. The most beautiful part of the costume is the knife-pleated fan which is either knee length or mid-calf length and links the two legs of the pyjamas. This fan opens up whenever the dancer takes the basic Bharata Natyam posture of aramandi.

Jewellery: The specific jewellery that is used for the dance is called as the Temple jewelry which is made of semi precious stones and metal.

It consists of Maattal and earbells for the ear, Kasumalai (coin necklace made of 'panchdhaatu'), Muthu maalai (long necklace), Necklace (small), Bangles, Talaisaamaan (head set, sun-surya prabha and moon-chandra prabha), Flowers (Jasmine ring and Kanakambaram (orange flowers), other hair decoration,

Nose ring, Chalang (Ghungroos-ankle bells-of brass meatl) and Waist band (kamar patta). The raakodi is worn at the top of the head which provides as an anchor for the flowers worn by the dancer. The hair is mostly plaited and tied to a beautiful fringe called the kunjulam.

SATTRIYA

Sattriya dance is a classical dance form of India. It is devotional in character and 'Bhakti Rasa' (spiritual aspect) is predominant in this dance form. This dance form was evolved in Assam in the 15th century by the great Vaishnavite saint Shri Sankardev who was a social reformer and a great performing artist. References of this dance form are found in the ancient Indian classical texts like Natya Shastra, Kalikapurana, Yoginitantra, Abhinayadarpana and also in sculptures, historical relics, etc.

Purity of Form

The efforts of Indira have helped turn Sattriya into a very aesthetic statement. Without disturbing the tradition she has introduced subtle changes that has given it an articulated strength.

> *"I have always insisted that the pure form of Sattriya be retained. Only after this can one experiment with music, text or costume. For instance, the monks used only white costumes. We use a two-piece dress in Assamese silk, which is made to order. The flower prints are all traditional, like the ornaments the dancer wears. In the 'sattras', only the `taal' and `khol' were used as music accompaniments. But now we use other instruments like the harmonium, tanpura, violin and flute. We have also experimented with various other texts."*

In 1982, Indira, along with her husband P.P. Bora, set up 'Kalabhumi,' a cultural organisation, in Guwahati.

"We have more than 500 students learning Bharata Natyam, Kuchipudi, Sattriya and other dance forms. Our aim is to revive and promote various traditional dance and music of the northeast, which is not very popular outside the region. Many of our students have started their own schools in different parts of the region." Carrying on the tradition is Indira's daughter Menaka.

"She is being trained at the Bharata Kalanjali, Chennai, under the Dhananjayans. She is also learning Kuchipudi," says a visibly proud mother.

Gentle and Hypnotic; a Dream-like Effect

Sattriya is a word derived from Sattra which means monastery. In the mid 15th century, Shankardev, a poet and religious leader united the various sects of Assam through his teachings and established a universal social brotherhood of Neo-Vaishnavism through congregational prayer. This included music, dance and drama based on the life of Lord Krishna. The monks who lived in these Sattras performed these dance dramas as a votive offering to their Lord. Shankardev composed Bargeet, Ojha Pali songs and numerous dances which were incorporated into the dance drama called Ankiya Nat.

The framework and content of these Sattriya dances were well preserved in the monasteries which were spread all across Assam. With texts like Sri Hastamuktavali which describes detailed used of hand gestures, the style has all the elements of Indian classical dance including a margam of eight sequences which encompasses the tandava and lasya elements. This eloquent ritual tradition has now been passed on to interested artistes who are vigorously engaged in performing and popularising Sattriya dance in India and elsewhere in the world. Sattras are the Vaishnava monasteries in Assam. The saint poet Shankar Deva of the 15th century AD started this institution to bring harmony to the region of Assam through religion, creating forms of dance—dramas, music, painting and collective prayer. The dance forms which have come to stay are called Sattriya dances, sharing all the characteristics of a classical dance form.

As a living tradition these dances are performed in the namghar, the prayer hall of the sattra by the celibate monks. Dressed in white costumes and turbans, head gears, they include kho lplaying, performing dance, creating soundscapes, floor patterns and choreographic designs. The numbers like "Sutradhari," "Chali," "Jhumura" partake of nritta, pure dance, nritya, expressional dance and dance-drama elements. The music is provided by khol-drum, patital, boratal-cymbals along with songs. The repertoire of Sattriya is vast. Now young female dancers also study these dances and they have come out of the sattra. They are presented on the metropolitan stages, with typical music of Assam, costumes and literary compositions viz borgeet. Both solo and group numbers enrich its presentation.

SOME FOLK DANCES OF INDIA

Dumhal of Kashmir is a dance performed by the menfolk of the Wattal tribe of Kashmir on specific occasions. The performers wear long colourful robes, tall conical caps which are studded with beads and shells. The party moves in a procession carrying a banner in a very ceremonial fashion. It is dug into the ground and the men begin to dance, forming a circle. The musical accompaniment comprises a drum and the vocal singing of the participants. Dumhal is performed on set occasions and at set locations.

Rouff is also a folk dance of Kashmir. It is danced solely by women on festive occasions. Rouff displays simple footwork.

Hikat is danced by women of Himachal Pradesh, and is a modification of a game played by children. Forming pairs, the participants extend their arms to the front gripping each other's wrists and with the body inclined back, go round and round at the same spot. With wide range and variety of the ethnic groups, Himachal Pradesh is blessed with natural beauty and artistic history. People living in this natural beauty, adorn themselves for the dance at all times of the year, in all regions, and continue to express themselves through music and dance.

In the Kulu valley, the festival of Dusehra is celebrated with great pomp and show. Images of Raghunathji are brought from the different shrines to a central place, and then there is singing and dancing. Dances of the region are collectively known as Natio, though each may be meant for a different purpose. No festive occasion, including wedding and similar social ceremonies, is complete without dancing. All regions of Himachal Pradesh have their own dances. Mostly men and women dance together, close to each other in the formation. Namagen dance is performed in September to celebrate the autumnal hues. The costumes are largely woolen and richly studded ornaments of silver are worn by women. The most picturesque amongst these are dances of Gaddis. The dances of the Doms. and the Bhotiyas in Uttar Pradesh range from simple performances of rejoicing to ritualistic dances. The most spectacular amongst these is the Dhurang which is connected with the death ceremonies. Its objective is to liberate the soul of the dead person from evil spirits. All the dancers hold swords and dance in a circle. The movements are virile and reminds one of the hunting dances of the Nagas on the eastern borders of India.

The Jhumeila, the Chaunfla of Garhwal and the Hurkia Baul of Kumaon, Uttaranchal, are seasonal dances. The Hurkia Baul is performed during paddy and maize cultivation. On a fixed day, after preliminary ritual, the dance is performed in different fields by turns. The name of the dance is derived from hurkia, the drum which constitutes the only musical accompaniment, and baul, the song. The singer narrates the story of battles and heroic deeds, the players enter from two opposite sides and enact the stories in a series of crisp movements. The farmers form two rows and move backwards in unison, while responding to the tunes of the song and the rhythm of the players.

A famous dance of Kumaon, Uttar Pradesh, is the Chholiya, performed during marriages. As the procession proceeds to the bride's house, men dancers, armed with swords and shields, dance spiritedly. Amongst the occupational groups, the most enthusiastic dancers are the dhobis, the chamars and the ahirs. The dhobis dance to celebrate any significant occasion. They sing and dance on the occasion of a birth or marriage, and during Holi or Dusehra. There are Rasa Dances that revolve around the early life of Krishna. The most interesting group of dances are the dances of the agricultural community which revolve round the annual seasons and which have a ritualistic and a functional dimension.

Dalkhai of Orissa is performed by women of the Sambalpur tribes at the time of seasonal festivals. The dance is quite vigorous, and is accompanied by a set of particular musical instruments, played by men, of which the drummers often join the dance. A dummy horse version is the Chaiti Ghorha, danced by a community of fisher folk. The performers are all men. Apart from dancing, the performers sing, deliver homilies of sorts, and offer brief dramatic enactments peppered with wit and humour.

Gendi or stilt dancing is fairly common among Gond children of Madhya Pradesh and Chhattisgarh. The dance is popular in the Vindhyas and the Satpura ranges. This is danced in the rainy season; from June to August. The dancer, who has the balance on the Gendi (stilts)) perform it even in water or on marshy surface. The dance is brisk, and ends with a dance in pyramid formation. This is generally confined only to children and the attraction consists in balancing and clever footwork. In the villages where the wheat seedlings festival, Bhujalia, is celebrated, children prance on their gendis, collect near the village pond or the river in which bhujalias are to be immersed. Other frolicsome children, dancing to the accompaniment of musical instrument join the group and they dance together. Sometimes, womenfolk also join them, but they do not use stilts. The Gendi season begins on the day of Bak Bandhi festival in the month of June and concludes after the Brita or Vrita of West Bengal is one of the most important traditional folk dances of Bengal. This is an invocational dance performed by the barren woman of Bengal who worship in gratitude after their wish being fulfilled. Quite often, this dance is performed after a recovery from a contagious disease like small pox, etc. Kali Nach is a dance performed during Gajan, in honour of the Goddess Kali. Here, the performer wears a mask, purified by mantras, and dances with a sword, and when worked up can make prophetic answers.

The Bihu of Assam is the most widespread folk dance in the state and is enjoyed by all, young and old, rich and poor. The dance is part of the Bihu festival, that comes in mid-April, when harvesting is done, and continues for about a month. The participants are young men and girls, who gather in the open, in daytime. They dance together, but there is no mixing of the sexes. The dance is supported by drums and pipes. In between, the performers sometimes sing, usually of love. The most common formation is the circle or parallel rows.

The Bihu demonstrates, through song and dance, the soul of the Assamese at its richest. The sense of fun and frolic of the Nagas is seen in many of their dances. The Zemis, Zeliangs and other tribes of Assam have a series of dances. Harvesting season is naturally the time for celebrations. All the Naga tribes have their particular harvest dances. The characteristic feature of all Naga dancing is the use of the human figure in an erect posture with many movements of the legs and comparatively little use of the torso, and the shoulders.

KATHAK

Kathak is one of the *classical dance* forms of India (originally from North India). It is a narrative dance form characterised by fast footwork (*tatkar*), spins (*chakkar*) and innovative use of *bhav* in *abhinaya*. It has today a form that has been influenced at various times in the past by mythological narratives by *kathakas*, temple dances, the *bhakti movement* (both Vaishnavism and Shaivite), and Persian influence of the Mughal courts in the 16th century onwards; and these elements are readily discernible. Performers today generally draw their lineage from two major schools of Kathak: the Jaipur *gharana* and the Lucknow *gharana* (born in the courts of the *Kachwaha Rajput* kings and the *Nawab* of *Awadh* respectively); there is also a slightly less prominent Benaras *gharana*.

Origin

This dance form traces its origins to the the nomadic bards of ancient northern India, known as Kathaks, or story-tellers. These bards, performing in village squares and temple courtyards, mostly specialised in recounting mythological and moral tales from the scriptures, and embellished their recitals with hand gestures and facial expressions. It was quintessential theatre, using instrumental and vocal music along with stylised gestures, to enliven the stories.

With the advent of Mughal culture, Kathak became a sophisticated chamber art. Patronised by art loving rulers, the practitioners of Kathak worked at refining its dramatic and rhythmic aspects, delighting elite audiences with their mastery over rhythm and the stylised mime.

The technique of Kathak today is characterised by fast rhythmic footwork set to complex time cycles. The footwork is matched by the accompanying percussion instruments such as tabla and pakhawaj, and the dancer and percussionists often indulge in a virtuoso display of rhythmic wizardry. The dance movements include numerous pirouettes executed at lightning speed and ending in statuesque poses.

The interpretative portion, based on tales of Radha and Krishna and other mythological lore, contains subtle gestures and facial expressions. Lucknow, Benaras and Jaipur are recognised as the three schools, or gharanas, where this art was nurtured and where the interpretative and rhythmic aspects were refined to a high standard.

Various Steps

All compositions are performed so that the final step and beat of the composition lands on the 'sam' or first beat of the time-cycle. Most compositions also have *'bols'* (rhythmic words) which serve both as mnemonics to the composition and whose recitation also forms an integral part of the performance. Some compositions are aurally very interesting when presented this way. The *bols* can be borrowed from *tabla* (*e.g. dha, ge, na, tirakita*) or can be a dance variety (*ta, thei, tat, ta ta, tigda, digdig* and so on).

Often *tukras* are composed to highlight specific aspects of the dance, for example gait, or use of corners and diagonals, and so on. A popular *tukra* type is the *chakkarwala tukra*, showcasing the signature spins of Kathak. Because they are generally executed on the heel, these differ from *ballet's* pirouettes (which are properly executed on the toe or ball of the foot).

The spins usually manifest themselves at the end of the *tukra*, often in large numbers: five, nine, fifteen, or more, sequential spins are common. These *tukras* are popular with audiences because they are visually exciting and are executed at great speed. Other compositions can be sub-divided:

1. *Vandana* the dancer begins with an invocation to the gods.

2. *Thaat* (the first composition of a traditional performance; the dancer performs short plays with the time-cycle, finishing on sam in a statuesque standing (thaat) pose);
3. *Aamad* (from the Persian word meaning 'entry'; the first introduction of spoken rhythmic pattern or *bol* in to the performance);
4. *Salaami* (related to Ar. 'salaam'—a salutation to the audience in the Muslim style);
5. *Gat* (from the word for 'gait, walk' showing abstract visually beautiful gaits or scenes from daily life)
6. *Kavit* (a poem set on a time-cycle; the dancer will perform movements that echo the meaning of the poem)
7. *Paran* (a composition using *bols* from the *pakhawaj* instead of only dance or tabla bols)
8. *Parmelu* (a composition using *bols* reminiscent of sounds from nature, such as kukuthere, jhijhikita, etc.)
9. *Tihai* (usually a footwork composition consisting of a long set of bols repeated thrice so that the very last *bol* ends dramatically on 'sam')
10. *Ladi* (a footwork composition consisting of variations on a theme, and ending in a tihai)

Gharanas

Kathak, passed down from *guru* to *shishya*, has developed different styles, called *gharana* especially during the pre-independence period. Some well known *gharanas* are:

Lucknow Gharana: The *Lucknow Gharana* developed in the courts of the Nawab of Awadh of Lucknow is characterised by its *nazakat* and *khubsurti*. *Abhinaya* plays a very strong role in this style. It is known for the improvised *abhinaya* of Birju Maharaj and Shambhu Maharaj.

Jaipur Gharana: The *Jaipur Gharana* developed in the courts of the Kachchwaha kings of Jaipur, is characterised by strong rhythmic elements. This style explores different *talas*, and provides a vigorous and forceful form.

Benaras Gharana: The *Benaras Gharana* is the style developed by Janakiprasad. It is characterised by the *natwari bols*, which are different from the tabla and the pakhawaj *bols*.

This style uses the twelve *natwari bol* based compositions exclusively. There are differences in the *thaat* and *tatkaar*, and *chakkars* are kept at a minimum. Though the style developed in Benaras, it flourishes today from Bikaner.

Innovation within Tradition

Kathak Yoga: Kathak Yoga is a technique created By Pandit Chitresh Das, within the tradition of Kathak, bringing harmony of mind, body and soul where the dancer recites the chosen Taalam, singing the melody of the chosen Taalam, and dances precise mathematical footwork and Chhakars (pirouettes) all at the same time. In traditional Kathak, there is a singer who recites the given bol to guide the dancer. But in Kathak Yoga, one has to dance the mathematical bol pattern without assistance and recite the basic taalam, which requires the dancer to know the mathematics of the dance bols precisely.

The Music of Kathak

Kathak can be danced with a wide variety of music. Here are some of them:

1. Slokas *(Sanskrit/Hindi)* and Bhajans (devotional songs for Hindu Gods and Goddesses).
2. Classical and Light Classical Songs *e.g.* Thumri, Dadra, Kajri, Hori.
3. Film songs preferably based on Ragas
4. Darbari and Ghazals *(mainly Urdu)*—songs based on love, admiration, infatuation, seperation, etc.
5. Pure Classical type *e.g.* Paran, Tukda, Gat Nikas, Jugalbandi (a friendly competition), Sawal-Jawab (footwork with tabla or pakhawaj) and demonstration of different Beats.
6. Tarana based on different Ragas.
7. Songs written by Ravindra Nath Tagore and Kazi Nazrul Islam *(Bengali)*
8. Folk Dances from different states of India *e.g.* Bhangra, Dandia, Garba, Machua, Chhau, etc. and also gypsy dance. They have a unique style but they can be blended with kathak.

9. Dance Dramas *(mainly Hindi)* example, topics chosen from the epic Mahabharata which was composed by Vyas Deva and describes the story of Vedic era. The other great composition is the epic called Ramayana written by Valmiki. It describes the story of Rama (a representative of God Vishnu), the king of Ayodhya. Rama's wife Sita was abducted by Ravana, the demon king of Sri Lanka. Rama fought a war against Ravana and defeated him. Ramayana presents the ideology of king Rama and his love for his country; Shakuntala, Krishnaleela, etc.
10. Any musical (classical) composition *e.g.* Sitar, Sarod, Violin, Sarengi, Israj, Dilruba *(String instruments)*, Sehnai, Flute *(Wind instruments)* and Tabla, Pakhawaj, Naal, Dholak *(Percussion instruments)* based on an ancient or modern theme *(preferably on* India*)*.
11. Kathak (specially footwork) can be blended with Tap dancing

Kathak Costumes

- Kathak is a wonderful blend of Hindu and Muslim culture. The costumes are very gorgeous for both Hindu (Lahenga-Choli) and Muslim-(Churidar-Kameez-Vest) called Angrakha.

KATHAKALI

Kathakali (Malayalam) is a form of Indian dance-drama. It originated in the Indian state of Kerala during the 7th century C.E. The Raja of Kottarakara is the earliest exponent of this art. It is considered to be one of the oldest dance forms in India. It is a spectacular combination of drama, dance, music and ritual. Characters with vividly painted faces and elaborate costumes re-enact stories from the Hindu epics, Mahabharatha and Ramayana. Kathakali is featured in the award-winning Indo-French-German produced film *Vaanaprastham*. Kathakali is traditionally performed in the Hindu temple, but nowadays may also be seen in theatre performances. Kathakali is considered to be a combination of five forms of fine art:

- Literature (Sahithyam)
- Music (Sangeetham)

- Painting or make up (Chutti)
- Acting (Natyam)
- Dance (Nritham)

Kathakali, literally meaning 'story-play', is a dance-drama originated in the 17th century in Kerala, one of the smallest states in India lying on the west coast of the Indian peninsula. However, its roots could be tracked back even to the earlier times. *Koodiyattom*, the only surviving form of Sanskrit theatre in India has been preserved in Kerala for centuries, now, by a small community called *Chakyar* as a part of their hereditary temple service. *Krishnanattom*, another form of dance-drama considered fore runner to Kathakali in its origin, is performed even today at the famous Sree Krishna temple in Guruvayoor as an offering to the Lord. Besides these two forms, elements from martial, ritualistic, socio-religious arts have also influenced in the making of Kathakali. Though Kathakali is only 300 years old, a great deal of enrichment and refinement has taken place in every aspect of its technique during this short period. Scholars are of opinion that Kathakali is the result of a fusion between all Indian theatre tradition represented by *Koodiyattom* and the indigenous tradition of folk dance forms.

It was one of the *Rajas* (Chieftain) of Kottarakkara, who wrote the first play intended for Kathakali performance. They form a cycle of eight stories based on *Ramayana*. The performance for each story was designed to last for six to eight hours. The performed stories were then known as *Ramanattom* (play pertaining to Rama), which later came to be called as Kathakali. Stories based on other epics and *puranas* were added to its repertoire in later period.

A vivid picture of the nature of performance of Kathakali in the past is not known. However, it is said that in the beginning the actors themselves used to sing the text while performing. Masks were elaborately used for some characters and percussion was limited to a *Maddalam* (two headed barrel shaped drum), a *Chengila* (metal gong) and *Elathalam* (a pair of cymbals).

Among the better known Kathakali play writes are Kottarakara Thampuran, the author of the above mentioned Ramayana Stories; Kottayam Thampuran, who wrote four stories based on *Mahabharata*; Irayamman Thampi, who was both a good poet and composer, accredited three stories; Unnayi Warrier, the author of *Nalacharitham* (Story of King Nala); and Vayaskara Moosad who wrote one of the popular stories—*Duryodhana Vadham*.

Structure of the Performance: In olden days Kathakali performance mostly took place on a temple premises or at the house of a local land lord. For a typical performance, a simple temporary *pandal* (canopy made of thatched roof) at a height of 101/2 feet will be erected. A minimum of 12 feet-square (144 sq. feet) is needed for the acting area. A green room will also be located close to the stage. The stage will be decorated with coconut leaves, bunches of areca nuts, etc. The only source of light is a big bell metal lamp placed down the centre stage. The level of the stage used to be the same as that of the ground where people used to squat while witnessing the performance.

Kelikottu at about 6 'o' clock in the evening will announce the performance of the evening. *Kelikottu* is a brief passage of drumming involving *Chenda* (a cylindrical drum), *Maddalam*, *Chengila* and *Elathalam*. The actual performance will begin only between 9:00-10:00 PM. *Arrangukeli* will announce the beginning of the performance.

This is a passage of drumming, which is followed by *Thodayam*, a piece of abstract dance at the same time are invocatory in nature. *Thodayam* is performed by junior actors in the group with simple makeup. Recitation of *Vandanaslokam* (Prayer Song), followed by *Purappad*—traditionally a preliminary item introducing the main character of the story in full costume and makeup. However, nowadays it is mostly Krishna and Balarama who are presented, sometime with their spouses in this introductory dance. Next is the *Melappadam*, which is a musical piece where vocalists and the drummers are given opportunity to show their skill without depending on the actors. Then the story or part of the stories proposed are enacted which may last till dawn. The end of the performance is marked by a piece of pure dance called *Dhanasi*.

Techniques: Kathakali is a dance-drama in which a high degree of stylisation is seen in the method of acting, presentation, makeup and costuming. Realism is limited only to certain characters. The acting mode of Kathakali in its totality can be better understood in terms of four fold scheme of historic representation given in Natya Shastra. They are:

1. *Angika*—pertaining to the body and its limbs.
2. *Vachika*—relating to the vocal including proper pronunciation, modulation of voice accents and percussion.
3. *Satvika*—representation of psychic condition.
4. *Ahraya*—costume, makeup, stage props, etc.

Angika Abhinaya: This involves the whole body of the actor and included an elaborate scheme of facial expression, mime, gestures, accompanied by their appropriate movements, poses and attitudes. Dance passages known as *Kalasams* have an important role to play in Kathakali. While sustaining as a pure dance, it is also meant to enhance the appropriate *bhavas*. Hand gestures is another integral part of *Angika* since the interpretation of the text is mainly conveyed through this. *Hastalakshna Deepika* is the regional text on the *Hastas* (hand gestures) mainly used in Kathakali.

Vachika Abhinaya: One of the distinguishing characteristic of Kathakali is that the actors do not speak. *Vachika* (drama text in the form of verses and songs) are recited and sung by vocalists. These songs are explained and interpreted in details by actors through an elaborate method of *angikabhinaya* which consists of highly codified gestures, facial expression, and body movements. The vocal music in Kathakali although based on the *Karnatic* (South Indian) system has developed a distinct regional style called *Sopanasangeetham*. Its main aim is the evocation of the appropriate, dramatic mood and sentiments.

Aharya Abhinaya: The makeup and costuming is another important factor of the dance-drama. Such an elaborate system is rarely found elsewhere. The characters in Kathakali are types. As such characters are classified under 5 major types. According to their nature. They are:

- *Pacca* (green)-heroic, divine *e.g.*:-Krishna, Arjuna.
- *Kathi* (knife)-heroic but lustful with arrogant. *e.g.*:-Duryodhana, Ravana.

- *Tadi* (beard)-red, villainous and evil. *e.g.*:-Dussasana
- *Kari* (black)-a demoness.
- *Munukku* (shining)-all females (expect demoness in their original form). Brahmans, sage, messengers, charioteer.
- *Teppu* (special make-up)-birds, bheeru (coward), etc.

A major part of the face makeup is done by the actor himself. However, specially trained artists are entrusted to apply *Chutty* (framing the face with white paper and rice paste). Design vary according to the type of a characters. A close observation on *Aharya* aspect of Kathakali would reveal the highest level of aesthetic imagination conceived by our predecessors. This short note on Kathakali could be summarised as such that the theatre form is a combination of dance, music, percussion, acting and painting thus make a total theatre in its completion.

Makeup: Kathakali makeup is an elaborate process lasting for 3 hours. It helps in giving a super human look to the actors. The make up of the male character other than the saint, is tedious. The Makeup is directly applied to the face and it does not obstruct the full expression of face and eyes.The colouring material used is made from various stones and powder which are mixed with water or coconut oil and ground into fine paste.

The actor lies flat on a matted floor and the expert starts drawing "the designs" on the face. The most elaborate part of the make up is the chutti (a series of white ridges built up from the chin to the either side of the cheek). After face part make up the actor stands up to put on the costume. The skirt is a well starched and pressed into frills garment. Before the skirt is put on, the actor ties 20 to 40 pieces of short cloth around the waist by the help of a large cloth twisted rope in order to give the skirt a oval shape. He then puts the jacket, etc. The actor is profusely ornamented with garlands of beast, armlets, cupped mirrors, etc. The head dresses are huge and large.

The make up colour also plays an important role in Kathakali. According to sastras colour symbolism has got significance. They reflect certain categories of emotions and gunas (attributes). The classification and nature of character are as follows.

Green represents Sattivika nature

Red represents Rajasic nature

Black represents Tamasic nature

Yellow represents Sattivika & Rajasic nature Green goes with godliness, white with spirituality, red with ambition and violence, yellow with passivity, and black with evil.

Mudras

Mudras are gestures of hands which imparts the expression of thought and emotion. This mudras are prevalent from the time of the vedas and still used by the priests while chanting manthras. In Kathakali stories conveyed by mudra from tragedy to exultation. Each mudra has got a different meaning. Depending upon the context the meaning changes. The actor should learn about 600 mudras during training. The alphabet of the hand, as mudras are, form a complete vocabulary of more than 500 words which most commonly occur in a dance story and which describe concrete objects or express an emotional situation or relate an incident in simple words.

Origin and Development of Kathakali

It was believed that *Kathakali* was conceived from *Krishnanaattam*, the dance drama on the life and activities of Lord Krishna created by the Zamorin of Calicut. The reason for that is said as follows: Once *Kottarakkara Thampuran* the Raja of Kottarakkara who was attracted by the tone of the *Krishnanaattam* requested the Zamorin for the loan of a troupe of performers on the eve of some festive occasion. Due to internal feuds and political rivalry between them, the Zamorin refused to send the performers and insulted with the remarks: "It is useless to depute the troupe, because Kottarakkara Thespian's court would be neither able to appreciate nor understand anything of the highly artistic *Krishnanaattam* and the high standard of the performance". Here the political rivalry between the two chieftains leads to the art rivalry.

So *Kottarakkara Thampuran* initiated a parallel mode of entertainment, which he called *Raamanaattam* which was later transformed into *Aattakatha*, and yet later into *Kathakali* while *Krishnanaattam* based on the story of Lord Krishna's activities,

Raamanaattam described the complete story of Lord Raman. *Krishnanaattam* was written in Sanskrit, "the language of the Gods". *Raamanaattam* was in Malayalam, the language of the people. By the end of the seventeenth century, the finished product of *Raamanaattam* was placed before the world under the tittle *Kathakali. The* costume of *Kathakali* has been much influenced by *Chaakkyaar koothu* and *Koodiyattam* the two older forms of dramatic representations in vogue in Kerala.

The history of their origins dates back to the period of *Perumals, i.e.* much earlier to the introduction of *Raamanaattam*. The whole scheme of *Abhinaya* (acting) and the use of *Mudras* (hand poses) and gestures were bodily adopted in *Kathakali* from them in addition to its borrowing and refinement of facial makeup and costume. The use of colour, costume, and makeup present a unique show and create an unearthly atmosphere. *Kathakali* became more attractive and popular than the *Chaakkyaar koothu* and *Koodiyattam*.

Moreover, its performance was not restricted to the precincts of the temples. *Kathakali* had a golden period between 1665 AD and 1743 AD. Remarkable contributions were also made by *Kaartika Thirunal*, the king of Travancore, to Kerala's literature, art and dance. His efforts were also directed to popularising *Kathakali* among the people. He instituted a tradition of arranging *Kathakali* performances at various festivals and on the Navaratri night. *Kathakali* employs the four abhinayas, viz *Sattvika*, expression of thoughts by the efforts of the mind (*Bhaava* and *Rasa*).

Aangika, conveyance of ideas by the movements of the various parts of the body (gestures).,*Vaacika*, spoken words, singing, shrieking, etc., and Aharya, the dress and deportment. As in earlier dramatic forms, *Raamanaattam* players also sang the *padas*. But for the vigorous *Kathakali*, demanding tremendous physical exertion, singing by the actors was exacting and tiring. A change in the practice was conceived by Prince *Vettathu Thampuran*, who introduced a few fundamental innovations. He provided seperate singers and introduced the *chenda*, a percussion instrument, to announce a performance and give background sound effect. This drum's powerful and penetrating sound heightened the acting of supernatural characters appearing on the stage in hideous and fantastic make-ups. The religio-theatrical reforms brought *Raamanaattam* performances outside the temples for the enjoyment of all sections of the community.

Masks were replaced by makeup; *Mudras* were accentuated, a variety of percussion instruments and characteristic costumes were introduced; singers and musicians formed an independent part of a show.Symbols of the hand have played an important role in the art of *Kathakali*. With the help of *Mudras*, the hand poses are called in Sanskrit, a whole literary expression is reduced to elementary notions. There are sixty-four basic hand poses which connote five hundred words, while the alphabet of the eyes express emotions. Their permutations can be employed to convey any number of meanings requiring any detailed explanation in the modern concept of story-telling. In the art of *Kathakali*, all emotional qualities, and psychic conditions acquire remarkable outward manifestation and *mukhabhinaya* (facial mime) is cunningly, sometimes lightly employed. While the *Kathakali* use elaborate similes and hyperboles, and fingers permute, into *mudras* to represent words of comparison such as like, as if and same as, the eye-balls roll evanescently to tell the miracles.

The face becomes the open drama in which the story is drawn in successive shades and touches of lineament.According to the theme, a *Kathakali* song suggests the use of a particular *Bhaava* and *Rasa* (aesthetic delights) and the dance and mimicry are rendered most effectively in harmony with these aesthetic appeals.

The powerful music heightens the moods of the actor and adds life to acting. He dances to the melodies of the song and executes the various passages with well-defined *Padaghats* (foot work). It provides scope for the amplification of an emotion and the abridgement of the climax of a story. The powerful footwork trembles the earth below and cuts short the final action. As *Kathakali* is a story-play, interpreting a *drisya kaavya*, its various contrasting characters are presented.

There are good and bad characters, demons and gods, wordly and unwordly role-types according to their castes, quality and nature. Each group is distinguished from the other by specific make-ups. The makeup of *Kathakali* character is peculiarily native to the Kerala folk-art. In folk theatrical varieties, huge marks and make-ups were as much prevalent during the historic span of time. Elaborate makeup heightens dramatic effects. Colour symbolism reflect certain categories of emotions and *gunas*.

The green colour represents *Saattvika* reveals godliness, white represents spirituality. Red represents *Rajasic* reveals violence. Black represents *Tamasic* reveals evil. Yellow represents the combined character of *Saatvika* and *Rajasic*. Thus *Kathakali* characters are grouped into five major role-types, each having a specific makeup and costume. These role types are *Minukku*, *Paccha*, *Katti,taadi* (has three varieties, *viz. Velupputaadi*, *Chuvannataadi* and *Karupputtadi*) and *Kari*. *Minukku* is the polished variety of facial makeup consisting in smoothening the actor's face with a coating of a mixture of yellow and red pigments.

The composition obtains 'a self' (or natural skin) complexion colour. It reflects the characters usually found in Brahmans, Rishis and Virtuous women. The eyes and eye-lashes are painted and contours elongated with the black unguent and greasy collyrium. Sometimes the face is decorated with white or cream colour dots, running from the cheeks to the fore-head in a bow-shape. The lips are reddened and the forehead is decorated with a caste mark. This colour scheme serves to give a symbolic glow of piety to a devotee character. Women role-types are given delicate touches of the make-up.Paccha or pre-dominantly deep green face role-types, are Gods, celebrated mythological heroes, and virtuous personages, symbolising inner refinement poise, heroism and moral excellence. This include heroes of a play and noble characters, Indra, Krishna, Rama, Lakshmana, Bharata, Satrugnan, Harischandra and Nala.

The front part of their faces is given smooth deep green base on which *chuttis* (white rice-paste curves) run from the centre of the chin,covering the lower jaw, to either side of the face. The eyes and the eye-lashes are painted black and the lips bright red. It assumes the shape of a broad-blade saber or of a sweeping curve of a bow. The forehead, above the bow-tie shaped painted portion, is covered by a red ribbon of the gilded head gear. Kattias compared to *paccha*, the makeup of *Katti* role-types is complicated. This term literally means the knife, because in its makeup the shapes of colour positions resemble sharply bent daggers. Evil, demoniac and fierce characters standing against the hero of a play. *Pratinayakaas* such as *Asuras* (the enemies of the God's) ambitious and arrogant *Ravana*, *Keechaka*, *Kamsa* and *Dussaasana* are distinctively treated with this makeup. Their faces are given a foundation with green colour, the sides of their noses are painted in red.

The red paint round the nose rises up to the forehead above the eye-brows. It is like a patch, an upturned moustache, covering the upper jaw. Its border lines are treated in white. On the green base of the rest of the face, a *chutti* runs along the jaw-bones from the middle of the cheek. Two white knobs, called *chuttippuvus*, are placed on the face. These vary in size with the degree of the fearsome appearance of some demoniac characters like *Ravana* and *Dussaasana*, two long protruding canine teeth(called *dhamshtras*)are perched on either side of the mouth. These drop over the lower lips. *Katti* makeup characters stand in a singular position. taadi (Beard)Thôse who have the *taadi* makeup are again, good godly and evil-demoniac.

To differentiate one from the other, three taadi make-ups are in vogue: *Veluppu taadi* (white beard), *Chuvanna taadi* (red beard) and *Karuppu taadi* (black beard) In these make-ups white chutti is not planted on the face. Veluppu taadiIt consists of a white beard and a fur coat. It is a realistic makeup for characters like *Hanumaan*, the son of God *Vaayu*, and other monkey sages and warriors. The upper half of the face-the neither part of the eyes-and lips are treated with a black ointment. The chin at the middle is decorated with a white rosette, bearing a red dot within. Red paint is applied to the lower part of the lower lip, up to the chin. A thin coating of *chutti* decoratively encloses the black-end part of the face and meets the *chuttinata*-the hem of the head dress.

Another white pattern develops on either side of the cheeks and circling the red spots, starting from the base of the green painted nose. On the tip of the nose and the forehead two oval-shaped spots are given in red. Chuvanna taadi is given to hideous characters. The face is painted red, with black contour lines drawn round the eyes, lips and chin. This adds to the ferocity of less evil characters like *Baali*, *Sugriiva*, *Kaalakeya* and *Dussaasana*. The eye-brows and lashes are not elongated, no *chutti* is applied to the *Chuvanna taadi*.

The face is dubbed in red and treated with black lines. Around the eyes, almost a square patch of deep black colour is provided to give to the eyes a fiendish look of a evil designer. Lips painted in black, are given a hilly curve to give the role type a lucid image of a beastly character. Running from the upper lip are two white paste bristled rows throwing the black patch round the eyes in bold relief and adding ferocity to the fiery red eyes, and demarcating the black portion from the remaining nether part of the face is red. *Chuttippuvus* (white blobs) on the tip of the nose and the fore-head are bigger in size than those put on by *kathi* characters. It is the most impressive of all make-ups in *Kathakali*. Karuppu taadi the third type of bearded characters makeup is with a black beard and coat. These characters include *Kali*, *Kaattaalan* (hunter), brigands and robber chieftains. In their makeup, the face is first coated with black unguent.

The eyes are bracketed within oval-shaped white border lines, the area between two such lines being painted in red. Small white bristles adorn the ridges. Lips are in red. The tip of the nose bears a *chuttippuuvu*. Kari reveals the vile and evil characters, such as *Suurpanakha* and *Simhika*. Their faces are painted in black and the cheeks have a red crescent in the middle. A pair of *damshtraas* are provided. Shiva in the role of *Kiraata* (hunter) is also given this type of the makeup. A remarkable feature of the *Kathakali* makeup is the reddening of the white of the eyes of all characters by putting in a few young seeds of *chunda puuv* (sollanum pubescence) crimson eyes stand in contrast to the colour scheme of the face. The practice is usually followed in *pacha* and *minukku* faces. Makeup in the 'Green room'*Kathakali* makeup is an elaborate process lasting for over three hours.

It helps in giving a super human look to the actors. Whether it is a man's makeup or the woman's, the work is conducted by a makeup expert. Paints used in Kathakali makeup are freshly prepared and applied to ensure correctness of rhythmic curves and precision. The makeup of the male characters other than saints is tedious. The role-type lies flat on a matted floor and the expert starts drawing 'the designs' on the face with a thin rod. The face part being complete, the role type gives the finishing touches himself. Thereafter he stands up for putting on the costume. The skirt is a well starched and pressed into-frills garments. But before the skirt is put on, the actor ties 20 to 40 pieces of short cloth round his waist by the help of a long cloth twisted rope in order to give the skirt an oval shape. He then puts on the jacket, etc.

The finishing touches to the costume are given by the costume attendant. The actor is profusely ornamented with garlands of beads, armlets, cupped mirrors, etc. Fully decorated, the actor gives the last minute touches to his makeup with the help of the cupped mirror. His head-dresses are huge and often unwidely. These are tied by an attendant. The last part of the costuming is the tying up of the anklet bells. Women fancy to have the silver paijaebs (an ornament) and then tie the bells. In the case of male characters a decorative woolen is tied immediately above the anklet and the bells fixed on a leather pad or tied right below the knee. *Kathakali* makeup traditions today widely differs from what it was in the seventeenth century. An intensive dance training is needed to make the body flexible and supple in order to respond to unusual forms weaved in the course of dancing. To achieve fluidity, a *Kathakali* pupil undergoes extensive and vigorous training from an early age.

A complete alteration in the behaviour of the body is effected. Massages and oil-baths are an essential aid to awaken muscles, joints and nerves and to control their behaviour. Between the age of 11 and 14 years the pupil goes to an *Aasaan*, the teacher of a *Kalari* (a kind of gymnasium) and offers to him *daanam* (a present) either in cash or in kind clothes and with his *guru-diksha* (benediction) he enrolls himself for training. *Kathakali* performances are not confined to a temple's courtyard; they are held in the open under the sky. Before a performance begins, *chendakkaaran* the instrumental musician, beats the drum to announce the news that a dance-drama will be held shortly. This nervous and insistent tattoo' is called *Ke'likottu*. The village folk-men, women and children begin to assemble and crouches on the land in a circle around *chendakkaaran*.

The night's 'stadium' has the covering of a clear, star-studded sky; cool breeze rustling through the jagged patterns of palm fronds, children wandering back and forth aimlessly or running to a hawker or pestering their mothers or aping a character of a previous play; people discussing a role-type, an actor, a character, a story or a matter of current or religious interest. And those among the audience who are tired from the day's hard work on their fields go back and sleep until they are awakened by a relative or a friend or by the noise from the stage, to witness the favorite hero play or a climatic battle scene. In its indigenous form, Kathakali has no stage in the modern sense. The centre of the stadium is the stage provided with a huge brightly polished brass lamp of coconut oil. The audience sits in darkness.There are no back-curtains, no stills, no sceneries. But behind the lamp there is a simply designed 'tirasila', a rectangular silk curtain, held by two members of the troupe.

Actors who have to appear first stand hidden behind it. During scenes the curtain is dropped to the ground and removed by the two men. The job over, these men go about on other errands of the stage, like pouring oil in the lamp-well, adjusting the thick wicks which constantly threaten to gutter and burn out, arranging the banana tree trunk support against the wicks gliding down in the well, and assisting the actors on odd jobs. The stage is also provided with a small stool. This is used for many purposes. For instance, in the 'curtain look' the actor stands on it; on other occasions an actor may rest on it. Musicians stand in a half circle behind the actors. They number four to twelve. Musicians do not wear any special costume.

They are normally bare-chested. The actors are profusely dressed mostly in billowing skirts, crowned with massive head-dresses and provided with the accessories of the face and finger nails. The 'actresses' are adolescent boys, for they are nearest to femininity and have simple dress. In the repertoric of its technique Kathakali has seven items to be presented in the following sequence: 1. *Todayam*-the basic nritt; 2. *Purappaadu*-debut of the hero and the virtuous character; 3. *Tirano'kku*-

'curtain look' by evil characters and demons; 4. *Kummi*-permeable for the female character's appearance; 5. *Kathakali*-the main play; 6. *Kalaasham*-a passage of vigorous dance which serves as a hyphen between two pieces of verse-play; and 7. The concluding benediction dance The dance drama begins with the call of the drum which has rent the air at night.

The audience is alerted. *Tirasiila* is drawn by two men. Music begins. Drummers display their cleverness. Religious songs are sung. They purify the atmosphere. And dancers are behind the curtain. The preliminary dance behind the curtain is commonly refused to as *Purva-ranga* by *Bharata* in the *Natya Shastra*, in the language of *Kathakali* it is called *Todayam*. The basic technique of *Kathakali* lies in *Todayam*. *Purappaadu* or the debut, signifies the first appearance of a character on the stage. It is a piece of a preliminary dance. It serves to announce the virtuous qualities of the hero. If a demon is to appear violent drumming of high pitch drums is incessant. The curtain is drawn as high as the arms of the attendants can stretch.

The whole atmosphere is surcharged with earth-shaking and hair raising activities. The sound of quick and heavy foot steps can be heard from behind the curtain. Its synchronisation with the sound effect of the drums heightens the climax. The entire climate forebodes that a terrific personality is about to appear. Suddenly a coloured canopy appears over the curtain and a rumbling growling noise is heard. Drums burst into shattering sounds. Here is a shrick, and there a groan. But before the eyes can catch the character, fingers are seen rising in the centre of the curtain. The left hand fingers are covered with long thimbles.

The two hands are kept about three feet apart. They clutch the curtain. Fingers glide across its top. There is deafening drumming; but no singing.To the accompaniment of the drums, the anti-hero shakes the curtain violently, and breathless the audience catches an occasional glimpse of the top of a glittering head-dress, which seems to be gyrating madly in some internal whirlwind. He pulls the curtain towards him; then plugs forward and fans flames. With gusto, the fire illuminates the character's face and enables the audience to spot him out by his weird makeup. The feverish pitch of excitement over, the curtain is dropped and the whole figure of the character emerges after a great deal of suspense. The curtain is pulled off the stage from its right wing.

Thus develop *tiranokku* or 'curtain look'. For male anti-heroes *Tiranokku* is prescribed and for female characters there is another standard dance called *Kummi*. In it gestures and movements are modified and smoothened to lend gentleness and elegance. so much necessary for feminine characters. Paces are slow; roles are passive and subsidiary. *Kalaasams* are pure dance passages performed in pure *taandava* style. They punctuate two verses; two scenes. It is here that in *Kathakali* an important role of *nritt*a is discovered. From the sequence detailed *Kathakali*'s basic characteristic of a dance-cum-drama is unfolded. How the various limbs of *sangiitha* have been synthesised to bring about an underlying unity of all Indian dramatic arts in *Kathakali* is unique. It is the only form of the histrionic arts in India, which adumbrates in principle, the three essentials of the Sanskrit drama, *naatya*, *nritya* and *nritt*.

Aivarnaatakam *Aivarnaatakam* is one among the popular rural dramas of Kerala. It is also known as *Aivarkali* and *Pandavar kali*, which means the play of the *Pandavaas*-the five heroes of *Mahabhaaratha*-and is performed by the *Viswakarmas* which enfolds five communities consisting of *Aasaari* (Carpenter), *Muusaari* (Brassmith), *Kollan* (Blacksmith), *Tattaan* (Goldsmith) and *Kalthachan* (Mason). This ritualistic art form is performed in almost all important temples of Kerala. Today it is found in central Kerala. In Trichur District *Vilkurupas* also enacted this art form. It is performed on a tara or a raised platform in a beautifully decorated pandal with a five-wicked *Nilavilakku* (bell-metal lamp) at its centre. The *Nilavilakku* is crowned with multi coloured flowers. *Kulaavazha* or plantain trees with full bunch of ripe plantains are erected on both sides of the Tara.

In some villages, they have permanent platforms for the performance of Aivarnaatakam. Permanent platforms are found in the villages such as Adattu, Olarikkara, Pallippuram, etc. near Bhagavathi temples. The performers describe to the audience the details of the stage and other decorations in their songs. The performers numbering five or more with their leader called *Kaliaasaan* enter the performance area after ritualistic bath, with sandal paste on their foreheads, chests and upper arms. They are dressed in white dhoti and have a towel wrapped around their heads. The dancers gather around the lamp carrying small sticks with small bells attached at one end called *Ponthi* and offer their prayer to their deities.

After *Ganapati Pooja*, they bow to their leader and the *Nilavilakku* and start the dance by singing devotional songs. Aivarnaatakam is divided into three parts namely *Vattakkali*, *Parichamuttukali* and *Kolkali*. *Vattakkali* means the dancing in a circular form round the *Nilavilakku*. *Parichamuttukali* is the second part of *Aivarnaatakam*, where sword and shield are used. The dance gradually grows vigorous and powerful and is accompanied by varied songs sung by all the dancers led by their leader. Besides *Ponthi*, only *elathaalam* is used for musical accompaniment with the singing, the dancing rises to a crescendo of rhythmic fervour and the dancers swish around, feet in step and the sticks striking perfect time. It is the third item of Aivarnaatakam. After this performance the group leader switches on to its prose version called kavitham which gives elucidation of the song sung. *Kavitham*, one of the highlights of *Aivarnaatakam* is a rhythmic prose rendering of the play.

The *Aasaan* ask questions to the audience to test their knowledge in the epics and he himself gives answers to the questions. *Aasaan* gives the synopsis of this story to the audience. *Aivarnaatakam* is performed during the night. Even three whole nights may not be sometimes enough to complete a story. The contestants have the freedom of choosing their actors for performance. At the conclusion of the performance, the people conduct pooja. Both the actors and spectators like fruits as a token of the blessings given by Saraswathy, the Goddess of wisdom. This ritualistic dance is reminiscent of an ancient legend connected with *Mahabhaaratha*. On hearing that one of her devotees, *Karna*, had been killed by the *Pandavaas* in battle. *Bhadrakaali* is determined to annihilate them.

Lord Krishna who is a friend of the *Pandavaas*, comes to know this and he directs them to sing praises of the goddess and to propitiate her, The legend has it that Lord Krishna transformed himself into a lamp and prompted his friends to sing and dance in praise of the Devi. The Devi finally becomes pleased and blesses them. *Aivarnaatakam* was an effective mass media for transmitting morally oriented stories of epics in the villages of Kerala, particularly to the artisan class and the Harijan community. 1. Chummar Choondal, Aivar Natakam, NBS, Kottayam, 1976.2. Festivals of Kerala, Tourist Dusk, Cochin, 1993.

Chaakyaar koothu *Chaakyaar koothu* is one of the plays performed in temples. This is enacted in the special dance hall called *Koothambalam*, connected to the temples. It is performed by people belonging to the *Chaakyaar* community. The word *koothu* is derived from the Sanskrit term, *Koordanam* which means 'dance'. The *Chaakyaar* community is a group which earns its livelihood by performing *Chaakyaar koothu* and *Koodiyaattam*. There are many versions regarding the origin of the term *Chaakyaar*, The *Chaakyaars* are believed to be people who have been ostracized from the Namboodiri Brahman Community. The women of the community are called *Illottamma*.

The *Chaakyaar koothu* consists of two parts of which one is action and the other narration. In the earlier days, the action part of it was known as *koothu*. There are different types of *koothu*, known by different names like *Mantraangam koothu*, *Anguliiyaangam koothu*, *Parakkum koothu*, *Matta Vilaasam koothu*, etc. When more than one actor performs on the stage, it is called *Koodiyaattam*. If the actors are not more than one, it is called *Chaakyaar koothu*. *Chaakyaar koothu*, is the narrration of Puranic stories by the *Chaakyaars* who wear the attire of a joker and tell the story humourously. Nobody knows how ancient this art form is. It is however clear from *Chilappatikaaram* that even during the reign of *Chenkuttava Perumaal*, *Chaakyaar koothu* was performed. The *Koothambalam* constructed for the perfomance are edifices built according to Bharata Muni's *Natyasaastra*.

It mentions three types of theatres which are rectangular, quadrangular and triangular. The *Koothambalam* of Kerala has a green room inside at one end. Just in front of the green room is the stage. The remaining portion is left for the audience to sit. The musical instruments used for *Chaakyaar koothu* are *Mizhaavu*, *Kuzhittaalam*, *Itaykka* and *Sankhu*. Of this *Mizhaavu* is the most important. It is said that *Mizhaavu* can be made from copper, bell-metal, or granite. Nowadays only *Mizhaavu* made of copper can be seen. *Mizhaavu* is a huge pot upto one's waist. Its mouth is tied firmly with animal skin. The sound of the *Mizhaavu* is more majestic as its size increases. The *Chaakyaar* adorns his face with the usual caste mark on the forehead (*pottu*), In addition soot and turmeric too are smeared on the face. There is a huge earring called *Kundalam* on one ear.

On the other ear, he wears betel leaves and geranium flowers as earrings. A pleated costume is worn. He wears girdle and bangles. The head is tied with a red cloth. *koothu* is a combination of dance and humour. As soon as the *Chaakyaar* comes to the stage and offers his salutations, a dance known as *Chaari*, starts. This dance is an offering. Hence there should be no mistakes in it. Later, prose and verse are recited and meanings given. Initially, *Chaakyaar koothu* was only story-telling. Each word is pronounced very slowly and in a special tune which is called Bharu Method. This special kind of pronunciation is found only in the speech of the *Chaakyaars* on stage. This special sound and clarity of speech are efficient to attract the attention of the distracted among the audience. It is audible, and the meaning can be grasped by the hearer. In the Sanskrit Dramas enacted in Malayalam, not only Sanskrit and its Prakrit are used but also Malayalam and its Prakrit.

In plays where there is the clown (*Viduushaka*) the *Viduushaka* speaks in Malayalam. He first pronounces the Prakrit sounds, which he is supposed to utter, and later speaks similarly in Sanskrit and again explains it in Malayalam. One can hear old Malayalam forms from the *Viduushaka*. The actor enlivens his narration with *Thaandava* dance, gestures and bodily postures derived from *Natya Shastra*. Combined with mime and gestures and interspersed with occasional dances, the narrative is made dramatic. The actor never misses an oppurtunity to make humourous and witty statements about political and social situations. He has the license to ridicule the audience according to his own imagination or discretion. Nobody could object or protest.Criticisms of contemporary events or personalities also figure in the narration. References 1. Narayana Pisharoti. P. *Kalaalo'kam*, Kerala Sahitya Academy Trichur 1989. 2. Vishnu Namboodiri M.V. Folklore *Nighantu*. State Institute of Languages, Trivandrum;2000. 3. Festivals of Kerala Tourist Desk, Cochin 1993.

Kaakkaarissi Naatakam Kaakkaarissi Naatakam is a popular entertainment among the backward communities of Kerala. This art can still be seen in its original flavour and style in the village of Nedumangadu in Trivandrum district. In the southcentral region of Kerala, it is found in Kurumpala, Karakkat, Karunagapally, Panthalam, Cheruvally, Ambalapuzha, Mankombu, etc. Here it is presented by the *Paanar* and *Kummaalar* communities. In Kilimanoor and Nedumangadu it is presented by *Kurava* and *Ezhavas*. Though there is a community called *Kaakkaalas*, they never take part in the performance or presentation of the play. Begging is considered as their legitimate profession with palmistry and lizardology – predictiing the future by interpreting a lizard's movements and sounds. This art form is spread all over the state, but they differ in certain respects from place to place. The main object of *Kaakkaarissi Naatakam* is to make the public aware of the poverty, misery and suffering of the communities. Legends about *Kaakkaalas* There are many legends about the origin of the *Kaakkaala* tribe.

One of them traces their beginnings to *Garuda*, the king of birds and the divine vehicle of *Vishnu*. Once *Garuda*, furious with mankind, gobbled up the entire human race, including all Brahmans. But later when his mother, *Vinata*, explained to him the sin involved in killing and eating up the Brahmans, he was filled with remorse. As a penance, he regurgitated what he had swallowed and threw up the Brahmans. Thus they were brought back to life. These Brahmans were called *Kaakkaalas*, from *Kaakkuka* – to regurgitate – in Malayalam. Another legend links this nomadic tribe with *Shiva* and *Paarvathy* – the parents of the world – who came on earth in order to redress the complaints of the suffering among the human race. They manifest as *Kaakkaalan* and *Kaakkaalathy*, the male and female respectively of the *Kaakkaakan* community.

The present–day *Kaakkaalas* are believed to be their descendants. The northern variation of *Kaakkaarissi Naatakam* is called *Paanarkali*, became it is performed by members of the *Paanar* community. Performance of *Kaakkaarissi Naatakam*. According to tradition the performer starts with the chief character named *Sundarak Kaakkaan* entering the arena and exchanging conversation with the audience. He invites the female players named *Kaakkaathimaar*, and when they enter, the play begins. Besides there characters, *Vedan*, *Thampuraan*, *Kuravan*, *Kurathy*, wild tiger, etc, also figure in the enactment.

Usually, the play takes place on a raised platform. The performance starts with *Naarada*, the celestial sage, informing *Shiva* and *Paarvathy* about the suffering humanity on earth. The *Kaakkaathimaar*, female characters, dance and invoke the presence of *Kaakaan*, the male character. He emerges from the crowd carrying a naked torch and enters the area with vigorous, rhythmic steps. He is accompanied by *Thampuraan*, representing an upper caste man, who shoots a volley of questions at the *Kaakkaan* who,through his crisp replies, tells the story and, at the same time, sarcastically comments on the arrogance of the higher castes.

The *Kaakkaan*, who is wholly absorbed in the rhythm of his steps, is interrupted by the *Thampuraan* who reminds him that he should first offer praises to Lord *Ganapati*. After the eulogy in accordance with the *Thampuraan*'s request, the *Kaakkaan* invites the two *Kaakkaattis* to the stage. The women quarrel and the *Kaakkaan* is totally lost. Through the dire helplessness of the *Kaakkaan*, the pitiable plight of a husband with two wives is humorously portrayed. In the second act, the *Kaakkaan* makes his reappearance as the *Sundara Kaakkaan*, a snake charmer. He goes snake – hunting into the deep jungle, blowing on and swaying his pipe to the rhythm of the snake's movements. Unfortunately the snake bites him, and he falls down unconscious. Meanwhile, the *Kaakkaattis* anxiously await the return of their *Kaakkaan*. Alarmed at the delay, they go searching for him with *Alakësan*, their brother. After they have travelled many a weary day through the thick woods, they find him at last, lying unconscious, and the *Kaakkaan* is saved.

The mastery of the staging lies in the fact that without any sets, the jungle, the Kaakkaan's abode, and the search are all conjured up through the performer's words and movements. The most important element in the next scene is the appearance of a *velichapaadu*, an oracle, and his prophetic pronouncements under divine dispensation. A band of professional thieves pray to their tutelary goddess before setting out on one of their nocturnal exploits. The spirit of the goddess enters the body of one of the thieves and thus he becomes a *velichapaadu*.

In that movement of divine enlightenment, he knows the truth about all the thefts that may have taken place in the near part. He reveals these secrets to the other thieves in the course of his inspired utterances. The aim of this episode in to warn the public of the doings of professional thieves haunting the area. During earlier days, these plays were enacted in the centre of a large level ground lighted with petromax lamps.

In many scenes, the actors went into the midst of the spectators thus giving them a feel and thrill of actual participation. Costumes are rustic, with the females wearing colourful clothes and the *Kaakkaan* in simple black. *Vedan* and *Kuravan* smear charcoal over their bodies. In the southern region, the *Kaakkaan* is painted jetblack and designs in white dots are executed on the surface. Turmeric and rice powder are also employed for makeup. Harmonium, *ganjira*, *elathaalam and mrudangam* are the musical instruments used. Stage props are not used in the performing stage.

There is no regular script for the performance of *Kaakkaarissi Naatakam*. Though essentially a ritual entertainment, its performance is not limited to rustic audiences. Puranic stories form the main themes of this drama but in presenting these stories, current problems are skillfully incorporated into the narration. Till 30 years ago, *Kaakkaarissi Naatakam* enjoyed considerable popularity. Then followed a period of gradual degeneration. Of late however the art form is being revived and is slowly regaining its place in the rural society.

MANIPURI

Manipuri one of the six classical dance styles of India, the others being *Bharata Natyam, Kathak, Kathakali, Kuchipudi,* and *Orissi*. It is indigenous to Manipur, the northeastern state of India and the indigenous people of this valley were said to be the dance-expert *Gandharva's*, mentioned in the epic Ramayana, Mahabharata and other religious scriptures.

Manipuri dance is purely religious and its aim is a spiritual experience. Development of music and dance has through religious festivals and daily activities of the Manipuri people. Not only is dance a medium of worship and enjoyment, a door to the divine, but indispensable for all socio-cultural ceremonies. From the religious point of view and from the artistic angle of vision, Manipuri Classical Form of dance is claimed to be one on the most chestiest, modest, softest and mildest but the most meaningful dances of the world.

The most obliging aspect of Manipuri culture is that, it has retained the ancient ritual based dances and folk dances along with the later developed classical Manipuri dance style. Among the classical categories, *'Ras Leela'*—a highly evolved dance drama, choreographed on *'Vaishnavite Padavalis'* composed by mainly eminent Bengali poets and some Manipuri Gurus, is the highest expression of artistic genius, devotion and excellence of the Manipuris.

History of Manipuri Dance Forms

It is stated that the indigenous people of the valley were the Gandharva's mentions in the *Ramayana* and Mahabharata. The dance patterns in Manipur must have a link with the Gandharva's Culture—which is mythological believed to excel over all other dance forms.

The Gandharva Culture of Mahabharata

Manipuri dance—as the name suggests, originated in Manipur, the northeastern state of India—a paradise on earth when the nature has been extra-generous in her beauty. Love of art and beauty is inherent in the people of this land from time immemorial. The people of Manipur are well-known for their high cultural sense. They are very religious minded exclusively attached to Sri Krishna and Sri Radhika, who are always in their thought. And it is difficult to find Manipuri girl who cannot sing or dance. Not only girls but boys too excel in art and culture. Dancing as a profession for few classes of people is unknown to the simple people. Every Manipuri can dance without additional effort and considerable time. A young Boy plays the rule of Krishna in the Ras Lila. This child seemed to be too young to dance. Surprisingly most of the dancers do not have a formal training.

It is stated that the indigenous people of this valley were the dance-expert Gandharva's, mentioned in the epic Ramayana and Mahabharata. The Aswamedha Parva of Mahabharata refer to the defeat of Pandava's at Manipur and the identification of Babhrubahana, the son of Arjuna and Chitrangoda, the soul daughter of the Gandharva king Chitrabahana.

Babhrubahana, the legendary King of Manipur played a vital role in the formation of the existing professional caste and races of Manipur. The dance patterns in Manipur must have a link with the Gandharva's Culture—which is mythological believed to excel over all other dance forms. Among the classical categories, 'Ras Leela'—a highly evolved dance drama, choreographed on Vaishnava Padavali's, is the highest expression of artistic genius, devotion and excellence of the Manipuris.

Manipuri Dance is Categorically Vedic-Aryan in Character

The history of Manipur says that different clans of the Indo-Vedic and Mongoloid people lived side by side in Manipur for centuries. Now it assembled in her the major folks of the east and the west-the Meiteis and the Bishnupriya Manipuris. Orthodox Bishnupriya Manipuris consider themselves to be the genuine Vedic decent, who according to them, came to Manipur valley from Dvaraka and Hastinapura, just after the Mahabharata war, which happening before the 9th century B.C. as generally accepted by modern research.

The Meitheis, on the other hand, differentiate themselves as mongoloid group of people. But some orthodox Meiteis believe that they are the descendants of group of people coming from

Mithila (Videha) which is the eastern frontier of Aryan culture for a long time.

Referring to the people of Manipur E.T. Dalton in his book "Descriptive Ethnology of Bengal", states that, "..And, this hordes overrun a country (Manipur) that has been previously occupied by the people of Aryan blood known in the western India and to the Bards." Also while explaining the appearance of the Manipuris, Dr. R. Brown says " although the general facial characteristics of the Mannipuris are of Mongolian type, there is great diversity of features among them, some of them showing regularly approaching the aryan type" (Imperial Gazetteer of India, 1908, Vol 17, page 126).

So certainly there was a bulk of Vedic people from the north-west of India had entered into Manipur valley in the pre-Christian era. If we talk of the history in respect of the Aryan population, their migration, settlements and cultural penetration and the development of political institutions in Manipur Valley, there are a little source of information's about this. Ancient temples like the Vishnu temple of Bishnupur, Govindaji temple in Imphal, the Kohima stone, old palaces and other related buildings and structures provide us little more historical information's. G. E.Geraini, in his work, Researches on Ptolemy's Geography, indicated the establishment of an Indo-Vedic state by the Bishnupriya Manipuris in the remote period in Manipur. He states, "From the Brahmaputra and manipur to the tonkin gulf, we can trace a continuous string of petty states ruled by those scions of the ksatriyo race, using the sanskrit or pali language in official documents and iscriptions, buildings, temples and monuments of old Hindu style and employing Brahman priests at the propitiatory ceremonies connected with the court, and the state".

The Manipuri Dance and Music of international repute basically centre round Krishna Bhakti and is indeed a great contribution of the Gandharva's and the Vedic immigrants to Manipur as per expressions found in Ashoka's Pillar inscriptions.

Mongoloid Elements

The other race in Manipur, the Meitheis, moved in from Chinese territory and this is reflected in the name. Meithei means, in Chinese, 'people of this country', *i.e.*, Chinese territory. "It is quite probable that the kalachaias are the first cultural race in possession of the Manipur valley," wrote Rajmohan nath in' The Background of Assamese Culture'. R.M. Nath also held that-"The Meitheis were the later immigrants." The Meitheis brought with them the experience and momentum of an ancient civilization.

They probably had superiority in numbers and gradually they gained ascendancy. Manipuri folklore tells of an adventurer named Poireiton who came form' the land of death' and taught the locals many wonderful things. This mythical figure may have been an enterprising Meithei. It is also possible that Poireiton wasn't a single person. It may have been a common name for the early settlers.

It is evident by a number of sources that China supplied some earlier racial elements that attributed to the development of the Indo-Chinese culture in Assam. The Accounts of Shung Shu (420-479 AD) recorded the Chinese's subduation of manipur valley, and also establishment of their suzerainty over Kapily valley which is to be located in Modern Nowgaon. Referring to the Chinese or Mongolian racial elements in the Manipur valley, Arther Pelliot (Deux Itineraries) stated that the Chinese invaded the valley in about 700 AD.

The Chinese called the people of the valley as Khalachas, *i.e.* the son of the wide lake (Loktak) and described them as highly civilized. Interestingly, the Meiteis of the Mongolian stock and later comers to Manipur used to call the Bishnupriya Manipuri as Khalachaya. E. T. Dalton held that by degrees the Meiteis became more powerful in Manipur. It encouraged them to introduce matrimonial relations with the indigenous people undoubtedly with the Vedic Aryan people, and it now merged into totally a new origin, *i.e.* Indo-Mongoloid Culture.

However, as mentioned in the Meitei sacred scriptures and texts, a most comprehensive dance form popularly known as *Lai-haraoba* mirrors the pre-vaishnavite culture and other types of solo, duet, group, etc., within its body. Lai-Haraoba (Merry Festival of the Deities) is the festival of the recollection of the creation stories played by all these deities with the first origin of this universe and evolution of the plants and animals through the will of *Atiya Shidaba*, the Supreme God of the Meitei sanamahi's.

A Remarkable Example of Cross-Cultural History

The people of Manipur and Bengal provide a most interesting example of cultural and aesthetic fusion. The story begins in the 15th century when religious developments from Bangladesh reached Manipur. By the mid-Seventeenth century a full repertoire of songs and dances of Bangla origin took root in Manipur. This was aptly named 'Bangladesh Pala'. Gradually the main centre of Bangladesh's distinctive school of the Kirtan-based songs and dances shifted to Manipur and has remained there ever since as an essential part of Manipuri culture.

The most obliging aspect of Manipuri culture is that, it has retained the ancient ritual based dances and folk dances along with the later developed classical Manipuri dance style. Among the classical categories, 'Raas Leela'—a highly evolved dance drama, choreographed on 'Vaishnavite Padavalis' composed by mainly eminent Bengali poets and some Manipuri Gurus, is the highest expression of artistic genius, devotion and excellence of the Manipuris.

Contribution of Rabindranath Tagore

Rabindranath Tagore, the world poet, was a great patron of the Manipuri dance and culture. He also deserves a honorable place in the style and regarded as the " pioneer of Manipuri dance and culture".

It was he who popularised the style with its high zenith among the people of the world. The world poet was fascinated with the lovely and charming Manipuri Rasleela at Machhimpur, a Bishnupriya Manipuri locality in the modern Sylhet District in Bangladesh in 1920. He immediately decided to open a new department of Manipuri Dance in his Shantiniketan in Calcutta.

Consequently, he invited Guru Senarik Singha Rajkumar,—a native of kalijar downtown Silchar of Assam and Guru Nileshwar Mukharjee of kamlganj thana of undivided Sylhet district. Both of the Gurus belonged to the Bishnupriya Manipuri Community, and with them the new department of It was an epoch making events in the history of Manipuri Dance and within a decade in crossed its regional as well national fields and became a reputed international style.

Ritualistic, Recreational, Religious and Temporal

The traditional Manipuri style of dancing preeminently embodies delicate, lyrical and graceful movements which enhance the audience in its beautiful and colourful costumes and presentation. The Manipuri dance whether folk, classical or modern, is devotional in nature. The folk dances of people captivate the beholders with their exotic costumes and simple but graceful rhythm. Their folklore is rich in quality. The dances are ritualistic and recreational, religious and temporal. The ritual dances are performed at a particular rite or ceremony or sacrifice and these dances naturally have a spiritual and religious basis. From the religious point of view and from the artistic angle of vision, we can claim that the Manipuri Classical Form of dance is one on the most chestiest, modest, softest and mildest but the most meaningful dances of the world.

The Gandharva's dance skills are mentioned in the Ramayana and Mahabharata and other Hindu Puranas. In Mahabharata, there is reference to Manipur in at least four different places – once in Adi parva, twice in Aswamedha parva and once in Mahaprashthanik parva. According to the Mahabharata, the ancient name of this country was 'Meckley' and this is the name that was used when King Gaursham signed a treaty with the British in 1763. In 1876, the king of Manipur used the same name referred to his kingdom which is documented in the treaty with the British Government.

Scholars have different opinions as well as views regarding the exact location of the Mahabharata Manipur with the recent Manipur. In the Allahabad stone pillar inscription of Samudra Gupta (4th century AD) there is no mention of Manipur, although the neighbouring kingdoms are named. In old assamese records, Manipur is mentioned as Magloo or Moglai. The Burmese call the country a Cassey or Kassay. McCulloch described that " The name Manipour accounted for by the Munniporie, who quote the Mahabharata in confirmation of its accuracy. They gave the same form Muni, a jewel. This jewel formerly in the possession of the Rajas of the country ages ago.

The country was at one time named Mahindrapore, but one Rajah by the name Manipur was in existence before the birth of Babhrubahana, and Mahindrapore or Mahindra Parbhata was the name of the hill, situated but a short distance to the east of the capital". On the other hand G. E. Geraini's Researches on ptolemy's Geography and The Gaits History of Assam compiled by Prof. Padmanath Battacharjee, stated that Bishnupur was the ancient capital of Manipur and Imphal come into existence in much later period than that of the city of Bishnupur.

Dr. Dinesh Chandra Sen (Brihod Bongo, 1935), Shri Ochchutcharan Chaudhury Tatvanidhi (Srihotter Itibritta, 1905,), Shri Janokinath Bosak (Manipur prohelika), L. Ibubghal Singha (Manipura), Sri Sena Singha (Prachinadhunik somkhipta Manipurer Itihas), Shri Mukundalal Chowdhury (Manipurer Itihas), Shri Mohendra Kumar singha (Manopurer Prachin Itihas), Shri Krishnamohon Dhar (Purbabango O Assam, 1909) and some other Indian scholars and historians idientified the present Manipur to be that of the epic as described in the Mahabharata, in their writings and articles.

The inhabitants of Manipur did identify them as "Manipuris" since past centuries. The land Manipur was formerly divided into small territories occupied by different clans, namely, the Khumals, the Moirangs, The Angoms, The Luwangs, the Ningthoujas, etc. The territories were after the names of the respective clans. Besides there are 70 Lokei (Ningthou–Khongya or members of Royel Family), Lempa Lokei (Thakcham), Moirango Lokei (Moirang –them) are the dominating groups. Each of the Lokei have their distinct ethnic identity (Gotros). So different clans of the Aryan and Mongoloid people lived side by side in Manipur for centuries.

Conversion of Meiteis in Hinduism by Shri Santidas Babaji in 19th century at the instance of the king Shri Pamhaiba was aimed at linking the with the Aryans, the mainstream of people of Manipur and their language too with Sanskrit. The Aryans, the followers of Lord Viṣhnu denied to accept the initiation by Shri Santadas Babaji and the others (accepted). And thus the Manipuri people – Aryan and Kuki-chin group have been classified and renamed as Bishnupriya and Meiteis their language too. Culturally, the Meiteis and Bishnupriyas cannot be distinguished from each other. Both these two clans developed a homogeneous culture, and the concept of the one community grew among them.

By analysing the root of establishment of Hindu dynasties in upper Burma, we can see that all the Hindu dynasties settled in Upper Burma had to come across Manipur from the western and northern India by road as Manipur was only the gateway of Far East. The beauty of the land Manipur, lake Logtak and its surrounding areas also might have attracted them and some of them settled there and reigned there for years together.

Manipur or Meckley is actually on a tableland surrounded by hills. In the plains beside the loktak lake lived a race of people who had sharp Indo-Aryan features and used a language which was similar to the Kamrupi tongue rather than the Burmese-Chinese group. For centuries these Aryan people have been called 'Khalachai' which in southern Chinese dialect means 'Children of the wide lake' (Kha=Lake; La=Wide; Chai=Children) as described by Shri R. M. Nath in "The Background of Assamese Culture", Page 86-87, 2nd Edn, 1978. Statement by Late L Iboonghal singha, Rtd.

District and sessions Judge of Manipur in a monthly Magazine "Ritu", 1959, page-21: " Arther Paliot in his History of China stated that the chinese invaded Manipur in about 700 A.D. and won over the war. They called Manipuris as khalachais or sons of the wide lake (Loktak) and described them as highly civilized". The Chinese inroads over the valley was authenticated in the writings of Hien-Tasng, the great Chinese traveller who has visited the court of Kumar Vaskar Varma of Kamrupa in the 7th Century A.D.

Manipuri is the classical dance from the Manipur region in the northeast. The past and origins of this dance are not clear as many myths and legends are associated with it. The Manipuris consider themselves the descendants of the Gandharvas who were the legendary musicians, and dancers in the celestial courts of Indira. The earliest records of this dance form date back to about 100 AD. It was King

Bhagyachandra of 17th century who established Manipuri dance on a scientific basis. It was he who innovated Ras Leelas (dance dramas) and Sankirtan (form of invocation). He also designed the beautiful Manipuri dance costume. Some other beliefs also exists like that of the Meitei tribes of Manipur, they believe that when the earth was newly formed it was lumpy and to make it soft and firm the seventh Lainoorahs danced on the earth by pressing their feet very gently. That is the secret behind the delicate steps of Manipuri dance.

Slow and gracious movements differentiate Manipuri from other dance styles. The delicate arm movements and gentle foot work characterise this dance. The Vaishnava faith brought along with it the origin of the Manipuri dance. The repertoire is dominated by the themes from the Vishnu Puranas, Bhagvata Puranas, and Geeta Govinda.

The female 'Rasa' dances, based on the Radha-Krishna theme feature group ballets and solos. The male 'Sankirtana' dances performed to the pulsating rhythm of the Manipuri Dholak are full of vitality. Manipuri dance is very much religious and associated to Vaishnava cult of Hinduism. The art form primarily depicts episodes from the life of Vishnu.

This style is multifaceted, ranging from the softest feminine to the obviously vigorous masculine. Dignified grace is to be found in every aspect and the range it offers in technique, rhythmic and tempo makes a Manipuri recital an absorbing and exhilarating experience.

Dance Style

The technique of Manipuri dancing is based on an interesting principle of compensatory movement with the objective of achieving rounded movements and avoiding any jerks, sharp edges or straight lines. The Manipuris are completely ignorant about the use of dance for the sake of dancing and contract system. From the sacred texts, we can point here some characteristic features of Manipuri dancing which are as under:

(1) The place where dance are held are sacred. It is considered to be a crime or sin to violate the rules. Anytime, anyplace is not good enough.

(2) Dances are devotional or ritualistic rather than entertainment of the eyes. It is a *Sadhan-Bhakti*-kind of devotion to God for both the dancers and onlookers.

(3) The dressing is so designed as to free them from any stimulus, excitement to the opposite sex. Dance is but the rhythmic expression of action and activities of life on the upper part of the body.

(4) The artist never looks at any person or audience as a mark of concentration to the Lord surrendering the outward world and illusions of *Maya* and also giving up all lust, greed, anger, envy, hatred and pride of the dancers.

(5) The steps of dancing are very much acute and complex and never show outward feeling of lust and amorous play.

The Techniques

The technique of Manipuri dancing is based on an interesting principle of compensatory movement with the objective of achieving rounded movements and avoiding any jerks, sharp edges or straight lines. If the right hand is outstretched towards the right, for example, the body is tilted towards the left in order to offset the right side thrust.

The movement towards the right has been balanced and subdued by one towards the left. This particularly contrasts with the technique of Bharata Natyam, in which, in the same example, the effort would generally be to emphasis the movement to the right. It is this aspect which imparts to Manipuri an undulating and soft appearance.

This impression of softness actually hides a very tough regimen of body control.

Feet Movement

Similarly, the feet never strike the ground with a sound on impact, as this would interfere with the delicate flow of the body movements. The knees and ankles cushion the landing so that no sound ensues. Manipuri dancers do not even wear ankle bells, whose purpose is after all to accentuate the beats tapped out by the feet.

Mudra's (Hand Movements)

The Mudra's or hand movements in Manipuri dance are quite different from other classical dance forms. From Bhagyachandra's *Govinda Sangit Leelabilas* and the book " *Laithok Laikha Jogoi*" the following Mudra's are found:

O-songyukta (single hand): *Potaka, tripotaka, ordopotaka, kotokamukh, sondongsa, mrigashirsha, hongsashya, olopollob, bhruksa, angush, ordhochandra, kurak, mushti.*

Songyukta (Double hand): *Shangkha, Chakra, onjoli, Taksa, Paas, korkot, Somput, rombhasum, pushpaput, kukil, shoshtik, sook.*

Musical Instruments

Dances are very much based upon the cymbals (*kartal* or *mangkang*) and the cylindrical drum known as *Manipuri mridang* or *pung*. Unlike other classical, dances where the instrument is merely used as an accompaniment, the *pung* and the *kartal (manjira)* are actually used in the dance. Manipuri is unique among the classical Indian dances in that the instrumentation is a central part of the dance, rather than as a side accompaniment. The main musical instrument in Manipuri dance is Kartal or cymbal. Another important instruments is the *Dhak* or *Pung* (mridanga or dram). *Dhak, Kartal, Mangkang, and Sembong* are the soul of Manipuri Sankritan music and Classical Manipuri Dance.

It assumes an important ritual character, an indispensable part of all social and devotional ceremonies in Manipur,- the instrument itself becoming an object of veneration. *Manzilla*, used by the female performers, is similar to *kartal*, but different in nature and smaller in size. There are of course may be considered as resultant instrument of traditional Manipuri and Hinduised Manipuri culture. The musical instrument which is Manipuris own is *Pena*, a string instrument which is played by fiddling somewhat similar to *Ektara* of Bengal. Often, The use of *Baashis* and *Harmoniums* are found in Manipuri Dance.

Dance Costumes

The Ras costumes and ornaments of Sri Radhika and the Gopies are colourful and handsome. The skirt the present day

Ras dancers wear is modeled on the one the Maharaja Bhagya Chandra (1763-1798) saw in his dream.

The costumes in Manipuri dance is very colourful, attractive and very richly bedecked. The female dancers wear a dress called "*patloi*". The lehenga is called "*Kumin*" with mirrors and zari work intricately woven into beautiful designs. It is layered with a transparent silk or "*Pasuan*". The choli is also embellished with zari, silk or gota embroidery. On the head, covering the face, they wear a transparent odhni, through which the expression and emotion on the face of the dancer can easily he seen. Gopis usually wear a red dress while Radha stands out in green attire. The male dancer, who is Krishna, wears a saffron dress.

Ras costumes and ornaments of Sri Radhika and the Gopies are colourful and handsome. The skirt the present day Ras dancers wear is modeled on the one the Maharaja Bhagya Chandra (1763-1798) saw in his dream.

Here is List of Costumes and some terms related to the costumes and ornaments used in Manipuri Dance:

- *Potlei:* Ras costume of *Sri Radhika* and the *Gopis*, designed by the *Potlei-setpa*'s who rent them for the performance at some rates.
- *Koknaam:* A gauze at overhead, embossed with silver *Jari*.
- *Meikhumbi:* A transparent and thin vail thrown over the head.
- *Kumin:* An Embroidered brightly colored silk skirt.
- *Pasuan:* A short flair of silver gauze over the kumin.
- *Khaon:* Rectangular embroidered piece with belt.
- *Koktombi:* Cap covering the head.
- *Thabret:* A griddle round the waist.
- *Khangoi:* Small rectangular belt over the Pasuan.
- *Leitreng:* Golden ring round the head.
- *Chura:* Made of peacock feathers, wired on top of head.
- *Feichom: Dhooti,* a saffron dress.
- *Ghungur:* Ornament for the foot.

Movements

The dancer begins with the movements known as the chali. It is a movement which suggests basic ways of walking and covering space. The dancer moves first to the front and back with hands held horizontally at the chest level and then moves these hands vertically in an up-and-down direction. She then covers space in side-ways walking, ending by weaving circles and spirals. In these basic movements, the various types of bhramaris are introduced, the two distinct varieties being the uplai and the longlai. These lais whether in lasya or in tandava as ways of covering floor-space; usually is side ways movement followed by a semi-circle.

They are the finale of the dance cadences and are often executed in multiples of three as in the tikai of the other dance styles. Sometimes a spiral movement in vertical space is executed, where the dancer treats her body like a screw and weaves a spiral vertically from a higher level to lower level. While doing so the dancer also takes a circle or a spin. This is very difficult movement has a graceful fluidity, sometimes mistaken for imprecision. The achongha of jumping movements are characteristic of the tandava portions of the dance.

The basic movements of the chali are connected together to form the various types of parengs. The parengs are cadences of movements in a given metrical cycle. The metrical cycles are many and in-beats and the cross-beats are complicated, requiring a high sense of precision. All the lais are used in parengs and different types of talas are employed, especially the rajmela, the seven beats (rupaka), 15 beats (panchamsvari) and the 16 beats (tintala). The first three bhangis and the bhangi pareng achongba, the Vrindavan pareng and the khurumba pareng are known as the lasya cadences.

They are used in common rasa portions of the dance. The three other bhangis have a common adjestive gostha which stands for the tandava bhangis. They are used by actors while presenting the character of Krishna in the rasa dances. Three such bhangis are prescribed, namely the gostha bhangi pareng, the gostha Vrindavan pareng and the gostha Khurumba pareng. The last one is rarely performed and seems to have gone out of vogue.

The dance has a highly complex technique of movement and tala. The dance is not restricted to solo numbers. Manipuri is the only classical style in which we find exquisite survivals of compositions, such as the hallisaka, the charchari and other forms mentioned in classical Sanskrit literature. In the rasa dances, we find that all the four types of pindis mentioned by Bharata can be seen.

Technique: Manipuri has a flow and a grace which contrasts from the precision of the South Indian styles. This impression of ease and fluidity results from an unusual treatment of the body. The vertical line of the body is never broken The body merely curves itself into a figure of 8. The positions attained are thus relaxed and controlled rather than sculpturesque. An effort is made to connect two parts of the body through beautiful curves. There are no sudden transitions from particular horizontal sutras as in Bharata Natyam. The knees are kept close together and the body is held upright but without any tension. The torso is not treated as a unit, but is divided into two distinct parts above the Katisutras, the chest and the waist.

Neither unit is used singly because the bend of any part by itself would mean creating an angle. Thus, the chest and the waist, although moving in opposition, are always connected. The effect is of the slow drawing of a curve in the shape of "S", but is never a simple bend. The neck and the head follow this principle but the head never moves horizontally. It also executes a figure 8 in space. The arms and hands follow the pattern of the lower limbs and the torso. They too are never tense nor are they even in acute flexion. They are held, in a naturally relaxed manner away from the body in a semi-circular curve. The wrists plays an extremely important part in the movement of the hands and the fingers, because it is the wrists which give the movements of the fingers a unique fluidity. A basic movement is the gradual closing in an opening out of the fingers; while the wrist attempts to execute a lateral figure.

The face is placid and without any exaggerated facial expressions. This controlled, but not unduly severe or austere, expression is sustained throughout the performance. In the Lasya portions the dancer does not and cannot lift her foot away from the ground above the level of the knee. The release from the ground is invariably characterised by a sweep of the ground, a gliding movement almost touching the floor rather than a movement where the foot is lifted high above the ground. The situation changes considerably in the tandava portion known for its agility, verve and high leaps.

The basic position in tandava is no longer the closed feet with knees bent in front leaving no space between them. There is nearly a four tala distance between the two feet and the knees are bent in front. In the tandava portions, the torso is occasionally treated as a separate unit and side bends are frequent. There are many sitting positions and many spirals and turns known to the dance styles, both in lasya and tandava. In lasya, the sthanakas or various positions once again attempt to limit space and although women dancers change the level throughout a performance, there is hardly ever much space between the two feet.

In the tandava portions, the sthanakas take the form of positions known as the Vrischika Karnas of the Natya Shastra tradition. There are few leg extensions in the lasya or tandava portions. Hip movements are not allowed in the tandava and lasya portions. There is one type of thigh or pelvic movement known to the dance style. It is an up and down movement and it is achieved through knee dips and through a suggestion of a hop on the toe. The manner of covering space in Manipuri, is expressive of its grace and delicacy. The dancer covers floor space also in figures of 8 and then the foot is lifted to cover space, it invariably touches the ground by a slight toe movement rather than flat foot or the heal. The Kunchita foot or the agratalasanchara foot of the Natya Shastra is seen repeatedly in this dance style.

Music, Costumes and Ensembles

The musical accompaniment to Manipuri dances is played on an instrument rather like a guitar called the khol, and the mridangam. But sometimes the singing is done by a group whose members do not join in the dance. When the drummer and the dancer together execute certain quick talas, each in his own medium, the tempo of the dance increases and the quick rhythmic pattern is enchanting to watch. The costumes are very picturesque. The women wear a tight-fitting conical cap of black velvet or other material, trimmed with a border of synthetic pearls, under a thin white veil. Modern dancers often discard the cap in favour of a bun on top and to the side of the head, and haloed with flowers. The choli or tight fitting bodice is usually of velvet with tight sleeves trimmed with gold embroidery. The gagra or flounced skirt is of a striking colour, yellow, red or green and usually of silk with a wide border at the bottom of the skirt consisting of a design of sequins. Tiny square, round or oval mirrors are scattered all over the skirt, which has a transparent Muslim garment over it, embroidered with silver thread. As the dancers swirl round, the flashing mirrors reflecting the light produce a striking effect.

The male dancer wears a dhoti with embroidered bands across his chest ending in flaps that fall over both hips. In the Ras-Leela, Krishna is gorgeously attired in a pleated dhoti of gold or yellow silk, the chest being covered with glittering necklaces while wristlets and armlets adorn the arms.

The Rasa dances go on for several hours at a stretch. The honeyed melodies Meera, Krishna's disciple are also greatly in vogue. The ritualistic dances have Krishna as the central figure. Manipuri dancers firmly believe that when they dance the gods descend to earth to join their revelry. The name Lai Horaopa signified 'sporting or making merry with the gods. Girls, gaily dressed, begin the dance with offerings of flowers and fruits. The men then join in and pick their partners. Actually this dance is the Shiva-Parvati done in the Manipuri technique. It is very robust.

The animism of the Manipuris, preceding their conversion to Hinduism, has left its stamp on their dance art and in the Lai Hairobi it is pronounced. This is an annual ceremony performed in every village for the purpose of propitiating its Lai, *i.e.* god's seat or the dwelling of Lam.

The Repertoire

The repertoire of Manipuri dances can be divided into three or four broad categories. This would not include the whole group of dances which one would call tribal or folk. The first group would comprise the pre-Vaishnava dance forms or dance rituals. Closely related to this group would be the Thang or the martial ritual dancers of Manipur, all these belong to pre-Vaishnava state of Manipuri culture.

The second group would constitute the dance and the dance music sections of the various jatras in Manipur. The Holi Pala, the Khumbak Ishei and other numbers today presented on the stage are part and parcel of these seasonal festivities.

The third group would constitute the different types of Sankirtana traditions. Part and parcel of these Sankirtana was the group dancing, the various types of walking or group forms executed either through clapping or through the playing of small cymbals called Manjira or large cymbals called Kartala.

A fourth group may be considered for the ballad forms which have both a vocal as also a miming aspect to them. Among these would be the presentation through solo duet rendering, in the forms known as the Wariliba, the Haiba Thiba, etc.

A most important part of Manipuri repertoire is recognised by the generic term Jagoi. At the artistic level, the Jagoi can be considered as the main type of art dance. Jagoi represents those sections of music and dance from amongst the Sankirtanas which could be presented outside the ritual parameters. The traditional gurus of Manipur have divided the Jagoi into several sub-categories such as the Pungalola Jagoi, the Motkanba Jagoi and just Lila. There is a further sub-division which is made by adding the adjectives Nupa or Nupi-Nupa standing for man and Nupi for woman. Amongst the further divisions are the Cholam, the Kartala Cholam, the Mridang Cholam, the dance of the Ghosta lila (also called the Shanshenba Jagoi) and the Spear dances.

Ras Leelas and Sankirtans are the highly developed dance-forms revealing the high aesthetic religious feeling of the people of Manipur. Ras Leelas go on for 8 to 10 hours in the temple courtyard from dusk to dawn. The religious people of Manipur shed tears of joy experiencing it as the real spirit of the Lord. All the technical elements mentioned in the Sangeet Shastras are found in Ras Leelas, such as Nritta (Pure Dance), Nritya

(Interpretative dance) and Natya (Theme expressed through four kinds of Abhinaya). In Sankirtan, male dancers with kartal and Mridang wear white dhotis and turban creating a serene and dignified atmosphere. In the festival dances, women wear the hand-woven and embroidered Phanek with strips and white thin scarf. There are various types of cholams. The cholams are both lasya and tandava.

Kartal Cholam: It is a Tandava dance of cymbals. It is performed, by the male dancers only. Their feats are in intricate talas or timing on the Kartals (large cymbals). An essence of harmony is achieved with the rhythmic tunes of mridang. The dancer shows the dexterity by making jumps radiating in semi circular ways, making strength-full movements with speedy whirls and turns with the exact Tala of the music. The dancer imitates the natural movements of Kapote (crane), Mayur (peacock), Khanjan (bagtail) and Hansa (swan) in perfect accuracy of movement and sound.

Manjira Cholam: This Tandava dance is performed in temples during Jholan Yatra. A beautiful dais is formed in the Mandapa hall of the Govindaji temple. The idols of Radha and Krishna are placed on the dais. The music party of the temple sits before the deities and then this dance is performed in their presence in reverence to the god and goddess.

Pung Cholam: It is a Tandava drum dance generally performed by a male dancer in the temple square on some special occasions. The dancer performs with a mad frenzy of speed with bends and turns holding the drum and producing the music simultaneously. Sometimes the drum sound is produced by imitating the sounds of Nature.

There are other cholam dances such as the Duff cholam and the Kanjira cholam. Amongst the Kartali dances are the clapping items performed only by women as the Nupi Khumbak ishei and the Nupa khumbak ishei. These are group dances in which a number of interesting group formations can be seen and the dance is built on clapping of hands at cross rhythms to be basics rhythm played by the accompanying pung. All the cholam and Kartali dances are pure nritta. There is not abhinaya, not is there any song accompaniment.

The Thang haiba and the Takhew sauba or the sword and the spear dances which belong to the tandava category have now become part of the artistic repertoire. Originally these were performed either in the contact of ritual magical performances or as a sequence in the Lai Haraoba. When incorporated as an artistic number, these are called thangta jagoi.

The Nupi Jagoi or the women's dance is the graceful variety and is divided into two main sub-divisions. The first Bhangi Jagoi and the second Punglol Jagoi. *i.e.*, that which is performed only to the mnemonics of the Pung the Manipuri Mridangam. The Bhangi Jagoi is marked by seriousness of purpose, a slow tempo and a very careful delivery of movements which are controlled and restrained. It comes under the category called the smitanga. The Punglol Jagoi is executed in a fast tempo, a metrical pattern and a repetition ending in triplets of three. All these should be considered both of the male and the female as pure abstract dancing without mime or abhinaya. This is the nritta repertoire of Manipuri dancing. It must be remembered that none of these numbers are dissociated from the repertoire which have mentioned in the context of the sankirtana and the jatra dances

Lai Horaoba: Lai Haraoba is performed all over Manipur, but chiefly at Moirang village in the memory of princess Thoibi and her lover Khamba. Lai Haraboa is an annual festival, a ritual and a dance-drama performance all rolled into one and lasting for many days. It is also performed to appease the local deities. It is performed on the outskirts of the village in front of the shrines of the deities of the forest called Umang lies. Lai Haraoba literally means "merry making of gods". The participants of this dance and music mela begin to assemble on the village green in the afternoon and enjoy the festival till sun set everyday in May. The main participants are the priests and priestesses called maibas and maibis respectively. The males disguise as ancient Manipuri warriors and heroes and the women as princess, dance together in a roaming fashion to reveal and re-enact the story of the creation and continuity of the universe. The dance movements present a strange mixture of suggestiveness, ludicrous and wed revelry.

The music that accompanies the dance consists of drums, flutes, gongs, manhiras and pena which has a bunch of tiny bells tied on one end of its bow. The bells produce a subdued tinkling sound in combination with the sombre and rather sad melody of the instrument proper, which resembles the music of a Sarangi. The dancer do not put on ankle bells. It seems the episodes of Khamba-Thoibi romance were incorporated in the dance-drama afterwards. These episodes have been narrated in the Manipuri epic.

Five different varieties of the Lai Haraboa are known and these are associated with different venues such as Kanglai, Moirang, Kakaching, Andra, and Chakpa. The festival begins with a procession going to a nearby river or a pond-like the leaders of the village invoke the spirits of the waters. The leaves-one placed facing the sky and the other covers the first leaf. The ritual symbolises the emergence of life from eternal water. Ritually, a seed is put within the two leaves. The procession returns with a filled pitcher from the pond and the leaves placed above it

Rasa: The Rasa dances of Manipur are lyrical narrative and not dramatic. The rasa dances have a structure and technique which can distinguish them from any other type of dance in Manipur. Bhagya Chandra Maharaj or King Jai Singh is considered the composer of at least three of the four Rasa dances known to Manipur. The Rasa dances are performed on particular occasion and in particular season.

First and the foremost is the Vasant Rasa for the full moon day of Holi. The Vasant Rasa is invariably preceded by the Natapala or the group of men dancers who play the drum and sing. Thereafter there is the presentation of a particular raga in this case, Vasant Raga by women singers now called sutradhari. Here the singing sets the tone of the presentation of the rasa. A particular mood is invoked and the players and the audience become prepared to transport themselves into the world of Lord Krishna in Vrindavan. Thereafter, there is the description of Vrindavan sung by the sutradhari and followed through dance by a group of young dancers.

The next sequence is Vaishnava Vandana. The most exciting part of the rasa is the entry of the young Krishna, normally played by a young girl. Thereafter is the presentation of the main themes in the case of Vasant Rasa. It is the theme of the gopis playing Holi with Krishna.

The Kunj Rasa is performed sometime in August coinciding with what is known as the full moon or rakhi or rakhi purnima. The theme of this rasa is drawn from the Srimad Bhagvata. It revolves round the mutual hide and seek of Radha and Krishna. The rasa is performed in a special group and it recreates the dance of the gopis with Krishna.

A third rasa called the nritya rasa which was created by Maharaja Chandrakirti in the nineteenth century can be performed at any time. Here dance, rather than the story or the theme is more important. These dances are performed generally at night in the dancing halls attached to the temples. The halls are profusely and tastefully decorated with garlands, flowers, flags, buntings, etc. on the occasion. Truly classical in spirit, the Rasa-dances are full of devotional fervour and are performed to the singing of songs and Kirtans and to the accompaniment of Khol or mridanga, manjira and bamboo flutes. Their liquid beauty lyrical quality, restrained and rhythmic swaying, swinging and spinning almost at one place, with hands, close to the body, coupled with soft vocal and instrumental devotional music lend the performance a uniqueness which defies description.

Besides these rasa dances, there are the Lilas. These Lilas also constitute an important part of the repertoire of the Manipuri dances. The Gostha lila recreates the play on Krishna and Balarama; Krishna and Yashoda and the dancers of Krishna with his companions. The main singer for the gostha lila is a man and not a woman.

In the ulukhala rasa, the birth of Krishna, Putna Vadh, etc. including makhan chori are presented. The Vaishnavite flavour lives and vibrates in the hearts of every Manipuri and truly through the rasa dances and the presentation of the lilas Vrindavan is called in every heart in far of Manipur. Their sophisticated pieces of opera with libretto musical scales, ragas, talas, giving enough scope for pure nritta abhinaya and the combination of both singing and dancing. The Maharasa concentrates on the love quarrel between Radha and Krishna.

The theme is based on the story of the Bhagvata Purana. The gostha or the Gopa Rasa is performed in Tandava style by Lord Krishna with Gopas. The killing of Asuras, etc. is shown in the dance.

MOHINIATTAM

Mohiniattam is derived from the words "Mohini" and "attam". Mohini means a beautiful woman and attam means dance. So this dance is an exquisite feminine style with undulating flow of body movements. The theme of the dance is generally "sringara" or love. Delicate themes of love are performed with suggestive abhinaya, subtle gestures, rhythmic footwork and lilting music.

After almost virtual extinction early this century, it is gratifying to note, that Mohiniattam survived its difficult phase and emerged as a full fledged dance form and credits itself to be one of the most exquisite dance styles of India.

Mohiniattam means Mohini's dance. Mohini according to Indian mythology, is a very beautiful woman who attracts people instantly and was an enchantress, thus it is the dance of the enchantress. It is also believed that Lord Vishnu had disguised himself as 'Mohini' with an intention to slay Bhasmasura and also during the churning of nectar from the ocean. But the basis of this dance is not seduction alone. It also signifies transformation of Lord Vishnu into a female form and also the concept of 'Ardhnareeshwara', *i.e.* male and female as one. Like many other dance forms, this was also restricted to the Devadasis.

The first reference to Mohiniattam is found in 'Vyavaharamala' composed by Mazhamangalam Naryanam Namboodiri, assigned to the 16th century A.D.

In the 19th century Swati Thirunal, the king of erstwhile Travancore, tried to encourage the development of this dance style. But after him, Mohiniattam suffered heavily owing to the exploitation by the Satraps and the Landlords. Poet Vallathol revived it and gave it a status throughout Kerala through Kalamandalam founded in 1930. Kalamandalam Kalyaniamma, and Chinnammu Amma, the last links of a disappearing tradition, nurtured aspirants in the discipline at Kalamandalm.

The theme of Mohiniattam is love and devotion to god. Vishnu or Krishna is more often the hero. The spectators could feel his invisible presence when the heroine or her maid details dreams and ambitions through the circular movements, delicate footsteps and subtle expression. The dancer in the slow and medium tempos is able to find adequate space for improvisations and suggestive bhavas. In format, this is similar to Bharata Natyam. The movements are graceful like Odissi and the costumes sober and attractive. It is essentially a solo dance, but nowadays Mohiniattam is performed in groups also. The repertoire of Mohiniattam follows closely that of Bharata Natyam. Beginning with Cholkettu, the dancer performs Jathiswaram, Varnam, Padam and Thillana in a concert. Varnam combines pure and expressionful dance, while Padam tests the histrionic talent of a dancer and Thillana exposes her technical artistry.

The basic dance steps are the Adavus which are of four kinds: Taganam, Jaganam, Dhaganam and Sammisram. These names are derived from the nomenclature called Vaittari.

Mohiniattam maintains realistic make-up and simple dressing. The dancer are attired in a beautiful white and gold bordered Kasavu saree of Kerala. Mohiniattam like many other form, follows the Hastha Lakshandeepika, as a text book for Mudras, or hand gestures. The style of vocal music for Mohiniattam as is generally seen, is classical Kamatic. The lyrics composed by Maharaja Swati Tirunal and Irayimman Thampi are in Manipravala (a mixture of Sanskrit and Malayalam). Till recently, Thoppi Maddalam and Veena provided the background music of Mohiniattam. These have been replaced in recent years by the Mridangam and Violin.

Some of the exponents of this dance form are Chinnammu Amma, Kalyani Kuttiamma, Kanak Rele, Sunanda Nair, Deepti Bhalla and Bharati Shivaji.

The Dance of the Enchantress

This Indian classical dance form—Mohiniattam—comes from one of the South States of India, Kerala. And the mere mention of Kerala brings up in one's mind the wondrous and incomparable beauty of its landscape. The scenic backwaters where the palm fronds fill up the Kerala skyline moving gently and gracefully in the breeze, the boats bobbing up and down gently, gracefully and in perfect tune with nature and its rhythm.

A Mohiniattam dancer immediately reminds you of this scenic beauty in her dance. The movements are beautiful and lyrical and they are always in an unbroken chain, from one movement very gently and gracefully merging into another. Though the movements are swaying and gentle the presentation comes out with a tremendous and strong impact leaving the spectator in an atmosphere of grace, charm, vitality and a forceful vivacity.

The graceful and long limbs of a Mohiniattam dancer brings before your eyes the vision of the palm fronds swaying and dancing in the breeze and the movements are like those of a boat bobbing up and down in the back waters. There is a tremendous amount of force that a Mohiniattam dancer brings out in her performance without which the performance would be lacking in its lustre but this tremendous energy is released in a very controlled and graceful manner which can be achieved only with discipline, hard work and (bhakti) or devotion to the art form.

Also, another feature that influences Mohiniattam is the simplicity of dressing by the people in Kerala which is visible in the costume of the dancer. White is a favourite colour of the people basically because of the hot and humid climate, and a Mohiniattam costume is always white or off white with gold or red border. The hair is tied in a bundle on the left side with white flowers (mogra) around it, with a simple ornament tied on the bun.

The jewellery used for the neck is a 'choker' and a kasimala (coin chain). For the ears a dancer wears a "toda' which is circular like a coin and has dangling earrings with it known as "jhumka". The face is done up with an exaggerated eye make up to help her express her emotions. The eyes reflect immediately the mental state of the situation or character the dancer is representing and a description of Mohiniattam cannot be complete without the mention of the nayanabhinaya or the use of the eyes, eyebrows and eyelids.

But at the end of it all the transformation is tremendous. The merrily dancing eyes and the fluttering of the eyebrows of the dancer all create a devastatingly mischievous atmosphere. The sweet smelling of the flowers, the gentle, swaying movement of the torso in perfect harmony with the music and the bewitching personality of a Mohiniattam dancer all take us to the highest aesthetic order "the atmosphere of enchantment.

The Indian mythology mentions a few times when Lord Vishnu (one among the trinity of Gods-Brhma, Vishnu, Mahesha) assumes the form of Mohini to save the Gods from their clash with the asuras or demons. In one instance when the Gods and demons were churning the mighty ocean for the pot of nectar (amrita), with the serpent Vasuki twined around the mountain Mandaragiri. The ocean brought out all the treasures buried in its depth, while the devas (gods) and asuras (demons) churned on and on. Finally when the pot of nectar appeared, the demons true to their nature grabbed it. The universe would be in total darkness if the demons had their way. It is at this moment the Lord, assumes the form of Mohini to save the Universe from the hands of the demons and total darkness.

The tinkling sound of bells, the sweet smell of flowers, the divine being, the beauty unparalleled-The Enchantress. The one, who could take your minds away from the present to another world of beauty and charm. The lotus eyed one dancing gently and gracefully filling the atmosphere with unsurpassed heavenly beauty. The demons true to her instructions shut their eyes to relinquish and behold the beauty they envisioned. She is Mohini the celestial dancer, one who has come to enchant.

Until, a few decades ago it was presumed that in India there were only four classical dances. Bharata Natyam, Kathak, Manipuri and Kathakali. But then due to the pioneering works of great gurus (teachers), dancers and scholars the dance forms of Mohiniattam, Kuchipudi and Odissi were discovered in their native settings and brought out into the urban stage, much to the delight and wonderment of the lovers of dance.

There is a considerable amount of disagreement among scholars regarding the antiquity of Mohiniattam. Most of them agree that it was during Maharaja Swati Tirunal's rule in the 16th century that Mohiniattam achieved its refined form. The

Maharaja of Travancore was a great patron of arts and he encouraged artistes, singers, dancers from all over the country to come and perform in his court. During this time he also invited the Tanjore quartets from Tamil Nadu who were great Bharata Natyam nattuvanars (or teachers) who brought with them dancers and thus influenced the already present local dance form. The Maharaja was a great bhakta or devotee of Lord Padmanabha and wrote and composed in Hindustani as well as Kamatic innumerable kritis, padams and varnams in his praise. The Maharaja's padams are always a part of a Mohiniattam dancer's repertoire.

But it was finally only in the 20th century that Mohiniattam got its fresh impetus that it actually deserved, and it has come to stay. It was when Mahakavi Vallathol set up the premiere institution for Kathakali, Kerala Kalamandalam in India that he invited three dancers practicing Mohiniattam at that time Kalpuratte Kunjukutty Amma, Tottacheri Chinnamuamma and Kalyani Kutty Amma to come and teach Mohiniattam in his institution. Till, little more than a decade ago the Mohiniattam repertoire ran almost parallel to the Bharata Natyam repertoire. But just as each region has its own individuality and identity it was natural that Mohiniattam had to find its own identity. Due to the relentless work of great researchers, scholars, performers of Mohiniattam, this dance form achieved its present classical standing.

Today, we have different schools of Mohiniattam just as you have schools for Bharata Natyam. But they all have one thing in common they all imbibe the beautiful lyrical elements of the social folk dances of the graceful women from Kerala. Every classical dance form from India has its beginnings in the local prevalent folk art forms and has also been very strongly influenced by the social, political, religious and behavioural pattern of the people of the region. The classical dance forms have imbibed these features to give them all a distinct flavour of its own, but they are still all bound by the great traditions set by the 'Natyashastra' around the 2nd century B.C.

The 'Natya Shastra' is a treatise on dance and drama and lays down rules regarding the practice and presentation of drama and dance. Each dance form adopts it to suit the regional changes in the social, religious, political and behaviour of the people. But it was around the 3rd century A.D that Nandikeshvara wrote the Abhinaya Darpanam which is very religiously followed by the practitioners of Bharata Natyam. It gives the usage of hastas (hand gestures), pada bhedas (feet positions), caris (gaits), gatis (steppings), etc.

Similarly a study of Mohiniattam wouldn't be complete without the study of Balaramabharatam. The author Maharaja Kartikatirunal Rama Varma was a descendant of the ancient Chera kings of South India who encouraged arts and literature in the 18th century.. The Maharaja was a great scholar and had an extraordinary talents not only for literature but also for music, dance and other allied arts and was also a great poet. His contribution to Kathakali (a dance drama tradition) of Kerala is incomparable.

The book gives a detailed insight into the technical performing aspects for Mohiniattam. There is a mention of the use of hastas (hand gestures), angas (major limbs) upangas (minor limbs) and pratyangas (neck, wrists, knees, thighs etc.). Reading through the text and the practical details mentioned in the book leaves a student of Mohiniattam with very few doubts on the technicalities. The Balaramabharatam is an accepted text by most leading dancers, scholars of India today for Mohiniattam.

Being associated for a very long time and having the opportunity to learn under one of the pioneer's of Mohiniattam, Padmashri (Dr.) Kanak Rele who is responsible for bringing Mohiniattam into the classical map of India, I would say is a blessing. Also the privilege of working with one of the leading theater personalities, scholar, poet and a great musical composer Shri Kavalam Narayana Panikker whose contribution to Mohiniattam also needs a special mention. Mohiniattam will flourish and go a long way. With due respect to all performers, scholars, and teachers of the art form, we shall have just one aim in mind to carry on this great art form from one century into the next. The responsibility put into us by the great performers of the last and present century to carry on this great tradition and initiate the uninitiated into another world of beauty, grace and charm.

The dance form of Mohiniattam was nurtured in the region of Kerala in southwestern India. The name Mohiniattam literally means 'Dance of the Enchantress,' and it does have a mesmerising quality. The white and gold costume, arresting hairstyle and the highly graceful movements in medium tempo, contribute to this aesthetic effect. Mohiniattam is characterised by swaying movements of the upper body with legs placed in a stance similar to the plie position. The eyes play an important role in accenting the direction of the movement.

Mention of Mohiniattam is found in some eighteenth century texts, but the practical aspect of the style was revived in the reign of Maharaja Swati Tirunal, a 19th century ruler who was a great patron of the arts. Under Swati Tirunal, Mohiniattam crystallised as a solo dance tradition with musical compositions set to the Kamatic style of music and a distinct repertoire. Later, in the twentieth century, the great poet Vallathol established the Kerala Kalamandalam to promote the arts of Mohiniattam and Kathakali. Here, further research was done and Mohiniattam was codified and revived.

Repertoirs of Mohiniattam

The Sopanam repertoir of Mohiniattam includes the following:

Ganapathy: Is customary to commence any performance with an invocation to Lord Ganesha. There are many varieties of such introductory offering to Lord Ganesha. Structured and presented from the tradition of Kerala like Marma Ganapathy from Agastia Muni's Marma Shastra. Ganapathy Tyani which is from the repertoire of the temple music.

Mukhachalam: The term Mukhachalam is borrowed from Kathakali in which it is used at the opening of a performance to signify the various ragas and talas used in the repertoire. The meaning of the word itself is the movement (Chala) or the opening (Mukha). There is scope to create a garland of Kerala rhythms and ragas, which are appearing in the ensuing programme.

Niram: Niram means colour or Varnam. Here Niram is an item based on the figure of Kali as drawn on the floor with five kinds of powder in five natural colours and the music sung on the side of such figure of Kali, which is traditionally called "Niram Padal".

Padam: Apart from Swathi Padams we have incorporated many krities from Manipravala literature and Sangham literature like Ardhanareeshwara dance from Chilapathikaram, lyrics from Kalithokai, Dandakam from Unniyadicharitam and the like.

Tatvam: Tatvam imbibes its philosophy from the circum-ambulation of the devotee around the temple. It also depicts the ritual offering to the sacrificial stones around the temple.

Jeeva: Jeeva represents the voyage of the devotee towards the sanctum of his favourite deity climbing through the steps known as Sopanam. The progress of this slanting journey signifies a growth towards salvation-a point of union with the ultimate. It is a growth from the athivilamba (the slowest) to the athidruta (the highest) speed, which is technically called in the Kerala percussion ensemble as progression towards the needle end of rhythmic experience.

The Sopanam style of Mohiniattam declares its adherence to the music of Kerala.

Contrary to the usual practice of employing the oft-repeated Kamatic rhythms, Sopanam Institute has introduced Kerala's own rhythms as defined and enumerated in the thullal works of Kunjan Nambiar, the fore runner of the aesthetic revolution in Kerala, who came out of the conventional concepts and established practices of the elitist arts and drew inspiration from the numerous folk musical and dance forms of the common people. His works are specially noted for their indigenous quality especially in the wide range of rhythms, which provide an organic vitality. Sopanam has used rhythms like Roopam, Champa, Karika, Panchari (Ayyadi), Muri Adanta, Adanta, Chempata, Kundanachi, Marmam, Lekshmi, Kumbham, etc., based on hridaya tala or the rhythm of the heart beats which gives its unique regional flavour.

Mohiniattam-Staging of Grace

Indian dance styles based on legends, mythologies and devotional themes are divergent in their technique. At the same time there is a central motif running through them: the theme of devotion expressed through the heroine that is the dancer to the hero who is none other than God himself. The human soul is conceived as a female yearning for union with the male.

Mohiniattam is one of the major classical dance styles of India. This art form from Kerala is perhaps one of the most graceful dances and totally identifies with the green environment, gentle singing of the palm trees and the calm ocean waters of this state. Kerala has always preserved all traditional arts and the people of the state consider it an integral part of everyday life.

The word *Mohini* means a maiden who charms the onlooker and *attam* means dance. Usually the legends in India links the name of Mohini to that of God Vishnu who had assumed the beautiful form of Mohini to entice Demon Bhasmasura and finally destroyed him. It is said that the demon had a boon which granted him immortality. He could die only if a hand was placed on his head. Mohini danced and made Bhasmasura also dance with her and suddenly for a moment placed her hand on her head. Bhasmasura too followed without thinking and then came his end. There is a common belief that perhaps the dance form got its names from this episode.

By the 16th century, Mohiniattam seemed to have established itself as a separate classical dance form of Karla but its popularity was confined to only some regions of the state. It is only in recent times in the 20th century that Mohiniattam has spread all over India and abroad. Mohiniattam is essentially a solo form of dance.

The royal family of Travancore gave the greatest encouragement to the dances performed by *Dasis*. *Dasis* are women who used to perform in front of the deities in the temples. There were dance schools or *nataka salas* preserved by the royalty where student used to be trained. The first reference to 'Mohiniattam' in literature is to be found in *Vyanatraramala* composed by M.N. Nambuderi assigned to 1709 AD. It tells about the Guru (teacher) of the *Devdasi* and the amount to be shared in balance by the whole troupe. It was only in the 19th century AD that Maharaja Swati Thirunal the then King of Kerala encouraged and patronised Mohiniattam and thus stabilised the art form. He was a true *raṣika* (connoisseur), who understood music and dance. He was a scholar, a poet and a great musician.

To make Mohiniattam a distinctive and attractive art form he composed a number of pieces called *varnams* and *padams* and made the music of this art form lyrically rich and attractive. He brought about reforms and improvements in the style and included Mohiniattam recitals in festive celebrations. He also had a dance troupe under his patronage. In his attempts to revive Mohiniattam, he took help of the famous Thanjavur quartet who were famous composers in the Bharata Natyam style of classical dance. Maharaja Swati Thirunal could undoubtedly be said to be the pioneer of Mohiniattam style.

Various teachers and Gurus kept the Mohiniattam dance tradition alive by their efforts In 1930, Mahakavi Valathol founded Kerala Kala Mandalam and along with Kathakali he included Mohiniattam so as to revive the dance form. The first dancer was Kalyaniamma. She also taught in Shantiniketan under Rabindranath Tagore's invitation. The other notable teachers in Kerala Kala Mandalam were Krishna Paniker and Madhavi Amma. In 1950 Thottasseri Chinnammu Amma Joined. It was from these Gurus that a new generation of dancers were born. These teachers maintained the classical patterns of teaching following text like *Natya Shastra* and *Abhinayyadarpana*.

As of now, Mohiniattam is a widely known and popular dance form. The contemporary well known artists, teachers and institutions are Kalamandalam Satyabhama, Ms. Kanaka Rele, Ms. Bharati Shivaji, Guru Thankamani Kutti's institution in Calcutta, Nalanda institution formed by Kanaka Rele and Nrityagram Bangalore established by Pratima Gouri provides training in Mohiniattam. The technique of Mohiniattam accentuates *lasya* and *Sringara* or romance is the prominent *rasa*. *Rasa* means the dominant emotion.

As mentioned earlier Maharaja Swati Thirunal devised a complete repertoire for Mohiniattam, and later Gurus and dancers added more items to that. The basic repertoire begins with the *Calkkettu* – which means stylised rhythm, beginning and ending with passages of invocation. It is followed by a

Jathiswaram which is a pure dance sequence. The *Varnam* is the *piece de resistance* which has the emotive as well as the pure dance sequences. A purely emotive piece is followed by another rhythmic composition. The *Tala* or system of rhythm in Kerala is unique. Special mention can be made of *Pancha Kumbha Tala* – which are a combination of Five patterns – the five representing the five flowery arrows or *Manmatha* – the God of love. The main percussion instrument used in Mohiniattam is *Eddaka*. The body of this drum is made of Jack wood and is about a quarter metre long. The skin of calf leather is stretched across a circular ring and placed against the mouth of the drum, one on each side.

The beauty of Indian classical dance is also its appropriate and relevant costume and jewellery. The traditional costume of Mohiniattam is white with gold. The dancer usually wears gold ornaments which symbolises, purity, truth and immortality – all these are attributed to the dance of the celestial maidens. The dancer wears a pair of large round ear studs known as Toda. The necklace is the traditional *Nagapadam* in the shape of a snake's hood, and the *powanmala* – a chain made of gold coins. The forehead is covered with an ornament called the *Nethichutti* and the nose is adorned by *Mukkuthi* or nose ring. The bangles are known as *Kappu*. The coiffure is unique as it is a gathered bun on the left side of the head. The *tilaka* or the red mark on the forehead represents conjugal fidelity of the Hindu women.

The distinctive style of Mohiniattam is the complete absence of heavy stamping and rhythmical tension. Footwork is gentle and soft and sliding. The movements are never abrupt, they are dignified, easy and natural, but the vertical line of the body is never broken. Hence, among the styles detailed by Bharata Muni in the ancient Indian treatise on dance, the *Natya Shastra*, Mohiniattam resembles the Kaisiki type meaning graceful. So, the style becomes most suitable for showing *Sringara Rasa* or the emotion of love.

Some thoughts on Mohiniattam

Mohiniattam is one of the most lyrical classical dance forms of India, originating from Kerala. The word *Mohini* stands for an enchantress, a beautiful woman who seduces others for a particular purpose. *Attam* means dance. So Mohiniattam is the dance of the enchantress.

The earliest known textual reference about Mohiniattam is found in a commentary on the Vyavaharamala, a Sanskrit text written by Mazhamangalam Namboodiri during the 16th century. In the commentary believed to be authored by a migrated Brahman scholar of Kerala, the word for dancers was translated as Mohiniattam artistes, etc. Another reference on Mohiniattam can be found in the Ottanthullal (a semi-classical and semi-folk dramatic art form of Kerala) script Ghoshayatra, authored by Kunchan Nambiar during the 2nd half of the 18th century.

Perhaps Mohiniattam is the only dance form of India that was subject to several revivals and renaissance. Some scholars believe that like Bharata Natyam, Mohiniattam too was associated with devadasi tradition and other scholars think Mohiniattam was a dance form performed by women but not associated with devadasi system.

Whatever it is, for several reasons the male members of the affluent and powerful Namboodiri and Nair families exploited the Mohiniattam dancers. Gradually the dance was considered inappropriate and there were few takers for it. The efforts of Maharaj Swathitirunal (1813-1846) and the attempts of Kerala poet laureate Vallathol Narayana Menon, in 1932, 1937 and in 1950, to revive Mohiniattam are important endeavors which are now considered as crucial chapters in the history of this art.

The tradition of this dance form sustained through the contributions of two veterans, Guru Kalyanikutti Amma and Guru Satyabhama. While Guru Kalyanikutty Amma's was an effort at her individual level, Guru Sathyabhama got the platform of the Kerala Kalamandalam, where since 1957, until her retirement as its Principal in 1993, she was faculty. While dance forms like Bharata Natyam and Odissi attained both national and international significance until recently Mohiniattam was sidelined. There are a few reasons behind this.

1. Kerala is a land blessed with classical arts unlike any other States of India. While Tamil Nadu is known as the land of Bharata Natyam and Orissa as the land of Odissi (Orissi), Kerala is better known as the land of Koodiyattam and Kathakali. While people and pundits of other states got either one classical form or nothing to pamper and nourish, Keralites are blessed with a few. The more stylised and classical forms got their due share. Parallel to the development of Bharata Natyam in Tamil Nadu, Kerala saw a development in sustaining Kathakali as a rich art form, followed by Koodiyattam. Hence Mohiniattam did not get much attention.
2. Mohiniattam too was revived and preserved through the efforts of Kerala poet Vallathol Narayana Menon through the institutionalisation of the art at the Kalamandalam. However, even at the Kalamandalam Kathakali enjoyed all sorts of priority, followed by Koodiyattam.
3. None took Mohiniattam seriously to the national performing scene, during the sixties and early seventies.
4. The repertoires of Mohiniattam were set similar to the Bharata Natyam. Like the Bharata Natyam, Kamatic music too was adapted for Mohiniattam. During those periods no serious research was done into the music of Kerala, the sopana sangeetam, which is most ideal for Mohiniattam.
5. Compared to Bharata Natyam, Mohiniattam is a slow, soft and graceful dance. It is basically lasya-oriented dance form. Further, no serious research was done at the esthetical appeal of the dance form and restricted to off-white dresses, though there is historical evidence that formerly Mohiniattam dancers used colored and check blouses.
6. Following or rather imitating the pattern of Bharata Natyam in terms of repertoire and music and being a slow dance form sans colorful dresses naturally pulled down Mohiniattam to treat it as a poor cousin of Bharata Natyam.

7. Mohiniattam is not yet completely free from controversy about style, excessive influence of Bharata Natyam;, etc. Certain self-adorned purists had contributed a lot of hindrances too to its development. Due to this several talented young dancers were compelled to refrain themselves from doing any serious work in Mohiniattam.
8. Generally, almost all the Kerala dancers practised three dance forms, including Mohiniattam. Their priority was Bharata Natyam, followed by Mohiniattam and Kuchipudi.

Now, slowly Mohiniattam started getting its due share in both the national and international performing scene. The identity of sopana sangeetam (Kerala music) as the music of Mohiniattam is recognised. New dancers made remarkable attempts to delineate the art from following the heels of Bharata Natyam, by choreographing new items. Jayadeb's ashtapadi got an eternally alluring charm in Mohiniattam stage.

Scholar-poet and theatre thespian Kavalam Narayana Panicker came forward with new compositions and researched theories to put Mohiniattam back to its rail, duly freeing it from imitating the Bharata Natyam repertoire, by emphasising on the aesthetics and ethnic influence of the art form. Artists like Kanak Rele and Bharati Shivaji took initiative to take it to more and more platforms. While thinking on the aesthetics of an art form, one cannot afford to overlook the ethnic or regional touches of the art form. No doubt, the change in the coiffure of the dance form to give it more a Kerala touch was a remarkable contribution in this direction. The change in the hairstyle to give the Mohini a typical Kerala touch was done at the platform of the Kalamandalam under the initiation of Guru Kalamandalam Sathyabhama.

Kondakettal (hair being bunched upon the left side of the head with strands of jasmine flowers circling it) was accepted as the coiffure of the art form. In any old picture of traditional Kerala women one can see this coiffure, let alone the royal women in Ravi Varma paintings. Generally, for Mohiniattam off-white dresses with golden/colored borders are used. Very limited attempts are made so far to make the costume more attractive which is one of the important aspects of any dance form to satisfy the visual needs of the rasikas (audience). Even though now a day all rasas have been used for Mohiniattam items, the basic Rasa of Mohiniattam are Sringara (eroticism) Bhakti (devotion). The basic tempo is lasya, highly feminine movements. Hence, as far as the body language of the art is concerned it is equally important to consider both what should be done and what should not be done.

Now, gradually, Mohiniattam started getting its due share both at the national and international performing scene. Art lovers and connoisseurs started recognising the performance potential and significance of Mohiniattam. Mohiniattam is getting the long deserving recognition in lead festivals of the country, especially outside Kerala.

ODISSI

Odissi is an Indian classical dance style from the eastern state of Orissa in India, being apart of the ancient Odra Magadha style of dance from the eastern region. There is evidence that Odissi was danced in the temples of Orissa as far back as the 2nd Century BC. Originally performed as a sacred ritual dedicated to the Gods, Odissi is marked by sensuousness and lyricism, soft, graceful and flowing movements that reflect the divine sculptural motifs of the temples of Orissa.

Odissi owes its origin to the temple dances of the devadasis or temple dancers, whose earliest mention dates back to 10th Century AD. Female attendants of the temple, known as Maharis, danced for the Gods at various times of day to accompany various rituals of the temple deity. This dance was to the accompaniment of Mardala or the pakhawaj, small cymbals, flute and veena, a string instrument like the sitar. Over time however, the Mahari tradition started declining and a new class of dancers was created to revive the Odissi dance tradition starting in the 17th Century. This class consisted of young boys or Gotipuas who danced in female costumes. Most of the present day Odissi gurus or teachers were Gotipuas in their youth. These two living traditions were researched on after India's independence from colonial rule and incorporated into what is today the Odissi style. Master teachers or Gurus, such the legendary Guru Kelucharan Mohapatra, Guru Pankaj Charan Das, Guru Mayadhar Raut, Guru Deba Prasad Das, etc., scholars and performers came together for research based on these traditions and ancient texts such as the Natya Shastra and Abhinaya Darpanam, to create this style in its present form. Odissi is a graceful style of classical dance that is inspired thematically by the literature, art and spiritual movements of the Vaishnava (worshippers of Vishnu) as well as Shaiva (worshippers of Shiva) sects of Hinduism, and in technique, by the ancient Hindu temple sculptures of Orissa

What is Odissi? Orissi, or Odissi, is a classical dance form from the state of Orissa. Orissi is characterised by fluidity of the upper torso (the waves of the ocean on the shores of Puri) and gracefulness in gestures and wristwork (swaying of the palms), juxtaposed with firm footwork (heartbeat of Mother Earth). All classical Indian dance forms include both pure rhythmic dances and acting or story dances.

The rhythmic dances of Odissi are called batu/sthayi (foundation), pallavi (flowering), and moksha (liberation). The acting dances are called abhinaya. Although incorporating a range of emotions and mythologies, the eternal union of Radha and Krishna (Gita Govinda) is central to the abhinaya in Odissi Dance. Either Odissi or Orissi may be considered acceptable in writing.

Sculptures of Odissi dancers adorn many temple walls in Orissa. Carving of a dancer playing flute in the tribhangi position for a rapt listener (right) exemplifies the Odissi pose now associated with Lord Krishna. Odissi traces its origins to the ritual dances performed in the temples of ancient northern India. Today the name Odissi refers to the dance style of the state of Orissa in eastern India. Like other classical arts of India, this ancient dance style had suffered a decline as temples and artists lost the patronage of feudal rulers and princely states, and by the 1930s and 40s, there were very few surviving practitioners of the art.

The current form of Odissi is the product of a 20th century revival. Dedicated scholars and dance enthusiasts carefully researched manuscripts and studied the sculpture, painting and poetry of the region. They also met and observed the performances of the few existing performers, in order to revive and restructure Odissi as a unique classical dance style adapted to the requirements of formal stage presentation. Over the years Odissi has become one of the most popular classical dance styles.

Like other Indian classical dance forms, Odissi has two major facets: Nritta or non-representational dance, in which ornamental patterns are created using body movements in space and time; and Abhinaya, or stylised mime in which symbolic hand gestures and facial expressions are used to interpret a story or theme. The divine love tales of Radha and the cowherd God Krishna are favourite themes for interpretation, and a typical recital of Odissi will contain at least one or two ashtapadis (poem of eight couplets) from Jayadeva's Gita Govindam, which describes in exquisite Sanskrit poetry the complex relationship between Radha and her Lord.

The technique of Odissi includes repeated use of the tribhangi, or thrice deflected posture, in which the body is bent in three places, approximating the shape of a helix. This posture and the characteristic shifting of the torso from side to side, make Odissi a difficult style to execute. When mastered, it is the epitome of fluid grace and has a distinctively lyrical quality that is very appealing.

The Backdrop

Like other forms of Indian classical dance, the *Odissi* style traces its origins back to antiquity. Dancers are found depicted in bas-relief in the hills of Udaygiri (near Bhubaneshwar) dating back to the 1st century BC. The *Natya Shastra* speaks of the dance from this region and refers to it as *Odra-Magadhi*. Over the centuries three schools of *Odissi* dance developed: *Mahari, Nartaki*, and *Gotipau*. The *Mahari* tradition is the *devadasi* tradition; this is the use of women who are attached to deities in the temple. The *Nartaki* tradition is the school of *Odissi* dance which developed in the royal courts. *Gotipau* is a style characteristed by the use of young boys dressed up in female clothing to perform female roles.

Odissi dance was held in high esteem before the 17th century. Nobility were known for their patronage of the arts, and it was not unheard of for royalty of both sexes to be accomplished dancers. However, after the 17th century, the social position of dancers began to decline. Dancing girls were considered to be little more than prostitutes, and the "Anti-Nautch" movement of the British brought *Odissi* dance to near extinction.

Before Independence, the position of *Orissi* dance was very bad. The tradition of dancing girls at the temple at Puri was abolished. The royal patronage of *nartaki* had been severely eroded by the absorption of India under the crown. The only viable *Odissi* tradition was the *Gotipau*. This had weathered the British Anti-Nautch movement simply because it was danced by males. Yet even the *Gotipau* tradition was in a very bad state.

Independence brought a major change in official attitudes toward Indian Dance. Like the other classical arts, dance was seen as a way to define India's national identity. Governmental and non-governmental patronage increased. The few remaining *Odissi* dancers were given employment, and a massive job of reconstructing the *Odissi* dance began. This reconstruction involved combing through ancient texts, and more importantly, the close examination of dance posses represented in bas-relief in the various temples.

There were a number of people who were responsible for the reconstruction and popularisation of *Odissi* dance. Most notable are Guru Deba Prasad Das, Guru Mayadhar Raut, Guru Pankaj Charan Das, Guru Mahadev Rout, Guru Raghu Dutta, and Guru Kelu Charan Mahapatra. Today *Odissi* dance is once again deemed a viable and "classical" dance.

Archaeological/Sculptural Evidence

The carvings in the Rani Gumpha Caves in Orissa from the 2nd century B.C depict the first traces of dance, much earlier than the writings of Natya Shastra according to scholars. Natya Shastra mentions 4 types of vrittis:anti, Dakshinatya, Panchali, and Odra Magadhi. Odhra Magadhi is identified as the earliest precursor of the present Odissi.

2nd Century B.C to 5th Century A.D: Orissa has been a home for many kingdoms, Buddhist, Jaina and Shaivite and others before the Vaishnavite cult began. Following Temples and Caves belong to the from 2nd century B.C to 5th century A.D.

Udayagiri and the Khandagiri Caves: These are the first records in stone of the historic period where in full dances scenes have been found carved in the caves.

Ratnagiri and Lalitagiri Caves: Later during the *Buddhism cult* we find dance figures in movement or poses which establishes a certain continuity between the dance styles seen in the Udayagiri. There are Buddhist deities such as Marichi and Aparajita.

Tantric Temples: such as the Hirapur Shrine, many of the yoginis especially are depicted in poses reminiscent of present day Odissi.

6th Century A.D to 10th Century A.D: *Shaivite Cults* took strong roots in the 7th century A.D. Although we do find some of the first dance reliefs of the Nataraja in the 4th century A.D. Like the Shiva image with 8 hands holding a veena, trishula and akshyamla, a damru with a pataka and a varda hasta. It belonged to the king of the Bhanja dynasty, Shatrubhanja, who constructed the shrines for Shiva.

Bhubaneshwar Temples

From the 6th and 7th century onwards, there is a massive evidence of dance as part of worship and presumably this has inspired the sculptures of the early medieval temples of Bhubaneshwar. Within 300 years, nearly 500 temples were constructed. The temples include the Bharteshvara temple (6th Century A.D.), Parsuameshvara Temple (7th Century A.D.), Vaitan Deul, Sisiresvara, Muktesvara Temple, and Raja-Rani Temple. Each of them is a jewel of architecture in themselves built with perfect balance and proportion. Also, the sculptors have not only carved the poses but also the execution of the dynamic movements. It includes deities like Shiva, Durga, Ganesha, Nayaka-Nayikas on the walls in beautiful dancing poses and dance compositions. By 8th century, dance had already achieved a very distinctive stylisation in Orissa. There were already the traces of the Tribhanga poses, Ardhamandali, sthanas, karanas, charis, etc.

This sculptural evidence of dance in the temples of Bhuvaneshwar belonging to the 7,8,9 and 10th centuries almost come to a close around 11th and 12th centuries when changes take place in Orissa.

11th Century AD to 12th Century AD and Onwards: By the 11th Century A.D. there was the emergence of a *Vaishnavite cult* distinctive to Orissa.

Temple of Jagannath at Puri: Between the rulers of Chodagandeva and Anangabhimadev, was built the Temple of Jagannath. The temple itself was outstanding in its architectural plan, its sculptural reliefs and its special hall of the dance called the *Nat Mandir*.

Maharis and Gotipuas

No definite date can be conclusively ascribed regarding the practice of dance as an indispensable part of the ritual of the worship. But from chronicle records of the temple called Mandal Panji, it is clear that it was certainly co-terminus with the Jagannath cult.

The consecration of females to the service of temple dancing began in the Shaivite temples and continued in the Jagannath temple in service of the Lord Jagannath. These female attendants have been known as maharis (great women) or devadasis (servants of the lord) and have been considered the wives of Lord Jagannath. Odissi developed through their art.

A class of boy dancers emerged in the 17th Century called gotipuas. Goti means single and pua means boy. They brought the dance style out of the temples and performed in public.

Konark

Built round the 13th Century, Konark was a masterpiece of architectural design and an excellence in sculptural relief. Conceived as a chariot or ratha on 24 wheels dedicated to Surya (Sun), the temple reverberates with the movement of the dance whether in relief or around the main shrine or the Jagmohan or the Bhogmandap and most of all Nat Mandir. By the time of the Konark temple, the dance style had been set and a very distinctive method of body manipulation is apparent.

Manuscript Evidence

From 15th century onwards, it is observed by scholars, that no architectural activity took place. But on the other hand, the artists canalised into writing of manuscripts, the illustrations of manuscripts and paitings on the walls of temples. Some of these manuscripts deal distinctively only with dance.

Abhinaya Chandrika: Abhinaya Chandrika written by Maheshvara Mahapatra is a detailed study of the various movements of the feet, hands, the standing postures, the movement and the dance reperoire. It also includes illustrations of the *Karanas* mentioned in *Natya Shastra*.

Shilpaprakasha: Manuscript Shilpaprakasha is among those illustrated manuscripts which deals with the Orissan architecture and sculpture as well as the figures of dance. In this one finds a elaborate analysis of the manner in which the *salabhanjikas* or the feminine figures caleed the *alasa kanyas* are carved in the temple. The illustrations of Shilpaprakãsha reinforces the evidence of sculpture in temples.

Jain Manuscripts: A rather an unexpected source, the Jain Manuscripts, especially the Kalpasutra and Kalkacharya Kathãs show traces of Orissan dance style although they were being executed in Gujarat. The marginal figures of dancers show women in poses and movements similar to the distinctive style of Orissa. One of the famous illustrated Jain Manuscript called the Devasanpada Kalpasutra (1501, Jamnagar), there is depiction of the samapada, the tribhangi and the chuaka.

This shows that there was a great deal of mobility between east and west and many migrations took place. According to some historians, there were groups of dancers who were brought to Puri from Gujarat and also from Andhra.

Textual Evidence

The evidence of dance is further supported by the texts available on music and dance written in Orissa. Some of them include “Sangitanarayan” by Narayan Dev Gajapti (consists one section on dance called as the *Nritya Khand*), Nritya Kaumudi and Natya Manorama by Raghunath Rath (18th century), Abhinaya Darpana by Yadunath Sinha (17th-18th century), etc.

Literary Evidence

Many of the Orissan Literature works contain description of dance like Oriya Mahabharta by Saral Das (15th century), Dandi Ramayana by Balarama Das (16th century) and Niladri Mahodaya of Lokanath Vidyadhara (17th century).

Not many literary works survive of the Shaivite tradition of Orissa (8th to 11th century).

Sanskrit Poetry, Gita Govinda by Saint Jayadev, which is an integral part of abhinaya in Odissi dance recital, was contemporary with the construction of the Jagannath temple. Some of the first commentaries on this great poem were written in Orissa and it was accepted as a text of worship in the Jagannath temple.

There were many other composers like Ramananda Rai (play-Jagannath Vallabh Nataka), Jayadeva-II (Piyush Lahari), King Kapilendra Deva (Parsuram Vijaya), the outstanding poet Upendra Bhanjadeo, Kavi Surya, Baladev Rath, Gopal Krishna Pattanayak and Banmalidas. The tradition of the compositions of the lyrical poetry and the dramatic works and the singing of the Gita Govinda both in Sanskrit as well as Oriya translations continued well into the 19th century.

Revival: During the Mughal rule of India, the duties of the maharis, the temple dancers, shifted as they were also employed to entertain the royal family and courtiers in the royal courts. They became associated with concumbinage in respect to the king and ceased to be respected solely as servants to Lord Jagannath. A decline and degradation occurred in all the Indian classical dance styles during the British period, especially when a bill was passed prohibiting temple dancing.

The nationalistic leaders instigated the cultural renaissance and regeneration of India including the revival of the Indian dances as girls from respectable families learnt the almost extinct dance styles. At independence time, only Odissi had yet to be rediscovered. With the help of many, including Guru Kelucharan Mohapatra, Odissi was revived as a classical art form in 1955. Therefore, the Odissi dance recital that we see today is an attempt of reconstruction from the fragments of the Mahari tradition, Gotipua tradition, Bandhnritya tradition of martial arts, Chhau tradition known to Orissa and an ofcourse the inspiration drawn from the sculptural relief and pictorial image.

Style

There are a number of characteristics of the *Odissi* dance. The style may be seen as a conglomeration of aesthetic and technical details. One of the most characteristic features of *Odissi* dance is the *Tribhangi*. The concept of *Tribhang* divides the body into three parts, head, bust, and torso. Any posture which deals with these three elements is called *tribhangi*. This concept has created the very characteristic poses which are more contorted than found in other classical Indian dances.

The *mudras* are also important. The term *mudra* means "stamp" and is a hand position which signifies things. The use of *mudras* help tell a story in a manner similar to the hula of Hawaii.

Themes

The themes of *Odissi* are almost exclusively religious in nature. They most commonly revolve around Krishna. Although the worship of Krishna is found throughout India, there are local themes which are emphasised. The *Ashtapadi's* of Jayadev are a very common theme.

Music

The musical accompaniment of *Odissi* dance is essentially the same as the music of *Odissa* itself. There are various views on how the music of the *Odissi* relates to the music of greater North India. It is usually considered just another flavour of *Hindustani sangeet*, however there are some who feel that *Odissi* should be considered a separate classical system.

There are a number of musical instruments used to accompany the *Odissi* dance. One of the most important is the *pakhawaj*, also known as the *madal*. This is the same *pakhawaj* that is used elsewhere in the north except for a few small changes. One difference is that the right head is a bit smaller than the usual north Indian *pakhawaj*. This necessitates a technique which in many ways is more like that of the *tabla*, or *mridangam*. Other instruments which are commonly used are the *bansuri* (bamboo flute), the *manjira* (metal cymbals), the *sitar* and the *tanpura*.

Movement Patterns

The movement technique is developed from the basic position. There can be the possibility of walking in space, in different directions, in different manner and at different levels. The most characteristic amongst these is the semi-circular walk or the covering of space by one leg, more specifically the calf in semi circles, returning back to centre. The other half of the body is static. The same as the Minadandi, *i.e.* covering space like a fish. There is then the manner of covering space in circles, half circles and concentric circles. This is known as ghera.

From the tribhanga position emerge another group of movement. One half of the body is kept static along the vertical median, one knee continues to be bent and the other leg is either extended to the side or to the front or to the back. It can cross the static foot at the back or the front, it can be elevated at different levels and it can be totally extended at the back with the knee bending or calf and thigh in a straight line. Through a sitting or a kneeling position another group of movements emerge. The most characteristic amongst these is the extension of one leg to the side or to the back while one foot and knee are in contact with the ground. These movements arise out of the sitting position known by the generic term baitha. Another group of movements emerge out of basic position of the chauka or the mandalasthana. Here either movement can be in place, *i.e.* the feet can be static and only the torso can move or a complete pirouette can be executed holding the chauka position. Weight rests on the bent leg and the free leg executes a pirouette.

The Odissi technique has developed many single leg movements called the ek pada chari or using both legs or the feet called the dvipada charis and innumerable other ways of depicting the pose which can be seen in the sculptures reliefs in the Orissan temples. The dancer controls her body in the manner in which the sculpture pose is held for a spilt second only to get back into a series of movements termed. The sculpturesque quality of Odissi dance is dependent on perfect execution of these charis.

Another group of movements termed as Bhramaris are equally important. These are the spins or the pirouettes. Pirouettes can be executed in the tribhanga position or the chauka, both clockwise and anticlockwise and they can be executed in the standing position. Pirouettes also emerge from the three basic positions of the samapada, the tribhanga and the chauka. There is a simple bhramari, a bhramari with a jump therefore called an ut-pluta bhramari or an anti-clockwise pirouette called Viparita bhramari. There is also the bhramari called the antara bhramari. Here one foot touches the knee of the other leg and a pirouette is executed. The movement patterns of Odissi dance emerges from the positions, the manner of covering space and the method of executing the bhramaris.

There are then the group movements which may be called elevations, jumps or Utpluta. There is whole group of movements in Odissi dance where jumps and hopes are suggested and there is lack of contact with the ground. There are the sculptural poses which can contained within the dance techniques. From the tribhanga can emerge many sculptural poses which have been given different names some suggesting the type of heroines, *i.e.* nayikas, others suggesting the type of movement, *i.e.* half bent, full bent etc. and yet others suggesting an approach movement in Odissi dancing are called bhangis or sometimes the thais.

Nava Rasa (Nine Moods)

There are 9 moods or sentiments in Indian classical dance, called rasas. They are: srngara (love), hasya (laughter), karuna (sadness), raudra (anger), vira (pride), bhayanaka (fear), bibhatsa (disgust), adbhuta (wonder), and shanta (peace). Rasa is two-fold, experienced by the dancer and the audience. Situations are depicted using the state of the rasa, called bhava.

More than Dance: A Feast for the Senses

Observing Odissi awakes all the senses. Performances intertwine drama and story telling, hypnotic music, richly hued silk costumes and, of course, the intricacies of the dance itself—a panoply of hand and eye gestures, facial expressions, rhythmic footwork and soft, sensual body movements. With so much going on, how is an audience to fully absorb and appreciate the art form?

"Watch visually and on an instinctive level, without intellectualising it," Dey recommends. "The main thing is to realise that Odissi is an ancient tradition that has evolved along with the traditions of visual art, music, theatre and literature. The song lyrics are themselves great pieces of literature. The music is classical. Everything that contributes to the dance is valid and strong in its [respective] traditions. Realise the interconnectedness—that it's not just about dance, even though it is dance."

> *"The other thing to realise is that classical Indian dance works on two levels. The dances are told through stories that could be about human beings or about Gods, but its always symbolic and always about fundamental philosophical truths that come from ancient texts such as the Vedas and Upanishads. We draw on sacred texts to create the basis for the dance. So, realise it's not just about what a particular choreographer or dancer feels like portraying, and usually it's not about commonplace things. There are many layers."*

To help audiences grasp all the layers, Dey provides programme notes and explanations before each piece.

> *"You may not be able to appreciate all the layers at first, but it's alright because even at a basic level, there is visual beauty that gives enjoyment. As you watch more and more and get used to what it is visually, you'll be able to grasp more of the deeper layers."*

The Discipline of Odissi

Odissi derives from the temple sculptures and, as such, its style is sculptural in nature. Typically, the upper body is fluid and graceful, and moves in isolation to the lower body, which is strongly rooted to the earth. Because of the sophisticated array of precise techniques for virtually every part of the body, it takes years of intensive training just to learn the fundamentals.

"Then, it all has to come together: the hands, arms, legs, head, facial expressions, torso, hips, each part of the body," Dey explains. *"There are thousands of movements, each with a different name. There is a systematic learning process. We start with body conditioning exercises, everything from eyebrows to neck to lips. Each focuses on a different aspect of what is to come later—basic steps, hand gestures, eye gestures, hip positions, ways of moving the feet, using facial muscles to express different emotions. There are specific ways to learn each of these things."*

"If you want to learn Odissi, keep in mind that it takes four to five years before you can do anything meaningful, not to say that you cannot enjoy the process and do it for pleasure. But it's not true that you can take a few classes and start performing. You have to give it time and dedication."

As one of Dey's students, Lisa Di Gioia Nutini can attest to the level of commitment required to fully learn the art of Odissi.

"It's taken me two and a half years to learn the postures and build up strength to feel comfortable doing them," Di Gioia Nutini comments. "It's a lot to absorb, but for me, it has a healing aspect, whether or not I'm good at it. Odissi is not just a dance. Every movement is a sacred language unto itself."

The Repertoire

The repertoire of Odissi not only consists of dance items to present in a solo program but also represents a process in training, a process in following the spiritual path of Odissi where the Guru (teacher) is like the spiritual mentor, and a process in maturity. Today, a full traditional solo programme consists of a Mangalacharan to begin the program, possibly Batu Nritya, one or two Pallavis, one or more Abhinayas and Mokshya to conclude.

Group dance dramas have gained increasing popularity in Odissi. In Odissi, as in the other Indian classical dance styles, the dances are classified as nritta (pure technical dance with no meaning), nritya (expressional dance having meaning), and natya (drama).

1. *Mangalacharan:* Mangalacharan marks the entrance of the dancer on stage in the Odissi style. The dancer invokes the blessings of the presiding deity, Lord Jagannath (the Lord of the Universe) for an auspicious beginning. The dancer offers salutations to Mother Earth, the teacher, the accompanists, and the audience. The central piece of the item is a prayer in praise of a Hindu God or Goddess. Mangalacharan begins as an invocational prayer in praise of the Hindu Lord Ganesh, the remover of all obstacles.
2. *Batu Nritya:* Batu Nritya or Batu, the second item of the Odissi repertoire, is a basic example of nritta or pure dance. In this dance, particularly, the interrelationship between temple sculptural art and Odissi dance is established with an array of sculpturesque poses taken directly from the innumerable dancing sculptures adorning the temples of Orissa. These poses are stringed together with steps in different rhythms. The Guru and student take an oath, Batu Mantra, for the training and molding of the student's body to perform the technique in the form of the first pure dance.
3. *Pallavi:* The third item, Pallavi, is a nritta or pure dance like Batu. However, Pallavi differs from Batu in that it is more music oriented. Pallavi means elaboration. It is applicable here not only to the dance but to the music which accompanies it. Pallavi is woven with a series of lyrical movements bringing out the elaborate grace and charm of Odissi.

   In Pallavi, the technique blossoms in the dancer as he/she shows mastery and artistry in the Odissi technique.
4. *Abhinaya:* Abhinaya, the fourth item of the Odissi repertoire, is mime or nritya using a most intricate language composed of facial expressions, hand gestures, and through the use of the body. The dancer vividly depicts a song or poem. Although some Abhinayas are devotional songs, often the love theme or srngara rasa is explored between a nayaka and nayika (hero and heroine) usually Lord Krishna and Radha. For many

centuries, the Odissi repertoire in the temple solely consisted of songs from the Gita Govindam, which the temple dancing girls (Maharis) would sing and dance to for the pleasure of the Lord. Gita Govindam is a famous poem, written in 12th century by poet Jayadeva, a great devotee of Lord Jagannath. Gita Govindam consists of 24 ashtapadis (8-versed songs), telling the story of Lord Krishna and Radha, showing their love in physical separation and finally in spiritual unification.

The dancer achieves expertise in expression through the vivid portrayal of songs in Abhinaya.

5. *Mokshya:* The fifth and final item of the Odissi repertoire, Mokshya, parallels the concept of Mokshya or liberation in Hinduism, in which the dancer attempts to attain liberation or salvation in the ultimate surrender to God through dance. Mokshya is a fast paced dance of ecstacy.

   In Mokshya, the dancer uses the technique to dance with ecstatic joy, eventually to release him/her from it and unify with God.

6. *Dance Dramas:* Since the revival of Odissi dance, the dance style has seen the addition of a new form—the dance drama. The glory of the Odissi dance drama form banks upon the style's expressive and sculptural characteristics. It is particularly effective in displaying the love of a nayaka and nayika (hero and heroine).

4

THE PHILOSOPHY AND RELIGIONS OF INDIA

INTRODUCTION

Buddhist philosophy is the branch of Eastern philosophy based on the teachings of Gautama Buddha, a.k.a. Siddhartha Gautama (c. 563 BCE-c. 483 BCE). Buddhist philosophy deals extensively with problems in metaphysics, phenomenology, ethics, and epistemology.

From its inception, Buddhism has had a strong philosophical component. Buddhism is founded on the rejection of certain orthodox philosophical concepts, in which the Buddha had been instructed by various teachers. Buddhism rejects atheism, theism, monism, and dualism alike. The Buddha criticized all concepts of metaphysical being and non-being, and this critique is inextricable from the founding of Buddhism.

Particular points of Buddhist philosophizing have often been the subject of disputes between different schools of Buddhism. Metaphysical questions such as "Is there a god?" and "Does the soul (Atman) really exist?" have divided the Buddha's followers even during his own lifetime, and epistemological debates over the proper modes of evidence have always been lively in Buddhism.

Readers should note that theory for its own sake is not valued in Buddhism, but theory pursued in the interest of enlightenment for oneself or others is fully consistent with Buddhist values and ethics.

Buddhism as Philosophy

Some have asserted that Buddhism as a whole is a philosophy rather than a religion. Proponents of such a view may argue that (a) Buddhism is non-theistic (*i.e.*, it has no special use for the existence or nonexistence of a god or gods) or atheistic and (b) religions necessarily involve some form of theism. Others might contest either part of such an argument. Other arguments for Buddhism "as" philosophy may claim that Buddhism does not have doctrines in the same sense as other religions; the Buddha himself taught that a person should accept a teaching only if one's own experience verifies it and it is praised by the wise.

Arguments against Buddhism as a philosophy might call attention to the way Buddhism's pervasive inclusion of supernatural entities (not "gods" in the sense of Western monotheism, of course), to what most scholars identify as worship practices (ceremonial reverence of saints, etc.), to Buddhism's thoroughly developed hierarchies of clergy (not usually characteristic of a "philosophy"), and its overall religious organization.

A third perspective might take the position that Buddhism can be practiced either as a religion or as a philosophy. A similar distinction is often made with reference to Taoism. Lama Anagorika Govinda expressed it as follows in the book 'A Living Buddhism for the West':

> *"Thus we could say that the Buddha's Dharma is, as experience and as a way to practical realisation, a religion; as the intellectual formulation of this experience, a philosophy; and as a result of self-observation and analysis, a psychology. Whoever treads this path acquires a norm of behaviour that is not dictated from without, but is the result of an inner process of maturation and that we-regarding it from without-can call morality."*

It should also be noted that in the South and East Asian cultures in which Buddhism achieved most of its development, the distinction between philosophy and religion is somewhat unclear and possibly quite spurious, so this may be a semantic problem arising in the West alone.

JAIN RELIGION AND PHILOSOPHY

According to Jain beliefs, the universe was never born, nor will it ever cease to exist. Time is divided into Utsurpinis (Progressive Time Cycle) and Avsarpinis (Regressive Time Cycle). An Utsurpini and a Avsarpini constitute one Time Cycle (Kalchakra). Every Utsurpini and Avsarpini is divided into six unequal periods known as Aras. During the Utsurpini half cycle, ethics, progress, happiness, strength, age, body, religion, etc., go from the worst conditions to the best. During the Avsapini half-cycle, these notions deteriorate from the best to the worst. Jains believe we are currently in the fifth Ara of the Avsarpini phase, with approximately 19 000 years until the next Ara. After this Avsarpini phase, the Utsurpini phase will begin, continuing the infinite repetition of the Kalchakra.

When this cycle reaches its lowest level (in the current half-cycle: the sixth Ara), Jainism, as well as all religions will be lost in their entirety. During this time, all humans will be sinners; with short life spans, ugly appearances, and no sense of ethics. Due to this, all individuals during this time will be born in Hell. The world will be a rotting wasteland with little food or water. Then, on the next upswing (start of the Utsurpini half-cycle), the Jain religion will be revived and reintroduced by new [Tirthankar]]s (literally "Crossing Makers" or "Ford Finders"), only to be lost again at the end of the next downswing.

In our era, the twenty-third Tirthankar was an ascetic teacher Parshva, whose traditional dates are 877-777 BC, *i.e.*, 250 years before the liberation of the last Tirthankar, Lord Mahavir, in 527 BC. Jains regard all Tirthankars as reformers who called for a return to beliefs and practices in accord with the eternal universal philosophy upon which the faith is based. The title Bhagavan ("Lord"), applied to Mahavir and all other Tirthankars, means Venerable.

Bhaktamara Stotra: A Tirthankara is a shelter from ocean of rebirths

The twenty-fourth and final Tirthankar of this Avsarpini is called, Mahvr, the Great Hero (599-527 BC). A wandering ascetic teacher, he recalled Jains to the rigorous practice of their ancient faith.

Jains believe that reality consists of two eternal principles, jiva and ajiva. Jiva consists of infinite identical spiritual units (life); while ajiva (non-jiva) is matter in any form or condition: time, space, and movement.

Both jiva and ajiva are eternal; they are never born or created for the first time and will never cease to exist. The whole world is made up of jivas trapped in ajiva; there are jivas in rocks, plants, insects, animals, human beings, spirits, etc.

Any contact between jiva and ajiva causes the former to suffer and Jains understand that worldly existence inevitably means some suffering. Neither social nor individual reform can totally stop suffering. Every human has jiva which suffers because of its contact with ajiva. To avoid suffering, jiva must leave the four gatis (stages) of Human Life, Heavenly Bodies, Plants/Animals/Insects/Fish Life, and Hell, while remembering the ultimate aim of liberation.

Karma and transmigration keep jiva locked in ajiva. Liberation from the human condition is difficult. Jiva suffers during its infinite reincarnations. Jains believe that every action, good or evil, opens up sense channels (sight, hearing, touch, taste and smell), through which [karma]] adheres to the jiva within, weighing it down and determining the conditions of its next reincarnation. The consequence of evil actions (Pap) is negative karma, which weighs the jiva down, forcing it to continue reincarnating at low levels. Good deeds (Punya) lead to positive karma, allowing jiva to rise higher in its next life, with less suffering. However, good deeds alone can never lead to liberation. The fylfot (a.k.a. swastika) is among the holiest of Jain symbols. Worshippers use rice grains to create fylfot around the temple altar.

The way to moksha (release or liberation) is withdrawal from the world. Karma means cause-and-effect and hence every action has inescapable consequences. All Karmas, good or bad, must be shed to attain moksha, since all Karma, good or bad, has consequences and keeps jiva chained in endless reincarnations which lead to suffering to a greater or lesser extent. Liberation warrants prevention and eradication of new karma.

At the end of his life, a liberated soul (in the Jain belief, a Siddha), with no karma to weigh it, will rise free of ajiva, free of the human condition, free of all future embodiments. It will rise to the highest state in the universe, Siddhashila, where jiva, identical with all other pure jivas, will experience its own true nature in eternal stillness, aloneness, liberation and eternal happiness.

The way to discard karma is to withdraw from worldly involvement and close the senses and the mind to prevent karma. Such eternal liberation by freeing Jiva from Pudgala (ajiva), so no new reincarnation occurs, is Moksha. Ignorance (ajnâna) causes attachment, while true knowledge (keval jnân) leads to liberation. Jains believe that moksha is possible for humans in the fourth Ara of each Utsurpini and Avsarpini.

Nine Tattvas: The backbone of the Jain philosophy, the Nine Tattvas show how to attain salvation. Without knowing them, one cannot progress towards liberation. Jainism explains that Karma theory is intertwined with these nine principles.

Beliefs and Practices: The hand with a wheel on the palm symbolizes the Jain Vow of Ahimsa, meaning non-violence. The word in the middle is "ahimsa." The wheel represents the dharma-chakra, to halt the cycle of reincarnation through relentless pursuit of truth.

Jain monks practise strict asceticism and strive to make this, or one of the coming births, their last. The laity, who pursue less rigorous practices, strive to attain rational faith and to do as much good as possible now. Following strict ethics, the laity choose professions that revere and protect life and totally avoid violentlivelihoods.

Jains believe that Devas (angels or celestial beings) cannot help jiva to obtain liberation. This must be achieved by individuals through their own efforts. In fact, devas themselves cannot achieve liberation until they reincarnate as humans and undertake the difficult act of removing karma. Their efforts to attain the exalted state of Siddha, the permanent liberation of jiva from all involvement in worldly existence, must be their own.

The Jain ethical code is taken very seriously. Five vows are followed by both laity and monks/nuns. These are:

1. Nonviolence (ahimsa, or ahinsa)
2. Truth (satya)
3. Non-stealing (asteya)
4. Chastity (brahma-charya)
5. Non-possession or Non-possessiveness (aparigrah)

For laypersons, 'chastity' means confining sexual experiences to marriage. For monks/nuns, it means complete celibacy. Nonviolence involves being vegetarian and some choose to be vegan. Jains are expected to be non-violent in thought, word and deed, towards humans and every living creature. Human life is deemed the highest and it is vital to never harm or upset another. While performing holy deeds, Svetambara Jains wear cloths over their mouths and noses to avoid spittle falling on texts or revered images.

Jain Symbols: The holiest symbol is a simple swastika or svastik. Another incorporates a wheel on the palm of a hand.

Major Jain symbols include:

- 24 Lanchhanas for Tirthankaras
- The Ashtamangals
- Om
- Triratna and Shrivatsa symbols
- A Tirthankar's mother dreams
- Dharma-chakra and Siddha-chakra

MUSLIM RELIGION AND PHILOSOPHY

Islam: Islam is an Arabic word meaning both 'Submission to God' and 'Peace'. The followers of Islam who are called Muslims are found all over the world. There are over 100 cores (over one billion-1,147,494,000 Source: The World Almanac, 1999) of Muslims all over the world and out of this around one-eirth live in India alone.

Islam is not only a religion but also a particular way of life. The followers of Islam are governed by their religious teachings. Muhammad, the prophet of Islam, was born in Mecca in about 570 AD. In about 610 AD, God sent his first message to

Muhammad. Messages came to him from god till his death in 632 AD. These messages were recorded by the companions of Muhammad. The collection containing these messages is called the 'Quran', the holy book of Muslims. The sayings of Muhammad which were distinguished from the words of god were collected and are known as 'Habit', the second most important source of Islam.

The Arabs called Muhammad, 'Al-Amen' or 'The trustworthy man' and respected him greatly. But when god sent through him the first message of Islam, there was stiff opposition against Muhammad from all sides. The opposition kept mounting, so Muhammad was forced to leave Mecca in 622 AD. It is from this year that the Muslim calendar starts. Muhammad arrived in Medina where people listened to Muhammad and accepted him as a true prophet. The people in other towns challenged those who had already become Muslims and war became inevitable. However, when Muhammad died in 632 AD, not only the whole of Arabia had embraced Islam but also his religion called the Perfect Religion was fast spreading in many lands.

The death of the prophet of Islam posed the problem of succession. One group of Muslims wanted a person from the family of the prophet to be his successor. This group was known as the 'Shia'. The other group, the 'Sunnis', wanted the successor to be chosen by majority opinion. The majority went in favour of Abu Bark, who was chosen as Caliph. The Sunnis won, but this brought about two broad divisions of Muslims. After Abu Bark, two more caliphs'Omar and Othman'—were chosen. Then Ali, the son-in-law of prophet Muhammad and a candidate chosen by the Shia from the very beginning became the fourth Caliph of Islam. These four Caliphs are known in Islamic history as the Pious Caliphs. Islam was revealed by god to the prophet of Islam at a time when Arabia was witnessing a period of ignorance and tribal wars. A common cause of wars was the dispute over which god was superior to the others. Each Arab tribe had its own god. Islam substituted one god in place of so many and brought the Arab tribes together under the supreme Islamic belief that there is only one god. From the belief in the unity of god, Islam went on to preach the unity of mankind.

The great force with which the message of the 'Quran' spread from Arabia to the whole of Mid-Asia and other far-off lands, gives proof that it had an easy appeal for the human beings. It was the Arabs who went for trade with various countries, carried the message of Islam forward along with their merchandise. The great increase in knowledge in all fields that followed the birth of Islam was a result of the great emphasis laid by the 'Quran' and by the prophet, on the acquisition of knowledge from whatever source, was available.

The 'Quran' states clearly the importance of people who seek knowledge when it asks: 'Say, shall those who have knowledge and those who do not have it be considered equal?' The great contribution of Muslims to literature is to be seen in books like the 'Arabian Nights' and their contribution to art and architecture in many thousands of buildings, from the giant and majestic palace of Al-Hamra in Spain to the Taj Mahal in India.

The mystics of Islam, known as 'Sufis', played an important part in spreading the message of universal love and toning down the aggressive trends in Islam. Islam's spirit of brotherhood helped in loosening the rigidity of the caste system. It will be observed that the cultures of the Muslims in various parts of the world have remained unchanged. This proves that Islam never attempted to uproot people from their own cultures. On the other hand, it has allowed them to nurture their culture within the broad framework of the basic beliefs and practices.

SIKH RELIGION AND PHILOSOPHY

Over twenty million Sikhs follow a revealed, distinct, and unique religion born five centuries ago in the Punjab region of northern India. Between 1469 and 1708, ten Gurus preached a simple message of truth, devotion to God, and universal equality. Often mistaken as a combination of Hinduism and Islam, the Sikh religion can be characterized as a completely independent faith:

Sikhism rejects idolatry, the caste system, ritualism, and asceticism. It recognizes the equality between both genders and all religions, prohibits the intake of any intoxicants, and encourages an honest, truthful living. Sikhs have their own holy scripture, Guru Granth Sahib. Written, composed, and compiled by the Sikh Gurus themselves, the Guru Granth Sahib serves as the ultimate source of spiritual guidance for Sikhs. While the Sikhs hold their Gurus in high reverence, they are not to be worshipped; Sikhs may only worship God.

Members of the Sikh community are mainly concentrated in their homeland, Punjab; however, substantial Sikh populations exist throughout the rest of India and the world. Punjabi, a variant of the Hindi language with some Persian influence, is the spoken and written language of the Sikh people. Male members of the Sikh religion use the name, Singh (lion), as their middle or last name, while females use the name, Kaur (princess). Sikhs tend to be industrious and pioneering; this accounts for their general success wherever they live and settle. The hard-working nature of the Sikhs is derived from their religion, which can be best characterized as a faith of unlimited optimism.

Basics of Sikhism

1. Sikhism is the youngest of the World religions. Its history dates back to 1469.
2. Its founder Guru Nanak Dev was born in a village called Talwandi, now known as Nankana Sahib in Pakistan, in 1469.
3. The Sikhs have ten Gurus. It is believed that they all had same soul though they had different bodies, and that it was Guru Nanak Dev's spirit which passed on into his nine successors.
4. The Sikhs call God as 'Waheguru', meaning that God is great. Their common salutation is Sat Siri Akal (God is supreme and is immortal).

"Waheguru Ji Ka Khalsa, Waheguru Ji Ki Fateh"

has a two fold meaning. It denotes a special relationship between God and those who dedicate their lives to His love and service. Also it is the expression of a devotee's faith in the ultimate triumph of Truth over Falsehood. This Sikh salutation means "Khalsa belongs to God and to God alone belongs the Victory".

5. Guru Granth Sahib is the holy book of the Sikhs. It is believed that the tenth Guru, Guru Gobind Singh bestowed upon the Granth the title of the Guru.
6. The Sikhs worship only one Almighty God in his abstract form. They are not allowed to worship any idols, images or photographs.
7. According to the Sikh belief, God is the eternal truth; he is beyond fear, enmity and death. He is unborn and is self illuminated. He himself is the creator, preserver and destroyer.
8. The Sikhs believe that all existence is controlled by one omnipotent, omnipresent and omniscient Lord called by different names: Ishwar, Jehovah, Allah and Waheguru.

Who is a Sikh: A Sikh is any person whose faith consists of belief in One God, the ten Sikh Gurus, the Guru Granth Sahib and other scriptures and teachings of the Sikh Gurus. Additionally, he or she must believe in the necessity and importance of 'Amrit', the Sikh baptism.

God and the Sikhs: According to the Sikh belief, God is all omnipotent, omnipresent and omniscient. The sun, moon/s, wind, fire, water, vegetation and all other things which exist are His witnesses. A Sikh must worship only the abstract form of God. The worship of images or any other object is strictly forbidden.

God is both the creator and the destroyer. He is beyond birth and death. He is both merciful and compassionate. He is beyond fear and enmity. He is self illuminated. He is the Master of all the treasures. All our possessions are a result of His grace. The Sikhs call God as Waheguru, meaning the most wonderful Master.

The belief of the Sikhs in Waheguru is similar to that of Judaism, Christianity and Islam *i.e.*, God is the greatest power, He is supreme, He is the king of kings, He pervades everywhere, He knows the inner thoughts of everyone, He is the giver, He existed before the start of the time, He existed when the time was started, He exists now and He will exist forever.

Relationship with God: The Sikh Gurus called Waheguru as Master and themselves as his servants. In some hymns they called Him as Father, Mother, Friend and Brother as well1. Like Jesus Christ, Guru Gobind Singh, the tenth Guru of the Sikhs, in one of his hymns, called himself as God's son.

Universality: Sikhism does not believe in asceticism, celibacy or living alone at mountains or in caves or in forests in the search of Truth and God. It also rejects the orders of monasteries. For a Sikh the true life is the life of a householder. Living in a family environment and by serving the community both Truth and God can be realised. Thus it rejects the order of monks (Buddhism and Jainism) and nuns (Christianity).

The Sikh teachings are based on the principles of Fatherhood of God and brotherhood of humankind. Sikhism rejects the concept of chosen people (as in Judaism) and caste system (as in Hinduism); it also rejects the concept of entering 'Nirvana' without the blessings of God (as in Buddhism and Jainism).

The Sikh Shrine:Gurudwara:

1. A Sikh shrine is called a Gurdwara, meaning the doorway to the house of God.
2. The first Gurdwara was built by Guru Nanak Dev at Kartarpur.
3. The Sikh Gurdwaras must have a religious flag, called Nishan Sahib in the front of the Gurdwara.
4. Guru Granth is placed on the far side centre of the hall.
5. There should be no photographs of the Gurus or others in the hall where Guru Granth Sahib is installed.
6. Gurdwaras normally have two halls/rooms. The main hall where Guru Granth Sahib is placed and the second hall where the community kitchen is served.
7. All entrants must take off their shoes, wash their feet and cover their heads before entering the main hall.
8. All Sikh services end with the distribution of parshad (sweet pudding) and langar (dinner/lunch).

Five historical Sikh gurdwaras have been declared as the Sikh Takhats (thrones). These gurdwaras are vested with the power and authority to regulate the religious life of the Sikh nation. The head priests of these shrines constitute a Sikh parliament and they are empowered with executive, legislative and judicial powers regarding the Sikh religious issues. All Sikhs are under the authority of the five takhats. The takhats are as follows:

PARSI RELIGION AND CULTURE

A Parsi is a member of the close-knit Zoroastrian community based in the Indian subcontinent. Parsis are descended from Persian Zoroastrians who emigrated to the Indian subcontinent over 1000 years ago to escape religious persecution after the Islamic conquest.

Definition and Identity

As an Ethnic Community: Although the Parsis of India originally emigrated from Persia, they no longer have social or familial ties to Persians, and do not share language or recent history with them. Over the centuries since the first Zoroastrians arrived in India, the Parsis have integrated themselves into Indian society while simultaneously maintaining their own distinct customs and traditions (and thus ethnic identity). This in turn has given the Parsi community a rather peculiar standing-they are Indians in terms of national affiliation, language and history, but not typically Indian (constituting only 0.006% of the total population) in terms of consanguinity or cultural, behavioural and religious practices. Genealogical DNA tests to determine purity of lineage has brought mixed results. One study supports the Parsi contention that they have maintained their Persian roots by avoiding intermarriage with local populations. In that 2002 study of the Y-chromosome (patrilineal) DNA of the Parsis of Pakistan, it was determined that Parsis are genetically closer to Iranians than to their neighbours.

However, a 2004 study in which Parsi mitochondrial DNA (matrilineal) was compared with that of the Iranians and Gujaratis determined that Parsis are genetically closer to Gujaratis than to Iranians. Taking the 2002 study into account, the authors of the 2004 study suggested "a male-mediated migration of the ancestors of the present-day Parsi population, where they admixed with local females leading ultimately to the loss of mt DNA of Iranian origin".

The *Rivayat* epistles suggest that at some point between the 15th and 17th centuries non-Zoroastrians were accepted into the fold.

Self-perceptions: The definition of who is (and who is not) a Parsi is a matter of great contention within the Zoroastrian community in India. Generally accepted to be a Parsi is a person who (a) is directly descended from the original Persian refugees; and (b) has been formally admitted into the Zoroastrian religion. In this sense, *Parsi* is an ethno-religious designator. Some members of the community additionally contend that a child must have a Parsi father to be eligible for introduction into the faith, but this assertion is considered by most to be a violation of the Zoroastrian tenets of gender equality, and may be a remnant of an old legal definition of *Parsi*. Nonetheless, many Parsi Zoroastrian priests will not perform the *Navjote* ceremony-*i.e.* the rites of admission into the religion-for children from mixed-marriages.

An often quoted legal definition of *Parsi* is based on a 1909 ruling (since then nullified) that not only stipulated that a person could not become a Parsi by converting to the Zoroastrian faith (which was the case in question), but also noted that *"the Parsi community consists of: (a) Parsis who are descended from the original Persian emigrants and who are born of both Zoroastrian parents and who profess the Zoroastrian religion; (b) Iranis from Persia professing the Zoroastrian religion; (c) the children of Parsi fathers by alien mothers who have been duly and properly admitted into the religion."*

This definition has since been overturned several times. The equality principles of the Indian Constitution void the patrilineal restrictions expressed in the third clause. The second clause was contested and overturned in 1948. On appeal in 1950, the 1948 ruling was upheld and the entire 1909 definition was deemed an obiter dictum, that is, a collateral opinion and not legally binding (re-affirmed in 1966).

Nonetheless, the opinion that the 1909 ruling is legally binding continues to persist, even among the better-read and moderate Parsis. In the February 21, 2006 editorial of the *Parsiana*, the fortnightly of the Parsi Zoroastrian community, the editor noted that several adult children born of a Parsi mother and non-Parsi father had been inducted into the faith and that their choice "to embrace their mother's faith speaks volumes for their commitment to the religion." In recalling the ruling, the editor noted that although "they are legally and religiously full-fledged Zoroastrians, they are not considered Parsi Zoroastrians in the eyes of the law" and hence "legally they may not avail of (fire temples) specified for Parsi Zoroastrians".

Demographic Statistics

Indian census data (2001) records 69,601 Parsis in India, with a concentration in and around the city of Mumbai. There are approximately 5,000 Parsis elsewhere on the subcontinent, with an estimated 2500 Parsis in the city of Karachi and approximately 50 Parsi families in Sri Lanka. The number of Parsis worldwide is estimated to be fewer than 100,000.

Indian census data also established that:

- the number of Parsis has been steadily declining for several decades: the highest census count of the Parsis was of 114,890 individuals in 1940–41, which includes the crown colony populations of present-day India, Pakistan and Bangladesh. Post-independence censuses are only available for India (1951: 111,791) and reveal a decline in population of approximately 9% per decade. They do not however take immigration into account. As of 2001, Parsis constitute 0.0069% of the total population of India.

According to the National Commission for Minorities, there are a "variety of causes that are responsible for this steady decline in the population of the community", the most significant of which were childlessness and migration.

Demographic trends project that by the year 2020 the Parsis will number only 23,000 or 0.0002% of the total population of India, which—with 1200 million inhabitants—"will have achieved dubious distinction of being the most populated country on earth." The Parsis will then cease to be called a community and will be labelled a 'tribe'.

India, the land of spirituality and philosophy considers religion as an integral part of its entire tradition. The worship of various religions and its rituals play a significant role in every aspect of human life in the country.

India is the birthplace of two great religions of the world, namely, Hinduism and Buddhism. It is also the birth place of one of the oldest religions of the world, Zoroastrianism, and home to an ancient religion, Jainism.

Sikhism is another very recognisable religion which began here bringing together the best aspects of Hinduism and Islam. Followers of religions originated in other countries such as Islam, Christianity, Bahaism and Judaism also form a part of the population of secular nation, India.

Hinduism is the dominant faith. According to 2001 Census, 80.5 per cent of the population of the country are designated 'Hindu'. It is one of the ancient religions in the world, which began about 6000 years ago. Besides Hindus, Muslims are the most prominent religious group and are an integral part of Indian society. There are approximately 13.4 per cent Muslims (over 100 million), 2.3 per cent Christians (over 20 million), 1.9 per cent Sikhs (18 million) and others including Buddhists (6 million), Jains, Parsis (Zoroastrians), Jews, and Bahais, less than 2 per cent.

Hindus and Muslims are spread throughout the country. Muslims are found mostly in the states of Uttar Pradesh, Bihar, Maharashtra, West Bengal, Andhra Pradesh, and Kerala. They represent a majority in Jammu and Kashmir and Lakshadweep.

Christian concentrations are found in the northeastern states like Nagaland, Mizoram and Meghalaya and the southern states of Kerala, Tamil Nadu, and Goa. Sikhs are a majority in the state of Punjab whereas Buddhists are found in large numbers in Arunachal Pradesh, Laddakh, Bengal and Sikkim. Though a tiny minority, Jains are found all over India. Majority of Jains live in the states of Maharashtra, Rajasthan, Karnataka and Gujarat.

HINDUISM RELIGION AND PHILOSOPHY

Hinduism is found in nearly every corner of the globe. Hindus are estimated at 500,000,000 worldwide.

According to the CIA, the largest concentration of Hindus are in India (81 per cent of population) and Nepal (86 per cent). Countries with the fewest Hindus include Thailand (95 per cent Buddhist), Malaysia, Singapore, Oman, Yemen, Pakistan (mainly Islamic).

A large number of Hindus also reside in South America and the Caribbean, including in the countries of Guyana, Suriname, Trinidad and Tobago. The small island of Mauritius off the coast of South Africa (near Madagascar) is 54 per cent Hindu. Britain and the United States have significant, but relatively small, Hindu populations.

What is Special in Hinduism?

1. Hindu Religion is the world's oldest faith. It was followed by the ancient civilization of the Indus valley, Ganges valley, Deccan and Kaveri delta, as well as other parts of India all over the Indian peninsula and surrounding areas of Asia. Hinduism, is as much a "way of life" as a religion and affects every aspect of life for Hindus from birth throughout their life. It is followed by the devout Hindu in every aspect of life and activity, and not just in a prayer only.
2. With Hinduism you can have whatever you want. If you want to live a hedonistic lifestyle Hinduism will show you a way to live it without hurting yourself or others.
3. If you want to dedicate your life to worldly successes Hinduism will show you the way to do so within limitations. If all you want to do is your responsible duty to your neighbours, go ahead and do it. If what you want is liberation you can be shown the way.
4. Hinduism is a very philosophically thought out religion that essentially gives an answer for any question that you might have about your life. With each answer Hinduism gives a reason and a possibility of strengthening your understanding of the answer.

5. Hinduism is guided by the teachings of the Vedas, also believed to be the Revealed words by the Divine Powers. The Vedas are said to be older than the creation of the Universe and were given to the Ancient Sages by God as their intuition during their meditation. The Great Seers and Rishis of ancient times recited these Vedas, obtained by their meditative powers, as the teachings of God. These teaching are very ancient and were memorised and recited by generations of Sages, Teachers and their disciples until they were written down as texts and codified as the Four Vedas by Sage Vyasa. It is further explained by subsequent texts written by Seers and religious leaders based on these Vedas. Hinduism is also guided by these Upa-Vedas, Vedangas, Upanishads, Itihasas and Puranas, which contain the prayers, Philosophy, rituals and mythology, all in one, to suit everyone's cultural and mental development. While the learned person reads about the qualities of the all-powerful Brahman, the illiterate one is taught the same principle by mythological stories and simple forms of prayers to His manifestations.
6. The philosophy of Hinduism, as Divine revelations, is for all times, as old as creation and as modern as tomorrow. The Vedas have given us the rituals in various forms as a ladder to raise our faith and understanding. The Agamas and Puranas give us the incarnations and manifestations of 'God' in popular forms to condition our thoughts to the faith. It allows and accepts varying forms of worship with a tremendous tolerance of other religious faiths and beliefs. Though one may not agree that the other paths are better or perfect, every one is allowed to follow his own path. Often a devotee is urged to study all the paths and variations to fully understand his own faith.
7. This is the most important and valuable speciality of Hinduism that it has not closed itself inside any contours, but is the realistic representation of the limitlessness of knowledge and experience. It is absolutely open minded. This is the religion that calls

Let the good things come from all the directions of the world (aa no bhadrah kratavo yantu vishvatah). Thus this religion nurtured the good concepts with a neutral mindset. Hinduism is a dharma (discipline) than a religion. Various religions stand over this dharma. In general this is not the religion of just postulations.

8. Very naturally this religion does not force even the acceptance of God to the followers. The Hindus are not threatened that they would be punished for not praying/believing the God, whereas the major scriptures advice the followers to hold to the God in order to get liberated from the rough road of pleasures and pains! Even those things undergo a very healthy debate. Nothing is unquestionable. The Hindu scriptures instead of defining the way, in which the Hindus should live, in a better way, act as supporting material for the individual to decide the course of life and stand by that.
9. Hinduism, unlike most religions, has no founder and no one scripture. Hindus do not have one "Holy Book" like many other religions, but many texts including the four Vedas along with their Upanishads, called the "Sruti", several Dharma Sastras or Smritis, Itihasas and Puranas including the Mahabharata and the Ramayana. The Bhagavad Gita, or "Song of God", comes as part of Mahabharata, is an essence of the message of the Upanishads and Hindu Philosophy and is considered to be a guide on how we should live as told by Lord Krishna to Arjuna.
10. Hindus believe that as all streams and rivers lead to the same ocean, all genuine religious (spiritual) paths lead to the same goal; worship of every form of "GOD" and celestial forces leads to the same good. So we do not try to convert others to our religion. (Another example-path to top of mountain may differ but the view from the top of the mountain will be the same.)
11. Hindus believe in one God, beyond form, space and time and beyond human comprehension. They believe that God is Transcendent and Immanent at the same time and will create itself according to everyone's desire

and needs to protect the pious, to destroy the evil and establish the Divine Rule of Law and Justice.

12. Most Hindus, needing a form on which to concentrate, worship that one God in different forms, worshiping one aspect of that One Divine Supreme Truth.—Hindus God in masculine as well as in feminine forms and also like a family. At the same time, they all understand the True nature of the Supreme.
13. In the masculine forms, Hindus One God as Brahma—the creator, Vishnu—the protector and maintainer, and Shiva as Shiva—Nataraja—the destroyer and recreator.—In the female forms, Hindus that One God as Sakti or Durga,-provider of energy and power, as Lakshmi,—provider of prosperity and wealth and as Saraswathi,—provider of knowledge and intelligence.
14. These are the major forms of Hindu "Gods" worshipped, which takes the form as created by the supreme God Paramathma for the benefit of the Human creations to easily comprehend Him as He is. Please understand that many of the sects of Hindus following the various forms of philosophy and worship, visualise this same Paramathma—the Supreme God—as Narayana [Vishu], or as Paramasiva [Shiva] and ParaaSakti [Sakti or Durga].
15. Here please note that unlike the other major world religions, Hindus also see the Supreme as Mother, including as Sri Meenakshi, as Visalakshi, as Kamakshi and as many other names of Sakti. He is also seen as Father as in Shiva in various forms in several Hindu Temples—The Temple in which they are worshipped is not just a congregation hall but a palace of the Supreme God.
16. Hindu Rituals and Worship take into account the capacities and inclinations of different individuals.—Types of worship include Ritualistic worship (temple or home), offering (directly or through the priest) flowers, coconut, fruits, incense, flames of oil lamps and camphor, chanting of prayers in Sanskrit (or their mother tongue), etc.

17. Also Hindu religion advocates Worship through service of one's fellow man (charity) and by one's activity;—Worship through the service to fellow human and devotion to the Supreme;—Worship through meditation with physical and mental discipline and through understanding first the inner self then the divine that is everywhere.
18. Hinduism has also defined concept of Yogas. Jnana yoga is for people who are reflective and seek knowledge find their divinity through rationality and spirituality. Bhakti yoga is the path to God through love and devoted service. It insists on God's otherness and teaches love of God through adoration. Karma yoga is the path to God through work. Be productive and strive to work towards high rewards and work unselfishly.Raja yoga is known as the path to reintegration, a way to God through psychophysical experiments. Self-searching could be one way of describing Raja Yoga. Looking inward to discern the humanness from the Godness and bringing them together. It involves meditation and self discipline.

These and many more specialties of Hinduism make it a harmonious and worth religion, which is suitable for any time in present or future, for any land or creed.

Hindu Philosophy gives a clear understanding to the questions of cycle of life and death, the nature of Soul, the Universe and its creator and reasons for joy and sufferings, happiness and sorrow, health and disease and the ultimate understanding of man's relationship with God. It also explains his duties during this birth as well as about his past and his future. It investigates and inquires the Truth and allows us to think and reason in our search for a solution. Even though the Agamas and Vedas appear to be professing different doctrines, they both are written on the same philosophy but for different population group.

The Agamas give us the Theological aspect of our practice with prayers to God in various manifestations. The Vedas give us all the rituals and also the philosophy of our religious practice.

All of them are based on the principle that the Soul is a part of the Divine spirit and is covered by the sheaths of "Upadhis" as an effect of ones Karma. It goes through endless rebirth according to ones Karma to purify itself. Every one should follow his Dharma and perform their duties or Karma without attachment, as an offering to God to receive eternal salvation and liberation as Moksha.

The Divine Laws that Holds True for Ever: The teachings of Hindu philosophy are given to us in the Upanishads which are the wealth of our knowledge. The ethics and tenets are obtained from them through the Six Darsanas and various later schools of philosophers. The glory of Hindu philosophy is seen in the teachings of Hindu dharma, the theory of karma and rebirth, the six darsanas, and the four yogas or spiritual disciplines. They not only create the questions in our mind to think but also give us the answers to the problems. Dharma means "that which holds" the people of this world and the whole creation. It is the eternal Divine law of God. That which brings well being to man and supports the world with prosperity is dharma. It is the absolute Truth and laws of righteous living. The four Vedas are the authority of Dharma. The truth about dharma can not be realised through any other knowledge and one's own reasoning through any analysis alone can not be that authority.

Ancient sets of Rules that Holds and changes with Time: Purushartha are the four kinds of human aspirations, which are dharma, artha, kaama and Moksha. Among these, dharma is the foremost and is the gateway to Moksha or immortality and eternal bliss. Practice of proper Dharma gives an experience of peace, joy, strength and tranquillity within ones-self and life becomes thoroughly disciplined. It is classified as [i] Samanya dharma or the general and Universal Dharma and [ii] Visesha dharma or specific personal dharma. Samanya dharma includes contentment, forgiveness, self-restraint, spiritual knowledge, absence of anger, non-greediness, non-stealing, truthfulness, purity, non-violence, control of senses and desire, discrimination between right and wrong and between real and unreal. Visesha or specific dharma includes duties due to one's birth, age and family and duties to society and family, due to one's career and job and spiritual life. They also include the specific dharmas for the four ashramas and four varnas. These are the regular duties including the rituals and services to the family, community, ancestors and God that every one is expected to perform. We have separate Dharma for each of the four Yugas or time periods.

Varying Rules of Duty for Different Times: The Vedas give different rules of Dharma for people of different age groups, different family traits and different periods of time. The ashrama dharma gives the standards of living for different age groups of individuals. The varna dharma is one that is most misinterpreted and misused. If properly interpreted and understood, it is the most efficient sociological system of the nation.

It is indeed a splendid theory with a flawless rule. But, the defect came from somewhere else. Various dharma sasthras, or smrithis, written by Rishis like Manu, Parasara, and Yaagnavalkya, have varied for different periods of time according to varying social and emotional surroundings of the Hindu society [Yuga-Dharma]. The Hindus often follow the teachings of various Dharma sasthras for the philosophical guidance for daily living.

An Unencompassed Light, Transcendent and Immanent: The Divine is both in us and out of us. God is neither completely transcendent nor completely immanent. He is divine darkness as well as 'unencompassed light.' The philosophers with their passion for unity emphasise the immanent aspect, that there is no barrier dividing man from the real. Those who emphasise the Transcendence of the Supreme to the human insist on the specifically religious consciousness, of communion with a higher than ourselves with whom it is impossible for the individual to get assimilated.

There cannot be a fundamental contradiction between the philosophical idea of God as an all-embracing spirit and the devotional idea of a personal God who arouses in us the specifically religious emotion. The personal conception develops the aspect of spiritual experience in which it may be regarded as fulfilling the human needs. God is represented as possessing the qualities we lack. Justice, love and holiness are the highest qualities we know and we imagine God as possessing them, though these qualities exist in God in a different sense from their existence in us. The difference between the Supreme as spirit and Supreme as person is one of stand point and not of essence, between God as He is and as he seems to us.

Panjchakshara Mantra: While there are plenty of mantras available, there are a few that are chanted with high esteem by the shaivas. Definitely those are highly powerful ones that can lead the chanter on the great path to mukti (liberation). pranava, panjchakashra, gayatri to name a few. For shaivites the Holy Five Syllables (panhichakshara) with or without combined with the pranava is the ultimate mantra.

Holy Five Syllables-Panjchakshara Mantra: Panjchakshara as popularly known is the holy five syllables (literally holy five letters) that is the supreme mantra of all devotees of Lord Shiva. As the name suggests it is made up of five syllables. This great mantra is namah Sivaya (namah Sivaya). The five syllables in this mantra are na-mah-si-va-ya.

The Core of the Vedas: The Holy Five Syllables namah Sivaya is the heart of vedas. It is the core of the very famous chapter of vedas that stands in the middle of the vedas-the shata rudrIyam or rudra suktam. This great mantra of veda samhita while hailing the God as the Lord of everything of the worlds, salutes the God as namah Sivaya cha Sivataraya cha.

Meaning of the Panjchakshara Mantra: The meaning of this matchless mantra is abound. The puranas and the philosophical texts talk in a very detailed and elabourate manner its meaning and significance and hail its ultimateness. Here only a simple meaning is presented to start with.

The word Shiva means auspiciousness and perfection. It refers to the God Who is Perfect without any kind of dependency on anything external to make It complete. Naturally because of this self-perfection, It is completely blissful and ever auspicious. (All other auspicious things are in one way or the other dependent on the external circumstances, etc.) The prefix namaH is the mantra of salutation. The mantra namah Sivaya salutationally invoke the Perfect God Shiva.

Various Panjchaksharas: Panjchakshara has five syllables, so is Lord Shiva with five faces. Depending upon which letter the panjchakshara is starting with, the panjchakshara gets the name of a face of the God. Namah sivaya is the sadyojata panjchakshara and Sivayanamah is the aghora panjchakshara or the aghora mantra. Similarly the other panjchaksharas also get the names.

As the panjchakshara namah Sivaya is at the centre of vedas, it is referred as Vedic way panjchakshara. Sivayanamah is the panjchakshara is used very much in the Agamic worship of the Lord. So it is referred as the agamic way panjchakshara.

Ways of Chanting the Panjchakshari: While many mantras have restrictions as to when and how it can be chanted, etc., there is no such restriction to the panjchakshara mantra. The great prodigy sambandhar says in thevaram, "When you sleep as well as when you do not sleep, think of the Holy Five Syllables with heartful of devotion! This is the mantra that terribly kicked out the death when chanted (by markandeya) with sincerity."

Whoever you are, whenever be the time, whatever be the situation chant the Holy Five Syllables. There are no restrictions of colour, creed, caste, gender or any other restrictions. All it requires is sincerity. This mantra could be chanted as it is as panjchakshara or could be chanted along with the pranava (Aum) as shadakshara mantra (om namah sivaya). In fact it is to be noted that pranava itself is panjchakshara mantra (akara, ukara, Makara, bindhu, natham).

Benefit of Chanting the Mantra: The thoughts make the person. The one who has the positive thoughts is happier and the one full of worries is the sad one. The thoughts not only have effect at that moment but they definitely make impression on the personality of the individual, which could have a very long lasting impact. In this background while the good thoughts itself would be making things better, what needs to be said about the super-powered mantras that are rich in meaning as well as energy! Given the fact that "we tend to become what we keep thinking about", when one chants the sacred panjchakshara that hails the God as Perfection and auspicious, it would take one towards that Blissful Perfection. It takes to the union with the Supreme God. What else can be more rewarding ! Even the worst sinner would get corrected and get to the glorious states if chants this mantra piously.

Widespread Glory of Panjchaksara in Scriptures: The importance and glory of this mantra is stressed across the shaiva scriptures, as the most important mantra the devotee has to keep like own soul. Listing them would be highly arduous task given the importance this mantra gets in the scriptures.

Learning the various scriptures and chanting thousands of stotras (praise) of God, is all given secondary importance to chanting this great mantra. The authentic scriptures very clearly state that for the one who chants this mantra, even if none of the other scriptures are known or even any other worship of God is undertaken, that person would definitely gets eligible for the immense grace of the Supreme Lord Shiva. For this the chanting of the Holy Five Syllables has been prescribed as a definite requirement for the devotee. While the rudraksha and Holy Ash are the ornament externally for the devotee the internal ornament is the panjchakshara mantra. The supreme mantra very simple to chant and comes with no restrictions attached in order for everybody to chant and get benefited. With no inertia in mind chant and keep chanting as much as possible namah Sivaya.

Pranava Mantra (AUM)-Simple Explanation: The mantra that is held very sacred by all Hindus is the mantra Om also called pranava mantra. This mantra is part of every worship. This mantra is hailed in scriptures of various languages. Vedas—the holy scripture—is chanted always after chanting this mantra and always concluded with this mantra. Each of the hailing in the archanai that is performed for the divine is preceded by this mantra Om.

Pranava is the primal sound that existed before the creation and the sound that stays after the parlay. This is the natharupa-the Form of sound, of the Supreme Luminance. This mantra om refer to none other than God. The great yogis meditate in this mantra as the path to Eternal Bliss of the Formless Nameless God!

The pranava has five parts. They are akara, ukara, makara, bindhu, natham. (aum). Consequently this is also one of the glorious panjchakshara mantra. The scriptures that explain the glory of this pranava mantra are quite many. However the significant one is from the skandha purana. It is a well known puranic event that skandha described the real meaning of the pranava mantra to God Shiva. In the above mentioned episode of skandha purana the sage vamadeva seeks the boon from Lord Skandha to tell him too that description. Lord Skandha who was pleased with the devotion of sage vamadeva told him that great secret.

Aum: Tirumular says that the one letter, A, represents the universe. The two letters A and U are Shiva and Sakti, the latter being the all-powerful manifest energy of Shiva. The three letters, A, U, and M are Shiva, Sakti and Light, the last being Jnana or knowledge. The letter M is also Maya. Tirumular calls AUM as one-letter mantra, representing Tandava, the Divine Dance of Shiva. Tandava is derived from Tandu, a dancer and servant of Shiva. Any act performed by Shiva is a dance. The dances are named according to his acts (creation, maintenance, destruction, veiling and Grace), places (Chidambaram, etc.), and competition (Urdhva), 25 Lilas (acts of play). The most celebrated dance is the 'Tandava' in Chidambaram.

Symbols of Hinduism: In Hinduism much importance is given to the symbols than most other religions. The Hindu symbols range from the mark one puts on the forehead to the idols of the deities that are worshipped by the ardent Hindu devotees. Each one has its own significance. Hinduism at its core maintains that there is one God and many see it in different ways (Ekam sad viprah bahuta vadanti). God is formless and is beyond the limitations of the comprehension. This is the basis on which many of the great sages meditate on this Supreme Being that is beyond any contours.

So why are so many forms? The God in its natural form being very difficult to comprehend, leave alone loving that God and worshiping with devotion, the simple minds would certainly need a way through which they could worship the boundless God in a fairly simplified manner. But at the same time it should not contradict the basis that the God is beyond forms in any way.

Hinduism maintains that because of the abundant Grace of the God, It revealed itself in the Holy symbols for the humans and other creatures to worship. These symbols are easy to comprehend for the minds of the normal human beings, but at the same time they are not just the symbols but they are the objects themselves, which means that they symbolically indicate the God, which is beyond the exploration of knowledge.

Hinduism Symbols are the pranava (Aum) which is held in high esteem by all sects of Hindus and the glorious Shiva lingam (meaning symbol of Shiva, the God) that is considered the most sacred symbol of worship for the Shaivites. The intention is that the Formless Supreme could be achieved by simpler means of these formless-forms, the symbols. In a way these Hindu symbols are abstract representation of the God. These are quite closer to the ideal as they form a bridge between the Formless one and the mind that expects a form.

The simpler minds benefit better if the God could be correlated with the day to day lives they interact with. The God certainly is Graceful to the upliftment of the creatures, it took various forms in various occasions blessing either in valorous or joyful or yogic postures. There are numerous of these forms that Hindus worship in their temples, which are built in a gigantic manner with the patronage of various emperors that stand as the glorious homes of art and architecture. The maheshvara murthams are good examples of such forms of God. The Hindus wear various marks on their forehead that also have spiritual significance. For example the ash that the Shaivites wear represents the ash that the Supreme Flame-Lord Shiva has smeared on Him always. The same way the shrichurna and the Tilak have their significance and indications. In essence Hindus achieve the Supreme Things, by simple ways following the symbols.

Pranava /Aum: Revered by all religions of Hinduism. This is the primeval sound Om. This mystic sound is so important that there is little worship without this. The archanas done at the Hindu temples include this for each of the mantra chanted. The holy vedas also start with this. This mantra is one of the renowned mantra for meditation. This sound represents the Supreme Divinity.

Lingam: The prime symbol of worship of Shiva. (In fact the name itself means symbol). This is broad in the middle and conical towards the top. This is the form of flame. In Shaivites philosophy the God is formless. Due to the Grace on the souls for the easy comprehension of the Divine and liberation the God appeared in the form of a Flame. This flame is what is worshiped as lingam in stone and other forms that make the worship easier. This is considered more sacred than form worship by Shaivites.

Holy Ash / Bhasma/ Vibuti: The three bands one could see on the foreheads of the gods and goddesses. These three bands are worn by the Shaivites and the other religions in that family. This symbol is called tripundra (three bands). As the God appeared as a Supreme Flame (This need not be confused with agni. Agni becomes one of the aspects of God but not the Supreme itself), in the Shaivites religion, naturally Ash becomes the symbol that indicates the association with that Parma jyoti (Supreme flame).

Rudraksha: Rudra + aksha translates to the eye of rudra. This is a beed from a tree. This is considered to have emanated from the eye of Lord Shiva when He burnt the tripura asuras. This is one of the holy symbols worn by Shaivites along with Holy Ash. This is worn as a single beed or as garlands of beeds.

Tilaka: This is the dot most of the Hindus have at the eyebrow junction. This could be of sandal or red kumkum or a mix of both. This junction is one of the very significant chakra, called in spiritual terms AGYA chakra. This is a very sensitive point. So the tilaka is kept at this point.

Shri Churna: The vertical three lines (or at times single red line) that is worn by the Vaishnavites are called shri churna. The two outer lines will be in the white colour and the middle one in the red. The red line is normally with kumkum or the red sand at the base of the tulsi plant. This custom has been introduced in the later parts of time by Ramanuja as vaishnavite symbolism. Vaiahvavas not belonging to Ramanuja sampradaya (for example madhvas) do not follow this custom.

Nandi: This is the Holy Bull-the vehicle and the disciple of Lord Shiva. So Nandi is the first Guru Shaivites. On the wall of the Shaivites temples, in the flags, in the message headers and many other articles this emblem could be found. The ancience of this emblem will be very evident from the fact that this emblem has been found in the excavations of Harappa mahenjadaro (the so-called Indus valley civilization sites). According to Shaivites scriptures bull represents the dharma (justice).

Trishula: The tri headed spear (trident)—one of the renowned weapon of Lord Shiva. So this is the second important emblem of Shaivites after nandi. As the Goddess shakthi also holds this trident, this is the symbol that is held high by the devotees of shakthi as well.

Shanka Chakra: The counch called panjchajanya and the disc called sudarshana in the hands of Lord Vishnu are the important symbols of Vaishnavites. These two are printed as emblems in the artifacts associated with Vaishnavas.

Spear: The spear is the renowned weapon of Lord Skanda. So this is a much respected symbol of the devotees of Lord Subramanya.

Oh God, Your Feet is beyond the worlds beneath
and Your Crown beyond the universes above!
You are Immeasurable, Unexplorable, and Unimaginable!
But how simple You have come as a Sivalinga in my hand !!
-Basavanna

HINDU CULTURE

Each of the religions of the world has its own culture, with many customs, traditions and refined qualities. The Hindu culture is a culture of love, respect, honouring others and humbling one's own ego so that the inner nature, which is naturally pure and modest, will shine forth. Here we have described some of the important faith and behaviours of Hindu community.

Respect and Reverence

1. *Respect for Elders:* Respect for elders is a keystone of Hindu culture. This genuine acknowledgment of

seniority is demonstrated through endearing customs, such as sitting to the left of elders, bringing gifts on special occasions, not sitting while they are standing, not speaking excessively, not yawning or stretching, not putting one's opinions forward strongly, not contradicting or arguing, seeking their advice and blessings, giving them first choice in all matters, even serving their food first.

2. *Name Protocol*: Younger never uses the proper name of their elders. In the Tamil tradition, a younger brother, for example, refers to his brother as annan, or periannan (older brother), not by name. The elder, however, may use the name of the younger.

   Children are trained to refer to all adults as auntie or uncle. Only people of the same age will address each other by first name. A Hindu wife never speaks the name of her husband. When referring to him she uses terms such as "my husband," "him" or, for example, "Athan, Mama, etc.,".
3. *Touching Feet in Respect:* One touches the feet of holy men and women in recognition of their great humility and inner attainment. A dancer or a musician touches the feet of his or her teacher before and after each lesson. Children prostrate and touch the feet of their mother and father at festivals and at special times, such as birthdays and before departing on a journey.
4. *Darshana:* "Vision, sight." Seeing the Divine. Beholding, with inner or outer vision, a temple image, Deity, holy person or place, with the desire to inwardly contact and receive the grace and blessings of the venerated being or beings.
5. *Dakshina*: It is tradition to provide dakshina, a monetary fee or gift to a priest given at the completion of any rite. Dakshina is also given to gurus as a token of respect for their spiritual blessings.

Purity: Purity and its opposite, pollution, are vitally important in Hindu culture. Purity is of three forms—purity in mind, speech and body, or thought, word and deed. Purity is the pristine and natural state of the soul. Impurity, or pollution, is the obscuring of this state by adulterating experience and beclouding conceptions.

In daily life, the Hindu strives to protect this innate purity by wise living, following the codes of dharma. This includes harnessing the sexual energies, associating with other virtuous Hindu devotees, never using harsh, angered or indecent language, and keeping a clean and healthy physical body. Here are several ways purity is preserved in Hindu culture.

1. *Purity and Food:* Purity is central to food and nutrition, as the nature of one's nourishment deeply affects the entire physical, mental and emotional nature. One cooking food for others would never taste of the dish from a spoon and then put the spoon back in the pot. If food is to be tasted while cooking, a small portion is placed in the right hand. Similarly, one would not touch the lips to a water vessel that is also used by others. Nor would one offer something to another from which one has taken a bite or a sip.
2. *Flower Offerings:* One does not sniff flowers picked for offering to the Deities; even the smell is for the Gods, not for us. Flowers that fall to the ground should not be offered.
3. *Offerings:* Offerings, such as an archana basket, flowers or garlands, are carried with both hands on the right side of the body, so as to not be breathed on. All items are washed in preparation and, if carried more than a short distance, wrapped or covered.
4. *The Left Hand:* In Hindu culture the left hand is considered impure because it is used (with water) in the place of toilet paper for personal hygiene after answering the call of nature. Handing another person anything with the left hand may be considered a subtle insult.
5. *Shoes:* Shoes are considered impure. The cultured Hindu never wears shoes or sandals inside a temple or shrine, nor in his home or the homes of other Hindus. Carrying shoes in the hands from one part of the premises to another is also avoided. An ultimate insult is to be struck with a shoe.

6. *Caution with Footwear:* It is very important to apologies immediately if one touches someone with his or her shoe or sandal. This is done by touching the right hand to where the foot touched the other person and then touching one's right hand lightly to his own left eye and then the right. This same remedy applies to inadvertently hitting someone with the hand or foot or bumping into him or her.

Exchange of Prana

1. *Giving and Receiving with Both Hands:* Giving and accepting things from one to another, presenting offerings to the Deity, etc., is most properly done with both hands. The reason for this is that with the gift, prana is also given through both hands, thus endowing more energy to the object. The recipient of the gift receives it with both hands along with the prana from the gracious giver. It is known that this exchange of energies is vital for friendship, harmony and the total release of the gift to the recipient. Hindus never accept gifts from strangers or unknown persons.
2. *Hugging and Embracing:* Hugging and embracing is found in Hindu culture; but it is restricted to close relatives, Guru/disciples and associates that too in a private place. In Mahabharata and Ramayana we find this very often. Hugging and Embracing improves pranic energy and this practice is not allowed with strangers.
3. *Not Pointing the Finger:* Pointing with the forefinger of the right hand or shaking the forefinger in emphasis while talking is never done. This is because the right hand possesses a powerful, aggressive pranic force, and an energy that moves the forces of the world. Pointing the index finger channels that force into a single stream. The harshness of this energy would be severely felt in the nerve system of the recipient. More properly, rather than pointing or shaking the index finger to give direction or emphasise a verbal statement, the entire hand is used as a pointer, with the palm up and the thumb held alongside the forefinger.

4. *Shaking Hands:* The traditional way that Hindu men greet one another is with the anjali mudra, then, with palms still held together, extending their hands to one another, in a two-handed handshake, in a deliberate transfer of prana. The hands of one man, usually the less senior, are gently clasped between the other's. Each looks smilingly into the other's face while bowing slightly in humility. This handshake is not firm, but relaxed and gentle.
5. *Not Throwing Things:* Throwing any object on another person is considered extremely improper, even if the persons know each other very well. Cultured Hindus consider this crude and even mildly violent, even if done in efficiency or jest.
6. *Care in Sitting:* It is improper to sit with one's legs outstretched toward a temple, shrine or altar, or even toward another person. This is a grave insult. Crossing one leg over the knee when sitting in a chair should be avoided, though crossing at the ankles is permitted. One must always try to follow the example of traditional elders. Worshiping, meditating or sitting in the kneeling pose is not acceptable among Hindus.
7. *Doorways:* Conversations are not held inside or through doorways. This is considered inauspicious. Similarly, to exchange or give or lend an object, one-steps inside the room first, or the recipient steps out of the room so that both parties are in the same room.

Modesty

1. *Modesty:* Interaction in public between men and women is much more restrained in Hindu culture than in Western culture. In Hindu culture, for the most part, men socialise with men, and women with women. Men never touch women in public unless the lady is very elderly or infirm.
2. *Displaying Affection:* Married Hindu couples do not hug, hold hands or kiss in public. Even embracing at airports and train stations is considered not wise. Men, however, frequently walk hand in hand.

The Three Paths to Salvation: Knowing that there is diversity in life and no single way of life as prescribed or ordained by God will be followed by everyone, the wise thinkers have put forward three different paths (marga) for achieving salvation. The first is the Jnana marga, mostly for the intellectuals who are able to study and comprehend scriptures. The second is the Bhakti marga, wherein meditation on a personal image of God will lead one to realising the Truth. The third involves social service. Work in the field of uplifting humanity and performance of duty without expecting anything in return is called the karma marga. Renunciation of all worldly possessions and pleasures and continuous meditation is the fourth alternative, which perhaps is beyond the scope of most human beings today.

On the surface Hinduism certainly looks like a confused, directionless religion to an outsider. But the inclusiveness of Hinduism with its doctrine of tolerance makes it universally appealing. It is not an organised religion and the method of practice is entirely left to the individual, who will take full responsibility of his or her conduct. Superficially, it is a hodgepodge of beliefs and practices, but its core belief of ONE GOD, universal, omniscient and omnipotent has stood the test of time.

Jagdish Hare: In simple words 'Aarti' means Prayer.

Aarti is the most important ritual performed by the masses of India. This prayer is said to have been penned by Pandit Shradha Ram Phillauri in 1888. The entire prayer is an attempt to praise the glory of the inexpressible God and surrendering oneself to Him. The Aarti can be a very soothing experience. Each person, however, will realise for oneself by listening, singing and contemplating upon this simple but divine prayer.

Om, is perhaps the only word that phonetically and logically signifies the primordial sound. The great masters and saints have for thousands of years contemplated upon this one Word. It has even been said that all the Vedas dissolve into Gayatri and Gayatri itself dissolves into Om. In the Yoga, experiments have been conducted extensively to assess the impact experienced by an aspirant by simply uttering Om in a particular manner or by chanting repeatedly (Simran). It is not a case of hypnotism or auto-suggestion, but an established fact that one's association with the word Om with understanding helps in attaining transcendence.

In this verse the worshipper is being motivated to contemplate on the Name. Reward is offered in the form of mental peace and healthy body, both essential ingredients to lead a harmonious life. It is my understanding that all our mental chaos and ill-health is projection of our own ego. It is due to the neglect or the lack of understanding of our own unique individuality that we find ourselves dragged into comparisons both subjectively and objectively.

God, the primordial seed, is the Creator. Thus God is both the mother and the father. This being so, I can only beseech You and surrender myself to You. Without God there is nothing, hence my highest aspirations can only be You. We notice in our daily life that we neglect God and rely upon transient sources for our existence. Resultantly, our lives are chaotic and full of frustrations.

HINDU ETHICS

Three documents, namely the Upanishads, Bhagvad Gita and Brahma Sutra form the basis of Vedanta (called Prasthana-traya). From these scriptures are drawn Hindu ethics that help in guiding the Hindu through his daily as well as spiritual journey. Though Vedanta currently is the favourite of English-speaking Hindu intellectuals, it was from the wisdom of the Upanishads and Bhagvad Gita that the ancient Hindus set forth their ethics in a practical way, expected to be followed by all Hindus. The Laws of Manu (Dharmashastra or Manuva Shastra) gave details of societal rules and Artha Shastra of Kautilya detailed the politics and economics.

Ethics of Upanishads: Upanishad means 'to sit down near' because they were explained to the students, who sat at the feet of their teachers. In general Upanishads proclaim salvation by knowledge and realisation, rather than by faith and works. Selfish desires are obstacles to the seekers of Truth (the Higher-Self, also called as Brahman). A seeker of true Divinity will attain salvation when he realises the Truth, the all-pervasive Brahman. The universe came into existence because of a primeval desire of Brahman. Now it is the duty of the humans to restore it to the state of things before creation. This can be done by sacrifice, benevolence, study and even ascetism, which in turn will permit the seeker of truth to attain bliss. Honesty is especially extolled. He who has not denounced evil will never obtain Brahman. The worldly perceptions of smell, taste, touch, hearing and sight makes one separate from the True Self. When one can transcend these perceptions there is no consciousness of anything other than Self. This is immortality.

There are six great sayings (Mahavakyas) from the Upanishads that give the basic insight into its philosophy. They are as follows with a brief analysis of each:

Aham Brahmasmi: "I am Brahman". Vedic knowledge teaches that our own "Self" is the true Divinity. The Truth is within us, in our own heart. This states the identity of the inner most consciousness of the individual with the supreme Divine.

Ayam Atma Brahma: "The Self is Brahman". This states that not only individual soul is Divine but all beings are identified with the Absolute Truth.

Tat Tvam Asi: "That art thou". Whatever we see or think about, we are That. We are the ultimate Thou and I in all.

Prajnanam Brahma: "Knowledge is Brahman". Supreme intelligence is present inherently within us and is capable of returning us to the Divine. Our understanding of the truth is the truth itself.

Sarvam Kalvidam Brahma: " The whole universe is Brahman". Not only the consciousness in you and I but also the 'principle of being' are all Divine. The entire universe is Divine, which includes our Self.

So Ham: "Here am I". This identifies the Divinity in our self in something that happens naturally like breathing. "So" is inhalation and "Ham" is the natural sound of exhalation. These are the six statements of the identity of individual consciousness with the Divine reality. They all merge into and derive from the word "Om (Aum)" or the Divine word "I Am All". All of these statements point to the fact that whatever or however we worship, be it an image, book, an idea or even a

God, it is the knowledge that the Truth is within ourselves that will ultimately lead to self-realisation. Self is the true Divinity. This is the essence of Upanishads.

Ethics of Gita: Gita is the highest expression of philosophical Hinduism. It is a chapter of the immense Indian epic, the Mahabharata, the saga of the war between the Pandavas and the Kauravas. Arjuna, hero of the Pandavas, is about to confront the army of the Kauravas on the battlefield of Kuruksetra. Among the opposing army are his friends and relatives. Convinced that it would be wrong to kill his own kinsmen, Arjuna is overcome by despair. He lays down his bow and declares that he will not fight. God Vishnu, incarnated as the charioteer Krishna, explains that Arjuna should do his duty (Dharma) and do battle.

The human soul, which is part of the universal soul, is immortal-therefore no one is actually slain. If people perform the duties appropriate to their station, without attachment to success or failure, then they cannot be stained by action. The rest of the poem provides the full philosophy underlying this insight. The essence of karma yoga and of self-abnegation through yoga of renunciation as well as yoga of meditation, mysticism and devotion are discussed in eighteen chapters as conversation between Arjuna and Krishna. Detached action along with the fruits of this action is consecrated to God and this forms the basis of karma yoga.

Bhagavad-Gita teaches the causation and the effects of karma and how to deal with its manifestations. It also teaches that the human being has a free will that permits him to make intelligent choices, which in turn may alter the manifestation of the karma. The ultimate goal of every Hindu is to reduce the bad karma that he may have to carry with him into his next cycle of birth.

The Gita is variously dated between the third century B.C.E. and the fourth century C.E. The reason for uncertainty is that the Gita is not always consistent and may be the work of several hands. A follower of the philosophy expressed in the Upanishads probably wrote one strand, in which Brahman is the highest unity underlying reality. A devotee of the supreme god Vishnu may have added another strand, focused on a more personal deity, later. The Gita may originally have been written as a separate document and later incorporated into the Mahabharata.

God is in all things, and all things are in God. But the visible universe springs from only a fraction of Vishnu's glory. There is also a hidden part of God, which extends beyond the universe. Nevertheless, the Gita contains probably the most powerful and thoroughgoing expression of pantheism in world scripture. The one God is the pinnacle of all things—the radiant sun of lights, the thought organ of sense organs, the intellect of beings, the ocean of waters, the Himalayas of mountain ranges, the Ganges of rivers. He is also the inherent essence of everything—including evil. He is the gambling of rogues, the courage of the courageous, the rod of disciplinarians, and the statecraft of politicians, the Knowledge of the knowing.

Hindu Ethics and Conduct: Elabouration of the social code is found in the Mahabharata. There are four great aims of human life (purusharthas), namely dharma or righteousness, artha or wealth, kama or enjoyment and moksha or spiritual liberation; the four stages of life, the student or brahmacharya, the householder or grahasthya, the forest-dweller or vanaprastha and the wandering ascetic or sanyasa and the four castes, the priest-teacher or Brahman, the warrior or Kshatriya, the trader or Vaishya and the worker or Sudra.

The Manuva-shastra (codes of Manu) gives details of social rules and practices. Kautilya's Artha-shastra discusses economics and politics. A Hindu finds the ethics of Hinduism in the poems of Bhagavad-Gita. These were written at a time when there was attack on the establishment by reformers in order to maintain the order of the society. Gita teaches that by fulfilling his class function to the best of his ability, with devotion to God and without personal ambition, a man can find salvation, whatever his class. The teachings of the Bhagvad Gita are summed up in the maxim "your business is with deed and not with the result".

Other texts that that give insight into Hindu ethics also shaped the life of a Hindu. There is the Manasollasa written by 12th Century Deccan king Someshvara III Chalukya that illustrates Hindu morals. Hospitality, charity and honesty are extolled. Piety, performance of religious worship and pilgrimage are also important. Eight virtues of the soul were mentioned in the law book of Gautama, namely compassion, patience, contentedness, purity, earnest endeavour, pure thoughts, freedom from greed, and freedom from envy. Tamil texts of Tiukkural and Naladiyar also stress on the moral codes. Earnest kindliness and tolerance to all human relations along with non-violence had real effect on Hindu life. Desire for the well being of all beings and benevolence in the form of almsgiving were encouraged especially when done with no expectation of rewards at least in this life.

The duties also changed according to the ages and classes of people. The ascetic should set his mind on unworldly things but a layman was encouraged to strike a harmony between religion, profession and material pleasures. Similarly students, householders, elderly and the aged had different functions and duties to fulfil. Especially the orthodox classes also followed taboos like not coming in contact with an untouchable, eating forbidden meat as well as left over food. However the more intelligent teachers realised that mere outward observance was not meritorious as inner goodness. Rules were not rigid and there was always a way to circumvent the most stringent of the rules.

A Hindu is advised to contain and restrain all the emotions that may lead to a sinful existence. Thus he is asked to control such emotions as Kama (lust), Krodha (anger), Mada (ego, pride) and Matsara (jealousy). The moral codes of various texts repeatedly emphasise the importance of being aware of these ordinary but strong human emotions that lead to the disruptions of a harmonious society. There are nine basic requirements that a Hindu should be aware of and follow. Personal discipline, good conduct, self-inquiry and meditation are important. Here briefly are the nine beliefs of Hinduism:

1. Belief in the divinity of Vedas.
2. The Supreme Being is both immanent and transcendent, thus both a Creator and Un-manifest Reality.
3. The universe is in an endless cycle of creation, preservation and dissolution.

4. One creates his own destiny by his thoughts, deeds and words. This law of cause and effect is called the Karma.
5. Every soul evolves through a series of births and deaths (janma and punar-janma) until all karmas have been resolved. The cycle of many births (samsara) is the opportunity to shed the effects of karma in order to attain liberation (moksha) form the eternal cycle. Not a single soul is deprived of this destiny.
6. Belief in the existence of divine beings in unseen worlds. Temple worship, rituals, sacraments as well as personal devotions create a communion with the devas and God.
7. A master or a guru is essential to follow the right path to know the Transcendent Absolute.
8. All forms of life are sacred and are to be loved and revered. All must follow the practice of 'non-injury' or ahimsa.
9. No one particular religion teaches the 'only pathway' to salvation. All genuine religious paths are facets of God's Light and Love, deserving tolerance and understanding.

BAUDH RELIGION AND PHILOSOPHY

Stages in the History of Buddhism: The history of Buddhism in India, which lasted about 1500 years, can be divided into 500 year periods, during which distinctive forms of Buddhism emerged. This is an idealized and schematic picture, but it is convenient, and it can be matched up with where Buddhism spread during these periods and what forms of Buddhism became dominant there.

Buddhist doctrine and practice in the earliest period were agreed upon in a series of Councils, sometimes reckoned to be three, or four.

1. The First Council was held shortly after the Buddha's death, at Rajagriha. Issues about the conduct of the Sangha, the monastic community, in the absence of the Buddha appear to have been settled.
2. The Second Council was held about a century after the Buddha's death, at Vaisali. Sometimes this is considered

the First Council, or is confused with the previous one. It began to agree on the content of the Buddhist Canon and on the monastic discipline, the vinaya.

3. The Third Council was called by the Emperor Ashoka and held at Pataliputra. The content of the Pali Tripitaka, "Three Baskets," is supposed to have been settled at this Council, or there abouts in this period, consisting of the Sutra-pit.aka [Sutta in Pali], the sermons of the Buddha, the Vinaya-pitaka, the monastic discipline, and the Abhidharma-pitaka [dharma is dhamma in Pali], the philosophical development of Buddhist doctrine. Buddhism was introduced into Sri Lanka (Ceylon) as the result of Ashoka's own efforts, and the Canon in Pali was preserved there.
4. The Fourth Council was called under the Emperor Kanishka I and held at Jalandhara. This is not attested in Pali sources, and so one often hears that there were only three Councils. The Council is supposed to have supervised the translation of the Tripit.aka into Sanskrit. The Canon apparently had not only existed in Pali, but in other Prakrits, which were all consulted for a standard Sanskrit version. It appears to be the Sanskrit texts that were subsequently spread to China. The sutras of the Mahayana may have existed only in Sanskrit from the beginning.

Theravada (Teaching of the Elders) Buddhism (called "Hinayana," the "Lesser Vehicle," by the Mahayana): In India, 5th century BC to 1st century AD.

1. Distinctive doctrines:
2. The Buddha (Siddhartha Gautama, Shakyamuni) is gone, and individual practitioners must work out their salvation on their own.
3. The Buddha was unique, and individual practitioners cannot become Buddhas, only *arhats* (saints). There will be a future Buddha, Maitreya, but not for thousands of years.
4. *Nirvaṅa* (liberation) and *samsara* (the place of death and rebirth) are definitely different. *Samsara* is a place

of suffering to be left behind. *Nirvana* is a liberation that is free of death and rebirth but is beyond description and rational understanding.

Mahayana (Great Vehicle) Buddhism: In India, 1st century AD to 6th century. is not gone, and individual practitioners are not on their own. Instead, the Buddha taught the dharma out of compassion, and his compassion would prevent him from being unavailable to practitioners now. Indeed, to emulate the compassion of the Buddha, practitioners become bodhisattvas, who vow to carry all beings with them into salvation. Bodhisattvas are also available, like the Buddhas, to help people work out their salvation. Maitreya is presently a bodhisattva, but the most important bodhisattva is probably Avalokiteshvara, who became identified with the Chinese goddess of Mercy, Guanyin (Kwan-in in Wade-Giles, Kannon in Japan).

The Buddha was not unique, and individual practitioners who have become bodhisattvas can become Buddhas. There are already multiple Buddhas besides Shakyamuni. Most important are Mahavairocana and Amitabha. Amitabha is famous for his Western Paradise, or Pure Land, where he has Vowed to cause anyone who calls on him for help to be born, so they will be free of the world of suffering to work out their ultimate liberation. In Japan Amitabha is known as Amida and Mahavairocana as Dainichi. Most of the famous Buddha statues in Japan are not Shakyamuni: the great outdoor bronze Buddha at Kamakura is Amida, and the Buddha enshrined in the Tôdaiji ("Great Eastern") Temple in Nara (the largest wooden building in the world), is another Buddha named Locana.

Nirvana and samsara are no longer definitely different. The "Fourfold Negation" is applied to the relationship between the two. Samsara and nirvan.a are thus neither the same, nor different, nor both the same and different, nor neither the same nor different. This allows some room for maneuver, which may have made Buddhism more palatable in China, where Confucianism never did approve either of the world-denying metaphysics or the monasticism of Buddhism. Distinctively Chinese schools of Buddhism developed, like T'ien-t'ai (Tendai in Japan) and Ch'an (Seon [Son] in Korea, Thien in Vietnam,

Zen in Japan), for whom samsara and nirvan.a were virtually identical, so that enlightenment and nirvan.a transformed the world rather than eliminated it. The paradoxical metaphysics of Buddhism could be assimilated to the similar paradoxical doctrines of the native Chinese philosophical school of Taoism.

- *Places where Mahayana spread:* Mahayana Buddhism is presently practiced in China, Korea, Vietnam, and Japan. Buddhism was propagated in China by missionaries from India, like Ku.narajiva (344-413), who arrived in China in 401, and Buddhabhadra (359-429), who arrived in 408, and by Chinese pilgrims who traveled to India, like Fa-Hsien (Faxian), who travelled to India between 399 and 414, and Hsüan-tsang (Xuanzang, 600-664), who went to India between 629 and 645. These were difficult journeys, either by sea around Malaya, where many ships were attacked by pirates or sunk by storms, or by land through Central Asia, on the "Silk Road" caravan route, through deserts and over some of the highest mountains in the world. The highest peaks of the Pamirs and related mountain chains, called Bam-e Donya in Persian, "the Roof of the World," are all over 24,000 feet [note]. One story of a Buddhist missionary crossing the Pamirs, Kumarayana, father of Kumarajiva, is that he carried a Buddha image during the day—and the Buddha image carried him during the night! Kumarajiva, Fa-Hsien, and Hsüan-tsang all brought Buddhist texts from India to China and translated them.

Vajrayana ("Thunderbolt Vehicle") Buddhism: In India, 6th to 11th century

- *Distinctive Doctrines:* Vajrayana Buddhism is Tantric Buddhism, often called "esoteric" Buddhism. Although it is sometimes also translated as "diamond" (*i.e.* "hard"), the vajra (kôngô in Japanese) was originally the thunderbolt of Indra; and in Vajrayana it symbolizes the magical power of Tantrism. Tantric magic could be worked through man.d.alas, sacred diagrams, mantras, sacred formulas for recitation (the most famous one being, "Om, mane padme hum"—"The jewel is in the lotus") and mudras, sacred gestures. This Tantric magic could be merely thaumaturgical ("wonder working") or could be regarded as means of achieving liberation in addition to or apart from meditative or meritorious practices. Just as Hindu Tantrism expresses its magical power through goddesses like Kali, Vajrayana emphasizes female figures. Vajrayana comes to balance male Bodhisattvas with female Bodhisattvas as attendants of the various Buddhas. And while Buddhas tend to be regarded as male in all branches of Buddhism, Tibetan Buddhism supplies female figures corresponding to each Buddha, like the "savioresses" Green Tara, White Tara, and Mamaki, who actually vow to always be reborn as women in the process of leading all beings to salvation. Vajrayana symbolism always balances male and female: the Vajra Man.d.ala (or the "jewel" above) corresponds to the Womb (or Matrix) Mandala (the lotus). The extent to which Vajrayana practiced real sexual union, been the physical male "vajra" and the physical female womb, as part of its Tantrism is unclear and disputed. Often "right-handed"

Tantrism is distinguished from "left-handed" Tantrism, in which the former practiced the union of male and female, in symbolic, iconographic form, while the latter practiced it literally. While the "right-handed" forms are mainly what remain in Tibet and in Japanese Shingon today, there is little doubt that real "left-handed" practices existed in the past and survive to an extent in the present, and Tibetan art sometimes still portrays the more violent and disturbing aspects of Tantric practice—rape, bestiality, etc.

- *Places Where Vajrayana Spread:* Vajrayana Buddhism most importantly spread to Tibet and then Mongolia. In Tibet it assumed distinctive forms that are usually called Lamaism, since the monks are called Lamas. The present Dalai Lama, who was the priestly ruler of Tibet until he fled the Communist Chinese in 1959, is from a line that is reputed to be successive incarnations of the Bodhisattva Avalokiteshvara.

Vajrayana Buddhism also entered China, Japan, etc. as special "esoteric" schools, like the Japanese Shingon school. The great temple at Borobudur, outside Jakarta on the island of Java, dates from this period (c. 800) and embodies Vajrayana man.d.ala forms; but in Indonesia Buddhism soon thereafter gave way to Islam.

The End of Buddhism in India: Buddhism may have died out in India in the 11th century because:

1. It had become almost indistinguishable from the Tantric forms of Hinduism. Sophisticated Buddhist doctrine did not appeal to most people, and the actual practices and iconography of Vajrayana could easily be assimilated into Hinduism. And,
2. Islam arrived in earnest in India with the Afghan prince Mah.mûd of Ghazna, who defeated a coalition of Hindu princes in 1008 and soon annexed the Punjab. As Buddhism was persecuted, conversions to Islam increased, and Buddhism declined. By the time the British arrived, about 25% of India was Moslem. That ultimately led to the partition of the country into India and Pakistan. The Gautama Buddha himself has ended up being regarded as the 9th Incarnation (Avatar) of the great Hindu God Visnu, although the unflattering take on it is that he deliberately taught a false doctrine (*i.e.* Buddhism) in order to deceive and destroy demons.

5

INDIAN FESTIVALS AND FAIRS

Muharram

Muharram is the first month of the Islamic calendar. It is one of the four sanctified months of the year. Fighting in this month is looked down upon and is often put to the side in respect for Islam. Since the Islamic calendar is lunar, Muharram moves from year to year when compared to the Gregorian calendar.

Id-ul-Zuha

Also called Bakrid, Id-ul-Zuha, is a festival of great rejoice. Special prayers and exchange of greetings and gifts marked the Id-ul-Zuha (Bakrid), the festival of sacrifice, celebrated with traditional fervour and gaiety in India. Id-ul-Zuha is a reminder of Prophet Ibrahim's readiness to sacrifice his son for God's sake. It also marks the completion of Haj (pilgrimage to Mecca). On this day, special 'Dua' is recited by thousands of muslims for peace and prosperity.

Id-ul-Fitr (Ramzan Id)

Coming with the new moon, this festival marks the end of Ramzan, the ninth month of the Muslim year. It was during this month that the holy Koran was revealed. Muslims keep a fast every day during this month and on the completion of the period, which is decided by the appearance of the new moon, Id-ul-Fitr is celebrated with great eclat. Prayers are offered in mosques and *Idgahs* and elaborate festivities are held.

Id-i-Milad (Barah-wafat)

The Prophet was born on the twelfth day of *Rabi-ul-Awwal*, the third month of the Muslim year. His death anniversary also falls on the same day, the word *'barah'* standing for the twelve days of the Prophet's sickness. During these days, sermons are delivered in mosques by learned men, focusing on the life and noble deeds of the Prophet.

Jamshed Navroz

Over 3000 years ago, Shah Jamshed of the Peshadian dynasty ascended the throne on the Spring Equinox. His descendants, the Parsi community, celebrate it as the New Year, the dawn of a new day (Navroz literally means "new day"). It is celebrated, even today, with prayers and feasting.

SIKH FESTIVALS

Baisakhi

The Mughal Emperor, Aurangzeb, installed himself as the Emperor of India in 1657. To achieve his aim he had annihilated almost all his family opposition. Immediately after consolidating his power he embarked on a policy of religious persecution and set upon the process of Islamization of India. The Brahmins were his primary target. He levied unethical religious taxes against Hindus, and shut their temples and places of learning. He had been convinced by his clerics that once the Brahmins accepted Islam the others would follow. The Brahmins, particularly the inhabitants of Kashmir, looked for some dynamic leadership to fight this subversion.

Guru Govind Singh Jayanti

Punjab, rightly claimed as the traditional sword-arm of Bharatvarsha, has valiantly borne the first brunt of all the pre-European aggressors on her. And one of the most luminous stars which rose in that north-western horizon and shed its lustre over the entire length and breadth of the country is undoubtedly Guru Govind Singh the tenth and the final Guru in the holy tradition initiated by that great saint Guru Nanak.Richly had Guru Govind Singh inherited the legacy of the fearless martyrdom of his father-Guru Tegh Bahadur. Guru Tegh Bahadur, with a view to instilling courage and confidence among the Kashmiri Hindus to withstand Aurangzeb's fanatical tyranny and threats to Islamize them, challenged the Moghal emperor to convert him first. And the great Guru preferred to have his head roll down in Chandni Chowk of Delhi rather than sacrifice his faith, Govind Singh was just a boy of nine years at that time. On coming to know of his father's terrible end he exclaimed: "He saved with his blood the honor of Hindu Dharma. Oh, what a remarkable act in this Kaliyuga! He preferred to give up his life, but not his faith!"

Gurupurb

Gurupurb is not a single festival or occasion. These are holy days and are associated with anniversaries of the many of the Sikh Guru's birth or death, martyrdom day and anniversary of the installation of the Adi Granth Sahib. People from Sikh religion celebrate Gurupurbs. Some Gurupurbs are local events celebrated only where the original event took place. Some are celebrated universally.

Christmas: Jesus "Christ" is known as the founder or central figure of "Christianity." Christmas is a Christian holiday on December 25 that commemorates the birth of Jesus. Ancient Romans also commemorated Jesus' birth by marking a division of the calendar still in use today. The years before Jesus' birth are marked as B.C. (Before Christ), and the years after Jesus' birth are marked A.D. (Anno Domini, which means, in the year of our Lord).

Mahavir Jayanti: According to the *Digambara* school of Jainism, Lord Mahavira was born in the year 615 BC, but the *Swetambaras* believe that he was born in 599 BC. Both sects however agree that he was the son of Siddhartha and Trisala. Legend has it that he was conceived by Devananda, wife of a Brahmin named Rishabhdeva. It is believed that the gods, ingeniously, transferred the embryo to the womb of Trisala. It is said that the expectant mother had sixteen auspicious dreams before the child was born (only 14 according to the Swetambaras). Astrologers intepreting these dreams, stated that the child would be either an emperor or a *Teerthankara*.

This religious event is largely observed by the Jains by visiting sacred sites and worshipping the *Teerthankara*. The event holds special significance in Gujarat and Rajasthan due to the ancient shrines at Girnar and Palitana in Gujarat. Mahavir Jayanti is also celebrated at Parasnath Temple in Kolkata and at Pawapuri in Bihar.

BAUDH FESTIVAL

Buddha Purnima: Buddha Poornima, which falls on the full moon night in the month of Vaisakha (either in April or May), commemorates the birth anniversary of Lord Buddha, founder of Buddhism, one of the oldest religions in the world. Notwithstanding the summer heat (the temperature routinely touches 45 degrees C), pilgrims come from all over the world to Bodh Gaya to attend the Buddha Poornima celebrations.

The day is marked with prayer meets, sermons on the life of Gautam Buddha, religious discourses, continuous recitation of Buddhist scriptures, group meditation, processions, worship of the statue of Buddha and symposia. The Mahabodhi Temple wears a festive look and is decorated with colourful flags and flowers. The Chinese scholar, Fa-Hien, has recorded celebration of this festival.

Sindhu Darshan Festival: The Sindhu Darshan Festival, as the name suggests, is a celebration of River Sindhu, also known as the Indus. Last year, the Festival was organised from 6-8 June 2000 at Shey livened up by the presence of a wide variety of cultural troupes from various corners of India. Troupes from States where the mighty Rivers of India run, brought with them water from those rivers in earthen pots and immersed the pots in the Indus, thereby mingling the waters from all over India with that of the mighty 'Indus', the river that gave India its name.

Taj Mahotsav: This ten day event, held at Agra, Uttar Pradesh, the city of the Taj, in February, is a celebration of the arts, crafts, culture and traditions of Uttar Pradesh. Folk music, *shayari* (poetry), classical dance performances, elephant and camel rides, games and a food festival are the highlights of the festivites.

Tansen Samaroh: The great classical vocalist, Mian Tansen, was one of the "nine jewels", in Emperor Akbar's court. His memorial in Gwalior is the venue for the annual festival of Indian classical music held in November. Renowned singers regale audiences with mesmerizing sessions of much-loved classical *raagas.* Before performing the singers chew the leaves of a tamarind tree by the tomb-this is believed to improve the voice.

Teesta Tea Festival: This festival, held in Nov/Dec, commences in Darjeeling and Sikkim, and ends in Dooars, the gateway to the neighbouring kingdom of Bhutan. It includes a number of cultural programmes that take place in the lush greenery of historic plains, tea gardens, rolling hills and dense forests.

Bikaner Festival: This festival, held in January, in Bikaner, Rajasthan, is dedicated to the ship of the desert-the camel. The festival starts with a magnificent procession of beautifully decorated camels. There's plenty of Rajasthani culture on show too, to enchant those present: music, dance and competitions.

Chapchar Kut: "Kut" means festival in Mizo parlance, and the state of Mizoram celebrates 3 of them: Chapchar Kut, Mim Kut and Pawl Kut. All are connected with agricultural activities, and all are celebrated with feasts and dances.

Chapchar Kut celebrates the arrival of spring. The festival begins with *Kut Puipate,* the inauguration ceremony, followed by the *Then Katna,* arranging of the dance groups in the stadium. Once the *Then Hnihna* begins, elders, dressed in traditional costumes to represent the various tribes of the region, take part in a fantastic procession called *Kut rore.* This is followed by various tribal dances, the most important being the *Cheraw* (bamboo dance). The function ends with the *Then Thumna,* an event where local singers present traditional popular songs, with the cheering crowd joining in.

Chennai Dance and Music Festival: Started back in 1927 to commemorate the anniversary of the Madras Music Academy, this month-long festival is held from mid December to mid January in the city of Chennai to celebrate (classical) Carnatic music and the dance traditions of South India.

For lovers of Carnatic music, this is a treat. Held at a number of venues around the city by various *sabhas* (organizations), this cultural extravaganza sees more than 2,000 people take part. There are vocal and instrumental music concerts, and solo and group dances, with upcoming artists getting a rare opportunity to perform along with well-established artists.

Elephant Festival: Elephants are the centre of attraction at this festival held every Holi, in Jaipur, Rajasthan. They stride majestically, parading their decorated trunks and tusks. The festival begins with a procession of elephants, camels and horses, painted and gaily decorated with glittering ornaments and embroidered velvets. The elephants greet visitors, offer garlands to guests and walk past a jury of experts and tourists, vying for the "Best Decorated Elephant" shield.

The animals are followed by lively folk dancers. Elephant races and elephant polo matches are special attractions. The highlight of the festivals is a hilarious tug of war between elephants and men. The *Gaj Shringar* exhibition displays everything connected with the elephant-ornaments, textiles (jhoo), howdahs and carriages, paintings, medicines and food. Tourists are encouraged to join in the dances, mount the elephants and play Holi.

Nine nautical miles from the megapolis of Mumbai, just across the harbour, is the Elephanta Island, home to the Elephanta Caves, that date back to the 2 nd and 6 the century and are a UNESCO World Heritage site. This turns into a huge open-air auditorium during the Elephanta Festival held every year. The feast of dance and music, celebrated under the stars is surely not to be missed.

Ellora Festival: This festival of dance and music is organised in the splendid surroundings of the magnificent Ellora caves in Maharashtra, a UNESCO World Heritage site.

Garden Festival: If you love flowers, you should at this spectacular flower show, held in the capital city, Delhi, each year. A humongous variety of flowers and exotic plants are on display.

Hampi Festival: The ruins of the magnificent city of Hampi (353 kilometres from Bangalore), Karnataka, once the capital of the Vijayanagar Empire (one of the greatest empires India has known) and now a UNESCO World Heritage site, come alive during this extravaganza, held in the first week of November. Dance, drama, music, fireworks, puppet shows and spectacular processions. All combine to recreate the grandeur of a bygone era. The ruins of stone temples, elephant stables, barracks and palaces offer a fascinating glimpse into the lives of the people who once resided there.

Hemis Festival: The courtyard of Hemis Gompa (monastery), the biggest Buddhist monastery in Ladakh, in the state of Jammu & Kashmir, is the stage for this festival, which celebrates the birth anniversary of Guru Padmasambhava, revered as a reincarnation of Buddha. The colourful two-day pageant falls on the 10th day (Tse-Chu) of the Tibetan lunar month. A raised dais with a richly cushioned seat is erected in the courtyard, and a small, finely painted Tibetan table is placed here. Ceremonial items-cups full of holy water, uncooked rice, tormas made of dough and butter, incense sticks-are placed on the table. Traditional music is played, with four pairs of cymbals, pan drums, small trumpets and large wind instruments.

Locals dress up in their finest traditional garb for the occasion. *Lamas* (monks) perform splendid masked dances and sacred plays to the accompaniment of cymbals, drums and long horns. The head lama presides over the function. Every 12 years, in the Tibetan Year of the Monkey, the two-storey high *Thanka* depicting Padmasambhava, richly embroidered with pearls and semi-precious stones, is displayed. The last display was in 2004. A colourful fair, displaying some beautiful handicrafts, is the special highlight of the festival.

Holla Mohall: This Sikh festival begins the day after Holi, in March, and lasts for 3 days. It is celebrated at the sleepy town of Anandpur Sahib (close to Chandigarh) in Punjab. Sikhs from all over the state (and outside) congregate at the Gurdwara Keshgarh Sahib, the place where the Khalsa (Sikh brotherhood) was founded. Early morning prayers herald the event. A large number of community kitchens offer *langar* (free food) to those present. Dressed in traditional costumes, the Nihang Sikhs (traditional members of the Sikh army founded by Guru Gobind Singh) delight those present with a display of their skills in archery, fencing, tent pegging, bareback horse riding (standing erect on 2 speeding horses) and shooting.

Mock battles are enacted with enthusiasm and the area resounds to the sounds of the firing of ancient cannons. Of course, this IS Holi, so there's a lot of spraying each other with colour. A fair comes up around the Gurudwara. Evenings are for cultural events, including music and poetry competitions. The highlight of the last day is a long procession led by the Panj Piaras which makes a round of all the gurudwaras in the area.

Hornbill Festival: Held in Nagaland in December, this festival pays tribute to the Hornbill-the most revered bird of the Naga tribes. The festival showcases Nagaland's heritage in all its diversity and grandeur.

Hoysala Mahotsava: The splendidly sculpted Hoysala temples of Belur and Halebid in Karnataka, a UNESCO World Heritage site, are the venue for this dance festival.

International Flower Festival: Held every summer during the peak flowering season, this festival showcases the exotic flora of the tiny North Eastern state of Sikkim. On display are flowers, orchids, gladioli, roses, magnolia, cacti, alpine plants, creepers, climbers, ferns, and herbs. There are seminars and lectures by experts. And, of course, momos and other delectable Sikkimese delicacies. If you like what you see, why not plan a trip to Sikkim? The best time to go is from March to May, when the plants (including 600 species of orchids, 240 species of trees and ferns, 150 varieties of gladioli, 46 types of rhododendrons) are in full bloom. Bonus attractions are river rafting and the yak safari.

International Mango Festival: Mango lovers, like wine lovers, are passionate about their favourites, and at this festival, you can savour the many myriad varieties of the king of fruits and find out why. Cultural programmes liven up the event still further.

Island Tourism Festival: This ten-day long festival of dance, drama and music showcases the arts and crafts, flora and fauna and marine life of Port Blair, capital of the Andaman & Nicobar Islands. Aqua sports, tele-games and parasailing are added attractions.

Jahan-Khusrau: Only Sufi music is played at this music festival associated with Hazrat Amir Khusrau, one of the great followers of Hazrat Nizamuddin. Performers from all over the world perform. The festival takes place in Delhi in the last week of February.

Jaipur Heritage International Festival: The Pink City of Jaipur, in Rajasthan, always fascinating, becomes even more so during this festival, spread over fourteen days in January and in locations difficult to find anywhere else in the world. Events include exhibitions, seminars, sports, children's programmes and of course, crafts bazaars.

Ka Pomblang Nongkrem: Also called Shad Nongkrem, this colourful 5-day long event is the most important and elaborate festival of the Khasi tribe. Held annually in November at Smit near Shillong, Meghalaya, it gives thanks to the Goddess Ka Blei Synshar for a rich harvest. An important part of this festival is the *Pomblang Ceremony,* at which goats are sacrificed and offerings are made to the ancestor and ancestress of the ruling clan and U-Lei Shillong (the deity of Shillong peak). Sanctification of the *tangmuri* (pipes) as queen of musical instruments, forms part of the ritual. After the religious rituals, on the fourth day, Khasi men and women, dressed in traditional splendour, perform the famous Nongkrem dance, with young women dancing within a protective ring formed by young lads. The festival ends on the fifth day with a prayer for prosperity.

Kala Ghoda Arts Festival: The spotlight of this festival, held in the megapolis of Mumbai in January, is on fine, folk and performing arts and ethnic cuisines. Events include movies, concerts, competitions, exhibitions, food courts, street performances, workshops.

Kalidas Festival: Nagpur, in Maharashtra, is the venue for this festival, dedicated to the great Sanskrit Poet Kalidas. Celebrated every November since 1995, it is a feast of Indian classical dance and music. Upcoming artists perform alongside experienced performers to make the festival a memorable experience.

Khajuraho Dance Festival: There's more to Khajuraho than erotic carvings on temple walls, and this week-long festival of classical dances, held in February/March each year proves it. All the classical dance traditions-Kathak, Bharathanatyam, Odissi, Kuchipudi, Manipuri and Kathakali-are on show, against the spectacular backdrop of the magnificently lit temples, a UNESCO World Heritage site. Modern Indian dance has also been added recently. The dances are performed by some of the best exponents in the field, in an open-air auditorium, usually in front of the Chitragupta Temple dedicated to Surya (the Sun God) and the Vishwanatha Temple dedicated to Lord Shiva, belonging to the western group. They bring alive the former religious capital of Chandela dynasty, one of the powerful Rajput dynasties of Central India.

Konark Dance Festival: The floodlit Sun Temple of Konark in Orissa, a UNESCO World Heritage site and one of India's greatest architectural sights often described as a poem in stone, is the backdrop for this festival of classical dance held every December. Eminent dancers present their interpretations of various classical dance forms-Odissi, Bharatnatyam, Manipuri, Kathak and Chhau-as t he sound of *ghungroo* bells, flute and *pakhawaj* fill the air. A marvellous crafts mela and delectable cuisine add to the festive mood.

Kurukshetra Festival: Kurukshetra, Haryana, is the battlefield of the epic Mahabharata, on which Lord Krishna gave Arjuna, the Pandava prince, the advice enshrined in the Bhagwad Gita, the Holy Book of the Hindus. It is believed that Lord Brahma created the universe from Kurukshetra after performing a great *yajna* (sacrifice) here. Manu is said to have written his Manusmriti here, and it the Rig and Sama Vedas (Hindu holy scriptures) are also believed to have been compiled here. Lord Buddha and the Sikh gurus came visiting. All-in-all, it is an ancient holy land associated with the origins of Hinduism.

The Kurukshetra Festival coincides with Gita Jayanti, which celebrates the birth of the Gita. It is expectedly an exhilarating and spiritual experience. Pilgrims gather to take a dip in the sacred tanks of Brahma Sarovar and Sannehit Sarovar. Religious festivities include week-long *Bhagwad Katha* (Story-telling sessions of the Gita), recital of *shlokas* (sacred verses), dance dramas and *deep daan* at Brahma Sarovar. Free medical camps, book exhibitions and recitals of *bhajans* (religious songs) in the classical tradition are also organized.

Ladakh Festival

A colourful kaleidoscope of cultures-Central Asian, Tibetan, and North Indian-come alive in this festival held in September in Ladakh, nestled in the Western Himalayas. On display are traditional sports (polo and archery), folk dances and songs, age-old social and cultural ceremonies, art and handicrafts.

Lohri: Celebrated in Punjab on 13 the January, Lohri celebrates the successful harvest of the Rabi crops-an extremely important event in a predominantly agricultural community. It is a community festival, and celebrated as one. Children go from door to door to collect funds for community bonfires that are lit up in the evening. The villagers gather around the bonfires and offer sweets, puffed rice, *til* (sesame) and popcorn to the flames. The evening is spent singing, dancing, and exchanging greetings with family and friends. After Lohri, the biting cold of North Indian winters begins to taper off.

Lucknow Festival: Held in November-December, in Lucknow, the capital of the state of Uttar Pradesh, this festival perfectly captures the undying elegance and splendours of the ancient city formerly known as Awadh.

The arts, crafts, and above all, heavenly cuisine, are yours to savour for 10 memorable days, bringing alive Lucknow's Nawabi past. Colourful processions, traditional dramas, Kathak dances in the Lucknow *gharana* style, music concerts (sarangi / sitar recitals, ghazals, qawalis, thumri), traditional village games (*ekka* races, kite flying competitions, cock fights). just choose what you want to be entertained by and surrender.

Mamallapuram Dance Festival: Dancers and musicians from across the country participate in this festival held at the UNESCO World Heritage site of Mamallapuram, Tamil Nadu, in December-January, with Arjuna's Penance as its backdrop.

Marwar Festival: Originally known as Maand Festival, this is held in Jodhpur, Rajasthan, and is devoted to the music and dance of the Marwar region. Folk artists bring the myths, legend and folklore of the area to life. The festival is held for 2 days on *Sharad Purnima*, the full moon, in October.

The city of lakes, Udaipur, in Rajasthan, is the venue for this festival, celebrated in April during the Gangaur Festival. An exhilarating welcome to spring, it is an audio-visual feast with Rajasthani songs, dances, processions, devotional music and firework displays. A procession of colourfully attired women carrying images of the goddess Gauri make their way to Lake Pichola. A procession of boats on the lake offers a fitting finale to the splendid celebrations.

Modhera Dance Festival: The Sun Temple at Modhera in Mehsana district, Gujarat, dedicated to Lord Surya, the sun god, acts as the backdrop for this festival of Indian classical dances, held every year in January for three days. The festival seeks to present classical dance forms in a milieu that is as close as possible to that in which they were originally performed.

National Kite Festival: This takes place in Ahmedabad, Gujarat, on Makara Sankranti (14 the January), the day when t he Sun enters the *Makar Rashi* (the zodiac sign of Capricorn, the goat), starting its northward journey. Makar Sankranti is the day of the equinox, when day and night are equally long.

Hindus believe that those who die on this day attain *moksha*, escaping from the cycle of birth and re-birth. T housands of colourful kites dot the skies as people vie with each other to win community kite-flying competitions. Special kites have little paper lamps attached and these fill the night sky with flickering lights. Special Gujarati cuisine, exhibitions of handicrafts, and folk art enhance the festive spirit.

National Theatre Festival: Held in Kolkata in December, this is one of the largest theatre festivals in India. Drama troupes come from all over the country, and neighbouring countries too, to participate.

Natyanjali Festival: This 5 day festival which takes place in the premises of the ancient Nataraja temple of Chidambaram, Tamil Nadu, pays special tribute to Lord Nataraja, the dancing Shiva. It is held in Feb / March and begins on the auspicious occasion of Mahashivratri. Leading dancers from all parts of India congregate and dance in the temple as an offering to

Nataraja, while the carved pillars depicting Lord Nataraja in 108 poses of Bharata Natyam look silently on. The festival promote the message of "Unity in Diversity", conveyed in the universal language of music and dance.

Nehru Cup Boat Races: Kerala's backwaters at Aranmula and Kottayam, are the picturesque setting for the annual snake-boat races held on the second Saturday of August every year. T ranquil lake fronts are transformed into a sea of humanity, as over 100 oarsmen in each huge (over 100 feet long) snake boat vie for the prestigious Nehru Trophy, named after independent India's first Prime Minister. An estimated 2 lakh people watch, while the beating of drums and cymbals, and songs add to the festive mood. Preparations for the event begin several weeks in advance, and celebrations continue long after, for the winning teams.

Nishagandhi Dance Festival: The Nishagandhi open-air theatre in the palace compound at Thiruvananthapuram, Kerala, is the venue for this classical dance festival held every April. Renowned dancers perform Bharathanatyam, Mohiniattam, Kathak, Odissi, modern ballet and other folk forms. Artist and connoisseurs of dance come from all over India to enjoy this cultural treat.

Pattadakkal Dance Festival: The delicately carved temples at the UNESCO World Heritage site of Pattadakkal (the ancient capital of the Chalukyan kings) in the state of Karnataka form the backdrop for this festival of dance, held to celebrate this marvellous heritage.

Pete De Pondicherry: This cultural pageant, held from 15 the to 17 the August, in Pondicherry, coincides with Pondicherry's Liberation Day. The Park monument is brilliantly lit.

Thrissur Pooram: "Pooram", the two-century-old festival held at the Vadakkunnathan temple in Thrissur, Kerala, in Apr / May, is the most colourful of all the temple festivals held in the state. All the temples in the state send their best elephants to participate. B edecked with golden headpieces coming down over the trunk, the elephants go round the temple in a splendid procession t o the accompaniment of drums, pipes and trumpets. Carrying ceremonial umbrellas and fanned by white whisks,

30 of these gentle giants amble out majestically through the temple gate, to line up in 2 rows, facing each other, in the open ground. An elephant in the center carries the image of Lord Shiva. Each "team of elephants" has its own *Panchavadyam* (literally "five instruments", *i.e.*, conch, cymbals, trumpet and two kinds of drums) orchestra. The umbrellas are unfurled to the beating of the drums and cheering of the assembled crowds. Specially appointed judges award a prize for the most spectacular display. The festival ends with a magnificient display of fireworks that continues till dawn. Truly, you can call it a mammoth spectacle!

Qutub Festival: Veterans of Indian classical music and folk dance hold audiences enthralled at this festival held in Nov./Dec. each year, in Delhi, against the historic ruins of the Qutb Minar, a UNESCO World Heritage site. Kuchipudi, Odissi, Manipuri, Ghazals, Qawalis, Sarangi, Sitar. choose your event and look forward to a memorable evening. Spice it up further with regional cuisines available at the food stalls at the complex.

Rajgir Dance Festival: Rajgir, the ancient capital of the Magadha empire in Bihar, is held sacred by both Buddhists and Jains for its association with the Buddha and Lord Mahavira. Every October, a colourful festival of dance and music is held here. Instrumental music, devotional songs, opera, folk dance and ballet.

Gangaur Festival: The *Gangaur Festival* is the colourful and most important local festival of Rajasthan and is observed throughout the State with great fervour and devotion by womenfolk who worship Gauri, the consort of Lord Shiva during July-Aug. It is the celebration of monsoon, harvest and marital fidelity in Jaipur.Gan is a synonym for Shiva and Gaur which stands for Gauri or Parvati who symbolises saubhagya (marital bliss). Gauri is the embodiment of perfection and conjugal love which is why the unmarried women worship her for being blessed with good husbands, while married women do so for the welfare, health and long life of their spouses and a happy married life.

The festival commences on the first day of Chaitra, the day following Holi and continues for 18 days. For a newly-wedded girl, it is binding to observe the full course of 18 days of the festival that succeeds her marriage. Even unmarried girls fast for the full period of 18 days and eat only one meal a day.Images of Isar and Gauri are made of clay for the festival. In some families, permanent wooden images are painted afresh every year by reputed painters called matherans on the eve of the festival. A distinct difference between the idols of Teej and Gangaur is that the Idol will have a canopy during the Teej Festival while the Gangaur idol would not have a canopy.

FAIRS OF INDIA

Kumbha Mela: The pilgrimage occurs four times every twelve years, once at each of the four locations. Each twelve-year cycle includes the Maha (great) Kumbha Mela at Prayag, attended by millions of people, making it the largest pilgrimage gathering around the world.

The observance of Kumbha Mela is based upon the following story: thousands of years ago, perhaps in the Vedic period, gods and demons made a temporary agreement to work together in obtaining *amrita* (the nectar of immortality) from the Milky Ocean, and to share this equally.

However, when the Kumbha (pot) containing the amrita appeared, the demons ran away with the pot and were chased by the gods. For twelve days and twelve nights (equivalent to twelve human years) the gods and demons fought in the sky for the possession of this pot of amrita. It is said that during the battle, drops of amrita fell on to four places: Prayag, Haridwar, Ujjain and Nasik.

Thus, Kumbha mela is observed at these four locations where the nectar fell.Kumbha Mela is attended by millions of people on a single day. A ritual bath at a predetermined time and place is the major event of this festival.

Other activities include religious discussions, devotional singing, mass feeding of holy men/women and the poor, and religious assemblies where doctrines are debated and standardized. Kumbha Mela (especially the Maha Kumbha Mela) is the most sacred of all the Hindu pilgrimages. Thousands of holy men/women (monks, saints, sadhus) grace the occasion by their presence. The suspiciousness of Kumbha Mela is in part attributed to the gathering of thousands of holy men/

women at one place on earthAccording to astrologers, the 'Kumbh Fair' takes place when the planet Jupiter enters Aquarius and the Sun enters Aries.

Ganga Sagar Fair: Gangasagar Mela is the largest fair celebrated in West Bengal. This fair is held where the Ganga and the Bay of Bengal form a nexus. Hence the name Gangasagar Mela.

The river Ganga which originates in the Gangotri glacier in the snow clad Himalayas, descends down the mountains, reaches the plains at Haridwar, flows through ancient pilgrimage sites such as Benares and Prayag, and drains into the Bay of Bengal. Sagar Island, at the mouth of the river Hooghly in Bengal (accessed from Diamond Harbor), where the Ganga breaks up into hundreds of streams, and drains into the sea, is honored as a pilgrimage site.

Baneshwar Fair: The name 'Baneshwar' is derived from the revered Shivlinga, which is kept in the Mahadev Temple in Dungarpur. "Baneshwar means the 'Master of the Delta' in the local Vagdi language and this name was given to the Shivlinga. The Baneshwar fair is held at a small delta formed by the river Som and Mahi, from Magh Shukla Ekadashi to Magh Shukla Purnima. Baneshwar fair in its present form is actually one of two fairs: one which used to be held in of Baneshwar Mahadev (Lord Shiva) and another fair, which started after the construction of the Vishnu Temple by Jankunwari, daughter-in-law of Mavji, a highly revered saint considered to be an incarnation of Lord Vishnu.

Sonepur Cattle Fair: A visual extravaganza awaits all at the Sonepur Fair, where multitudes congregate on Kartik Purnima to offer obeisance to Harihar Nath and participate inwhat is the biggest cattle fair in Asia. Festivities stretch over a fortnight, giving visitors a feel of the pulse of Bihar. According to the Indian Almanacalmanac, the full moon day of Kartik Purnima,or Purnima of the month of Kartik, which usually falls in November, is one of the most auspiciousof days.

A number of big fairs are held at important paces of pilgrimage. The Harihar Chhetra Mela near Sonepur is one of the biggest fairs held in India and is also the biggest cattle fair pilgrimage and the Harihar Kshetra Mela, as the Sonepur Fair is also known, is one of the biggest.

Sonepur is located in the Saran district in the northern part of Bihar. This district shaped like a triangle is demarcated by three mighty rivers-the Ganga, Gandak, and Ghagra, demarcate this district, which is shaped like a triangle. Sonepur stands on the confluence of the Ganga and Gandak.

Tarnetar Fair: The Tarnetar Fair is one of the most important fairs of Gujarat. Various tribes like the *Kolis*, the *Rabaris*, the *Bharwards*, the *Khants*, the *Khanbis*, the *Charans* and the *Kathis*, get together to celebrate the famous legendary marriage of Draupadi with Arjuna, thereby retracing its origin to the times of the Mahabharata. Arjuna was the third of the five Pandavas of Hastinapur, who got married to Draupadi-the princess of this region, in the great Hindu epic, the Mahabharata.

Banganga Fair: The Banganga Fair is held annually on the full moon day of Vaishakh (April-May) near a rivulet 11 kms from the historical township of Bairath in Jaipur district. The stream is believed to have been created by Arjun, one of the Pandavas. Visiting the Banganga Fair, taking a bath and paying homage to the holy sites in the vicinity at this time is therefore considered very auspicious by the pilgrims who come from Alwar, Behror, Jaipur, Bharatpur and many other places. Devotees gather at the Shri Radha Krishnaji's temple in the morning, they take a bath at the ghats (a flight of steps leading to the water) of the Banganga river with the belief that it has powers to purify the soul. The people then proceed to the nearby shrines of Hanuman and Ganga Bihari and also visit the Shiva temple and the Math of Goswamiji.

Camel Festival: A lively and colourful event, the Camel Festival is organised by the Department of Tourism, Art & Culture, Rajasthan in Bikaner every year. January is just the right month for a desert spree, and Bikaner just the right place to see the Ships of the Desert. In the camel country Bikaner, these desert leviathans pull heavy cart loads, transport grain and even work at the wells. The Camel Festival begins with a colourful procession of bedecked camels against the red sandstone backdrop of the Junagarh Fort, the festivity advances to the open sand-spreads of the grounds, followed by the best breed competition, the tug-of-war contest, camel dance and acrobatics, etc.

The camels display amazing footwork, dancing gracefully to the slightest direction of their trainers. Bridal, bridles, bejewelled necks, jingling anklets and long, lanky camel shadows on dusky sands cast a magical spell. Hundreds of tourists and thousands of locals and dignitaries revel in this man-and-animal affair organised especially for the tourists.

The evenings close with a different tenor and tempo altogether: a traditional rendezvous of renowned artists of Rajasthan and the local folk performers.

The jubilant skirt-swirling dancers, the awe inspiring fire dance, and the dazzling fireworks light up the fortified desert city of Bikaner. Bikaner is connected by rail and road with all the major cities. The nearest airport is at Jodhpur (243 kms.)

Kaila Devi Fair: The annual fair of Kaila Devi, (Mahalakshmi or the goddess of wealth), is held at the village Kaila (24 kms to the south west) in Karauli district in the month of Chaitra (Mar-Apr), lasting for a fortnight. The temple of Kaila Devi is located on the banks of the Kalisil river in the hills of Trikut, 2 kms. to the north-west of Kaila village. Another attraction is the small temple dedicated to Bhairon, situated in the courtyard and facing the shrine of Kaila Devi is a temple of Hanuman locally called 'Languriya'.

Approximately 2 lakh devotees gather during the fair. The ritual of Kanak-Dandotis is observed by staunch devotees. They cover a distance of 15 to 20 kms to reach the temple, not on foot but by lying prostrate, making lines with their hands in that position, advancing up to the line drawn and repeating this procedure till they reach the temple.

While some eat food and take rest during the journey, others endure the rigours of the ritual without these. Groups of Mina tribesmen arrive in a spirit of gaiety dancing, singing and creating a lively atmosphere. The spacious courtyard becomes the venue for dances and songs sung in praise of the guardian deity.

The nearest rail-head is Hindaun at a distance of about 48 Kms. Shri Mahavirji is another rail-head of the Western Railway near Kaila. The site is approachable by well maintained roads from Karauli, Hindaun and Mahavirji. During the fair, the State Transport as well as private operators provide bus services keeping in mind the huge inflow of pilgrims.

Shekhawati Fair: The Shekhawati Festival held on 10th and 11th February every year is organised jointly by the State Department of Tourism, District administrations of Sikar, Jhunjhunu and Churu.

Shekhawati, already famous for its frescoes, is fast becoming a rural tourism destination too. Travelling on horse back, the tourists get a closer view of the countryside and the people.

And they return with an indelible imprint of not only the friendliness of the people but also of the agricultural revolution sweeping the villages—the region now exports 80 per cent of its crops whereas only a few years ago it could meet only 10 per cent of its requirement through local production. For a broad-based discovery of Shekhawati's culture, the festival is spread over a number of venues-Nawalgarh, Sikar, Jhunjhunu and Churu.

The programmes include a one day tour of the region, camel and jeep safaris, farm visits, rural games, cultural programmes, haveli competitions and fireworks. Nawalgarh is the central venue of the festival and can be reached comfortably by train and road from Jaipur (140 kms by Road).

Nawalgarh also has some of the finest frescoes of Shekhawati. The Clock Tower is a famous landmark and the Roop Niwas Palace hotel occupies a place of pride in the town.

Rath Yatra (Car Festival): This spectacular chariot festival celebrated for 8 days, is held at the famous Jaganath Temple at Puri (Orissa). Thousands of devotees flock to Puri during the occasion as they believe that a glimpse of Lord Jagnnath in his chariot gives salvation. Images of Lord Jaganath-the Lord of the Universe, his sister Subhadra and brother Balbhadra are taken out in a procession in three immense chariots. The main chariot is 14 meters high and 10 meters square with 16 wheels.

The deities are brought out of the temple to the chariots by rhythmic movement called 'Pahandi' in a royal procession to the accompaniment of the beat of the 'cymbals' and drums and chanting of prayers by devotees. The pushing and shoving to seat Lord Jagannath on his chariot continues for hours. The god it seems is testing the perseverance of his devotees.

The devotees in turn coax, cajole, they promise sweetmeats and other delicacies, when all this fails they call the Lord names and even give blows to the idol, all the while the surging crowd chants, sings and dances. It is believed that on these days Lord Jagannath will descend from his pedestal and mingle with his devotees with no barrier between them. After seating the idols, the traditional King of Puri sweeps the Chariots with a golden broom. Thousands of devotees pull these chariots to Gundicha Mandir, a temple 3 km away.

After a week, on 'Ashadha Sukla Dasami', the 10th day of the bright fortnight of Ashadha (June-July), return journey or 'Bahuda Yatra' of the deities commences in the same manner from Gundicha temple to the main temple like Rath Yatra. When two months of Ashadha fall in one year, Rath Yatra is observed as the festival of 'Nabakalebar' the old deities are buried within the temple premises ('Koilibaikuntha') and are replaced by new deities, carved out of Margosa trees for which there are set procedures. Double Ashadha occurs at intervals of 8 to 19 years. Construction of the chariots begin as early as April.

Orissa is a land of innumerable fairs and festivals celebrated round the year but the most spectacular of them is the Rath Yatra, hitherto known as the Car Festival to western world. This chariot procession on the main streets of Ahmedabad city features a lot of colourful chariots, trucks and other vehicles. The procession commemorates the journey of Lord Krishna to Mathura, leaving behind grieving Gopis. The massive procession begins at Jagdish temple in Jamalpur. The main chariots are dedicated to lord Krishna, his brother Balaram and sister Subadhra, followed by colourfully decorated elephants, trucks, motor vehicles, pilgrims on foot, acrobats and gymnasts.

Republic Day of India

26th January, 1950 is one of the most important days in Indian history as it was on this day the constitution of India came into force and India became a truly sovereign state. In this day India became a totally republican unit. The country finally realized the dream of Mahatma Gandhi and the numerous freedom fighters who, fought for and sacrificed their lives for the Independence of their country. So, the 26th of January was decreed a national holiday and has been recognized and celebrated as the Republic Day of India, ever since.

Independence Day

With the decision by Britain to withdraw from the Indian subcontinent, the Congress Party and Muslim League agreed in June 1947 to a partition of India along religious lines. Under the provisions of the Indian Independence Act, India and Pakistan were established as independent dominions with predominantly Hindu areas allocated to India and predominantly Muslim areas to Pakistan.

After India's independence on August 15, 1947, India received most of the subcontinent's 562 widely scattered polities, or princely states, as well as the majority of the British provinces, and parts of three of the remaining provinces. Muslim Pakistan received the remainder. Pakistan consisted of a western wing, with the approximate boundaries of modern Pakistan, and an eastern wing, with the boundaries of present-day Bangladesh.

August 15th, 1947 is the birthday of free India. It marks for her the end of an old era, the beginning of a new age. It's a day of freedom from the arduous British rule, 15th August is celebrated in India as Independence Day. To commemorate the sacrifice of martyrs Indians celebrate this day to pay homage to the brave patriots who gave Indians a reason to smile. The celebration begins in the morning with unfurling of Indian flag at Red Fort, New Delhi.

Gandhi Jayanti

The birth anniversary of Mahatma Gandhi, the father of the nation, is celebrated with reverence all over the country. He is the man who played a significant role in achieving independence for India from the British Empire with his simplicity and strong will power. Mohandas Karamchand Gandhi, also known as 'Bapu' or 'Father of the nation', was born on the 2nd of October in 1869, in Porbunder, Gujarat. He studied law in U.K and practiced law in South Africa. But he left his profession and returned to India to join the Indian freedom struggle.

Makar Sankaranti

The festival of Makar Sankrant traditionally coincides with the beginning of the Sun's northward journey (the *UTTARAYAN*) when it enters the sign of Makar (the *CAPRICORN*). It falls on the 14th of January every year according to the Solar Calendar. This day has a very special significance because the day and night on Makar Sankrant are of exactly of equal hours. This day is celebrated as a festival right from the times of the Aryans and is looked upon as the most auspicious day by the Hindus.

Pongal

Pongal is the first festival beginning off each new year in the Indian state of Tamil Nadu. As the dates for this festival are calculated by the solar calander (ie. Western), the dates of January 13-16 never change. Each day of this festival has a special significance, however, it is celebrated more grandly in the villages, while the city folk mainly celebrate on the second day only.

Vasant Panchami

Vasant Panchami is the festival dedicated to Saraswati, the goddess of learning. (Deepavali is dedicated to Lakshmi, goddess of wealth, and Navaratri Durga is dedicated primarily to Kali, goddess of strength, might and power.) Magh Sud 5 (5th day of the bright fortnight of the lunar month of Magh) is the day of Vasant Panchami. Hindus all over the world celebrate this festival with great enthusiasm. This Panchami is also known as Saraswati Day. It is believed that this day is Saraswati's birthday. Hindu temples are full of activities on this day.

Maha-Shivratri

Maha Shivratri is celebrated throughout the country; it is particularly popular in Uttar Pradesh. Maha Shivratri falls on the 13th (or 14th) day of the dark half of 'Phalgun' (February-March). The name means "the night of Shiva". The ceremonies take place chiefly at night. This is a festival observed in honour of Lord Shiva and it is believed that on this day Lord Shiva was married to Parvati. On this festival people worship 'Shiva-the Destroyer'. This night marks the night when Lord Shiva danced the 'Tandav'.

In Andhra Pradesh, pilgrims throng the Sri Kalahasteshwara Temple at Kalahasti and the Bharamarambha Malikarjunaswamy Temple at Srisailam. About *The Lord Shiva*-the word meaning auspicious-is one of the Hindu Trinity, comprising of Lord Brahma, the creator, Lord Vishnu, the preserver and Lord Shiva or Mahesh, the Destroyer and Re-Producer of life. Shiva is known by many names like "Shankar", "Mahesh", "Bholenath", "Neelakanth", "Shambhu Kailasheshwar", "Umanath", "Nataraj" and others.

Holi

The festival of Holi is celebrated on the day after the full moon in early March every year. Originally a festival to celebrate good harvests and fertility of the land, Holi is now a symbolic commemoration of a legend from Hindu Mythology. The story centres around an arrogant king who resents his son Prahlada worshipping Lord Vishnu. He attempts to kill his son but fails each time. Finally, the king's sister Holika who is said to be immune to burning, sits with the boy in a huge fire. However, the prince Prahlada emerges unscathed, while his aunt burns to death. Holi commemorates this event from mythology, and huge bonfires are burnt on the eve of Holi as its symbolic representation.

Ram Navami

The birthday of Lord Rama, the celebrated hero of the famous epic, 'Ramayana', is enthusiastically celebrated all over India. Lord Vishnu is worshipped in his human incarnation as Rama, the divine ruler of Ayodhya. Celebrations begin with a prayer to the Sun early in the morning. At midday, when Lord Rama is supposed to have been born, a special prayer is performed.

Temples of Rama are decorated, religious discourses are held and the Ramayana is recited for ten days. People sing devotional songs in praise of Rama and rock, images of him in a cradle to celebrate his birth. Rathyatras or chariot processions of Rama, his wife Seeta, brother Lakshmana and devotee Hanuman are held from many temples. The chariot is accompanied by several devotees dressed up in ancient costumes as Rama's soldiers. The procession is a gusty affair with the participants shouting praises echoing the happy days of Rama's reign. People gather in thousands on the banks of the sacred river Sarayu for a dip. Some observe a strict fast on this day.

Teej Festival

Held during the monsoons, July-August Teej is also dedicated to Lord Shiva and Parvati and this time it is married women who pray for a happy and long married life. Though celebrations are held all over the state, it is particularly colorful in Jaipur where a procession winds its way for two days through the Old City. It is the festival of swings which are decorated with flowers and hung from trees. Young girls and women dressed in green clothes sing songs in celebration of the advent of the monsoon. The Teej idol is covered with a canopy whereas the Gangaur idol is open.

Raksha Bandhan

Raksha Bandhan (*the bond of protection* in Hindi) or *Rakhi* is a Hindu festival which celebrates the relationship between brothers and sisters. It is celebrated on the full moon of the month of Shravana. The festival is marked by the tying of a rakhi, or holy thread by the sister on the wrist of her brother. The brother in return offers a gift to his sister and vows to look after her. The brother and sister traditionally feed each other sweets.

Nagpanchami

Hinduism as a religion is many-sided yet bound by a common search for Truth and to Hindus it means a way of life and a fellowship of faiths. With the advent of the Aryans, it originated as a simple form of worship of the forces of Nature, drawing in its system action in social organisations, local cults, deities diverse beliefs and modes of worship.

Nag-Panchami is an important all-India festival and is celebrated on the fifth day of the moonlit-fortnight in the month of Shravan (July/August). This is the time when serpents invariably come out of their holes that get inundated with rain-water to seek shelter in gardens and many times in houses. As such they pose a great danger to man. May be therefore, snakes are worshiped on this day. Right from the times when mankind started acquiring some sort of culture, Sun and Snake have been invoked with prayers and ritual worship in most of the countries. In India even before the Vedic times, the tradition of snake-worship was in vogue.

Krishna Janmashtami

Shravan vad 8 celebrates the birth of Lord Shri Krishna, one of the most venerated incarnations in the Hindu Dharma. Five thousand years ago, he incarnated, at the end of the third cosmic phase, 'Dwapar Yuga' and the beginning of the present, 'Kali Yuga'.

Janmashtami is the birthday of Lord Krishna, the re-incarnation of Lord Vishnu who gave us the vital message of the Bhagwat Gita-the guiding principles for every Hindu. Janmashtami is celebrated with full vigor all over the country. Janmashtami is celebrated in various parts of India to mark the birth of Lord Krishna. It is observed on the Ashtami day of the Shravan month according to the Hindu calendar. The temples of Vrindavan witness an extravagant and colourful celebration on this occasion. Raslila is performed to recreate incidents from the life of Krishna and to commemorate his love for Radha.

Ganesh Chaturthi

Ganesh Chaturthi is one of the most popular of Hindu festivals. This is the birthday of Lord Ganesha. It is the day most sacred to Lord Ganesha. It falls on the 4th day of the bright fortnight of Bhadrapada (August-September). It is observed throughout India, as well as by devoted Hindus in all parts of the world.

Dashaharaa

This festival is observed twice a year, once in the month of Chaitra and then in Aswayuja. It lasts for nine days in honour of the nine manifestations of Durga. During Navaratri (the word literally means "nine nights") devotees of Durga observe a fast. Brahmins are fed and prayers are offered for the protection of health and property.

The beginning of summer and the beginning of winter are two very important junctions of climatic and solar influence. These two periods are taken as sacred opportunities for the worship of the Divine Mother. They are indicated respectively by the Rama-Navaratri in Chaitra (April-May) and the Durga Navaratri in Aswayuja (September-October). The bodies and minds of people undergo a considerable change on account of the changes in Nature. Sri Rama is worshipped during Ramnavmi, and Mother Durga during Navaratri.

Diwali

This is perhaps the most well-known of the Indian festivals: it is celebrated throughout India, as well as in Indian communities throughout the diaspora. It usually takes place eighteen days after Dusshera. It is colloquially known as the "festival of lights", for the common practice is to light small oil lamps (called *diyas*) and place them around the home, in courtyards, verandahs, and gardens, as well as on roof-tops and outer walls.

In urban areas, especially, candles are substituted for diyas; and among the nouveau riche, neon lights are made to substitute for candles. The celebration of the festival is invariably accompanied by the exchange of sweets and the explosion of fireworks.

As with other Indian festivals, Diwali signifies many different things to people across the country. In north India, Diwali celebrates Rama's homecoming, that is his return to Ayodhya after the defeat of Ravana and his coronation as king; in Gujarat, the festival honors Lakshmi, the goddess of wealth; and in Bengal, it is associated with the goddess Kali.

Everywhere, it signifies the renewal of life, and accordingly it is common to wear new clothes on the day of the festival; similarly, it heralds the approach of winter and the beginning of the sowing season.

Diwali (also called Deepavali) is a major Hindu festival. Known as the "Festival of Lights," it symbolises the victory of good over evil, and lamps are lit as a sign of celebration and hope for mankind. Celebrations focus on lights and lamps, particularly traditional diyas (as illustrated). Fireworks are associated with the festival in some regions of the country.

Chhath

The Chhath festival of sunworship is celebrated mainly in Bihar, Eastern UP and other parts of India where large of Bhojpuri speaking populace is present. It is a festival in which mothers pray for long and healthy life of their children.

The Mothers observes fast for the full day and in the evening when moon rises she gives worships moon. Again in the morning mother worships Rising SUN by standing in the river water or pond.

Chhath Puja is an Indian thanksgiving festival dedicated to the Sun God. During the celebrations of Chhath Puja, people gather on the banks of the River Ganges to bathe in its sacred water, pray and make ritual offerings to the Sun God.

Chhath Puja is a highly elaborate festival noted for its impressive display of colorful costumes, music, singing and extravagant rituals. When *Chhath* Puja takes place, sometime during the months of October and November, immediately following the six-day festival of lights known as Diwali. Chhath Puja lasts for one night and one day.

Sarhul

Sarhul which means the sal-blossom festival is a semi-religious festival of the inhabitants of Chota Nagpur. This festival is celebrated by several tribes of the region such as the Orions, Mundas and the Santhals, the Santhals call it *Baha* and celebrate it in end February-March whereas the Orions celebrate it a little late in March-April.

Karwa Chauth

The fast of Karwa Chauth is kept 9 days before Diwali. It falls on the fourth day of the Kartik month by the Hindu calendar (fourth day of the waning moon or the dark fortnight).

Karwa Chauth is considered one of the most important fasts observed by the married Hindu women. On this day the women pray for the welfare and long life of their husbands. The festival is followed mainly in the northern parts of the country.

Bihu Festival

The breathtaking hills and valleys of Assam come alive with the sound of Bihu thrice a year. A festival that marks the change of season, Bihu is accompanied both by prayer and great rejoicing. One of the seven northeastern states of India (which are also known as the Seven Sisters), Assam is renowned for its picturesque landscape, exotic fauna and fun-loving people.

6

THE ROLE OF WOMEN IN INDIAN LIFE

INTRODUCTION

In traditional Hindu culture, women are held in the highest regard—far more respected, in truth, than in the West. But this does not imply the kind of equality or participation in public interactions that are common in the West. The qualities traditionally most admired in a Hindu woman are modesty of manner, shyness and self-effacement. Self-assertive or bold tendencies are regarded with circumspection. Feminine refinements are expressed and protected in many customs, including the following:

1. *Womanly Reserve:* In mixed company especially in the presence of strangers, a Hindu woman will keep modestly in the background and not participate freely in conversation. This, of course, does not apply to situations among family and close associates.
2. *Walking Behind One's Husband:* The wife walks a step or two behind her husband, or if walking by his side, a step or two back, always giving him the lead. In the West, the reverse of this is often true.
3. *Serving at Meals:* At meals women follow the custom of serving the men first before enjoying their own meal.
4. *Chaperoning:* It is customary for a woman to always be accompanied when she leaves the home. Living alone, too, is unusual.
5. *Women in Public:* Generally it is improper for women to speak with strangers on the street and especially to

strike up a casual conversation. Similarly, drinking alcohol or smoking in public, no matter how innocent, are interpreted as a sign of moral laxity and are not acceptable.

Guests in the Home

1. *Home Visits:* Close friends can visit one another anytime without being announced or making arrangements first. When they drop in, at least a refreshing drink is always served.
2. *Hosting Guests:* Children generally leave the room, with a smile, when guests enter. The mother remains close by to serve as needs arise. The father, if present, will speak with the guest. If he is not present, the mother and a mature son will fulfil this role; and if no son is present, the mother may act as hostess, but only with the accompaniment of someone close to the family.
3. *Wife Home Alone:* If the lady of the house is in home alone and a male visitor comes to see her husband, it is not proper for her to invite him in, nor for him to expect to enter. Rather, he will leave a message and depart.
4. *Giving Gifts:* Gifts are always given when one visits a home or stays overnight as a guest. The value of the gift varies greatly, depending upon circumstances. It is proper to give a separate gift for the wife and the husband. The wife is given the nicest item.

Body Language

All Hindus know that "Life is meant to be lived joyously!" All is God, and God is everywhere and in all things. This understanding and appreciation is exemplified in every aspect of Hindu deportment.

1. *Kindly Words and Countenance:* Hindus strive to keep a pleasant expression on their face, a gentle smile and a kind word for everyone they meet through the day. They know in their heart of hearts that God is everywhere and that all in the universe is perfect at every point in time. This knowledge gives them strength

and courage to face their daily karmas positively and graciously.

2. *Refined Gestures:* Hindus know that every movement of the body, the face, hands, eyes, mouth, head, etc., has a meaning. Youth are taught to be sensitive to the thoughts and feelings of others in their body language.
3. *Eyes:* Eyes are also a primary means of communicating, and the meanings are fairly straightforward. They usually indicate degrees of interest in what the speaker is saying. Smiling with your eyes as well as your mouth conveys sincerity. There are three levels of smiling (and infinite shades and degrees in between). Having the eyes open only slightly indicates mild interest. Eyes more open and a bigger smile indicates more interest and enthusiasm. Having the eyes open wide with a big smile or nod, possibly accompanied by some verbal expression, indicates greater interest or great happiness.

Hindu Women and Religion

In ancient India, women occupied a very important position, In fact, a superior position, to men. "Sakti" a feminine term means "power" and "strength". All male power comes from the feminine. Literary evidence suggests that kings and towns were destroyed because the rulers troubled a single woman.

For example, Valmiki Ramayana teaches us that Ravana and his entire kingdom were wiped out because he abducted Sita. Veda Vyasa's Mahabharata teaches us that all the Kauravas were killed because they humiliated Draupadi in public. Elango Adigal's Sillapathigaram teaches us Madurai, the capital of the Pandyas was burnt because Pandyan Nedunchezhiyan mistakenly did harm to Kannaki.

In Vedic times women and men were equal in many aspects. Women participated in the public sacrifices alongside men. One script mentions a female rishi Visvara. Some Vedic hymns, are attributed to women such as Apala, the daughter of Atri, Ghosa, the daughter of Kaksivant or Indrani, the wife of Indra.

Apparently in early Vedic times women also received the sacred thread and could study the Vedas. The Haritasmriti mentions a class of women called brahmavadinis who remained unmarried and spent their lives in study and ritual. Panini's distinction between acharya (a preceptor) and acharyani (a lady teacher or a preceptor's wife), and upadhyaya (a preceptor) and upadhyayani (a lady teacher or a preceptor's wife) indicates that women at that time could not only be students but also the teachers of sacred Vedas.

There were several noteworthy women scholars of the past such as Kathi, Kalapi, and Bahvici. The Upanishads refer to several women philosophers, who disputed with their male colleagues such as Vacaknavi, who challenged Yajnavalkya.

The Rig Veda also refers to women engaged in warfare. One queen Bispala is mentioned, and even as late a witness as Megasthanese (fifth century B.C.) mentions heavily armed women guards protecting Chandragupta's palace.

Hindu religion has been occasionally criticised as encouraging inequality between men and women, towards the detriment of Hindu women. This presumption is inaccurate. In the Vedic period, we come across female scholars like Ghosha, Lopamudra, Romasha and Indrani. In the Upanishad period, names of women philosophers like Sulabha, Maitreyi, Gargi are encountered.

In religious matters, Hindus have elevated women to the level of divinity. One of the things most misconstrued about India and Hinduism is that it's a male dominated society and religion and the truth is that it is not so.

It is a religion that has attributed the words for the strength and power to feminine. "Sakti" means "power" and "strength". All male power comes from the feminine. The Trimurti (Brahma, Vishnu, Shiva) are all-powerless without their female counterparts.

Devi is the Great Goddess.

This echoes Devi-Mahatmiyam prayer:

By you this universe is borne, by you this world is created;
By you it is protected,
By you it is consumed at the end,
O Devi! You are the Supreme Knowledge, as well as intellect and contemplation...

Women were held in higher respect in India than in other ancient countries, and the Epics and old literature of India assign a higher position to them than the epics and literature of other religions.

Hindu women enjoyed rights of property from the Vedic Age, took a share in social and religious rites, and were sometimes distinguished by their learning. There was no seclusion of women in India in ancient times.

Professor H. H. Wilson says: "And it may be confidently asserted that in no nation of antiquity were women held in so much esteem as amongst the Hindus."

In Ancient India, however, Hindu women not only possessed equality of opportunities with men, but enjoyed certain rights and privileges not claimed by the male sex. The chivalrous treatment of women by Hindus is well known to all who know anything of Hindu society.

Knowledge, intelligence, rhythm and harmony are all essential ingredients for any creative activity. These aspects are personified in Saraswati, the Goddess of Learning, Music and Fine Arts. Without the grace of Saraswati, or Saraswati Kataksham, as it is called, Brahma cannot do a worthwhile job as the Creator. Any maintenance activity needs plenty of resources, mainly fiscal resources. So Lakshmi, the Goddess of Wealth, is an essential companion to Vishnu. Shiva, as Destroyer, derives power and energy from Parvati, or Durga as she is called Sakti.

It is only the Hindu tradition, which provides, even at the conceptual level, the picture of the male and female principles working together, hand in hand, as equal partners in the universe. This concept is carried further to its logical climax in the form of Ardhanariswara, formed by the fusion of Shiva and Sakti in one body, each occupying one half of the body, denoting that one is incomplete without the other.

Just the sloka that is commonly recited during daily prayers is enough to show the status of the Goddesses. A sloka on Devi contains the following line: Yaa Brahma Achyuta Sankara Prabhrudibihi Devaissadaa Poojithaa, which means, 'O Devi! Brahma, Vishnu, Shiva and other Gods' always adore you.

In Hinduism, all power, Sakti, is female. Sakti is the fundamental strength of the feminine that infuses all life. Sakti is the divine feminine power found in everything. She is the Goddess. So that, actually, in India, Kali is the great divinity.

Hindus hold rivers in great reverence. The rivers are female divinities, food and life bestowing mothers. As such, they are prominent among the popular divinities represented in the works of art of the classical period. The most holy of rivers, the best known and most honoured, is the Ganga or Ganges. She is personified as Goddess Ganga. The river rises from an ice bed, 13,800 feet above the sea level in the Garhwal Himalayas. The river Saraswati is regarded as the mother god.

One of the most important of all Vedic hymns, the Devisukta, is addressed to Vak (speech, revelation), the goddess who is described as the instrument that makes ritual efficacious: "I am the queen, the gatherer-up of treasures..." It is not unimportant, that Earth (prithivi) is considered female, and the goddess who bears the mountains and who brings forth food that feed all.

Education for girls was regarded as quite important. While Bramhavadani girls were taught Vedic wisdom, girls of the Ksatriya girls were taught the use of the bow and arrow. Patanjali mentions the spear bearers (saktikis). Megasthanese speaks of Chandragupta's bodyguard of Amazonian women. Kautilya mentions women archers (striganaih dhanvibhih).

Similarly, Kautilya in his Arthasastra, which is also taken to be a document of Mauryan history, refers to women soldiers armed with bows and arrows. Buddhism kept up the traditions of Brahmanical religion in according to womanhood an honoured place in social life. Women were made eligible for admission to what was known as the Bhikshuni-Sangha, the Order of Nuns, which opened to them avenues of culture and social service and ample opportunities for public life.

In Gurukulas, the ancient Universities of India, boys and girls were educated together. Atreyi studied under Valmiki along with Lava and Kusa, the sons of Rama. Fine arts like music, dancing and painting was especially encouraged in the case of girls.

Girls had Upanayana performed for them and carried out the Sandhya rites. A young daughter who has observed brahmacharya should be married to a bridegroom who is learned like her. (Yajur Veda VIII.1). Seclusion of women was unknown in the Vedic times.

The Atharva Veda refers to daughters remaining with their parents until the end of their lives. A part of the ancestral property is given to them as dowry, which becomes their own property, and is called stridhana in later writings. "Home is not what is made of wood and stone; but where a wife is, there is the home." (Sanskrit: Na grham kasthapasanair dayita yatra tad grham-Nitimanjari, 68)

It is significant to note that only Hindus worship God in the form of Divine Mother. In Hinduism the deities for knowledge, learning and material wealth are female and not male. The past social inconsistencies and injustices that did not arise from Hindu scriptures, but from humans who failed to correctly incorporate the teachings of the scriptures, such as the Upanishads and the Bhagavad Gita, into their social philosophy.

This concept of the spiritual equality of souls naturally influenced the status of women on an individual and social level. Secularists make the predictable allegation that Hinduism as represented by Manu is anti-woman. Actually on reading this text one would realise that neither dowry (dahe) nor self-immolation of widows (sati) figure in it.

"Where women are honoured there the gods are pleased; but where they are not honoured no sacred rite yields rewards," declares Manu Smriti (III.56) a text on social conduct.

"Women must be honoured and adorned by their fathers, brothers, husbands and brothers-in-law, who desire their own welfare." (Manu Smriti III, 55)

"Where the female relations live in grief, the family soon wholly perishes; but that family where they are not unhappy ever prospers." (Manu Smriti III, 57).

"The houses, on which female relations, not being duly honoured, pronounce a curse, perish completely as if destroyed by magic." (Manu Smriti III, 58)

"Hence men, who seek their own welfare, should always honour women on holidays and festivals with gifts of ornaments, clothes, and dainty food." (Manu Smriti III, 59)

In an old Shakti hymn it is said-Striyah devah, Striyah pranah "Women are Devas, women are life itself."

"If a husband dies, a wife may marry another husband.

"If a husband deserts his wife, she may marry another." (Manu, chapter IX, verse 77).

"A woman's body," says Manu the law-giver, "must not be struck hard, even with a flower, because it is sacred." It is for this reason that the Hindus do not allow capital punishment for women.

In the Vedas, she is invited into the family 'as a river enters the sea' and 'to rule there along with her husband, as a queen, over the other members of the family.

The idea of equality was most forcibly expressed in the Rig Veda (Book 5, hymn 61. verse 8). The commentator explains this passage thus: "The wife and husband, being the equal halves of one substance, are equal in every respect; therefore both should join and take equal parts in all work, religious and secular." No other Scripture of the world have ever given to the woman such equality with the man as the Vedas of the Hindus.

A Hindu woman whose name was Romasha revealed the 126th hymn of the first book of the Rig Veda; the 179 hymn of the same book was by Lopamudra, another inspired Hindu woman. There are a dozen names of woman revealers of the Vedic wisdom, such as Visvavara, Shashvati, Gargi, Maitreyi, Apala, Ghosha, and Aditi, who instructed Indra, one of the Devas, in the higher knowledge of Brahman, the Universal Spirit. Every one of them lived the ideal life of spirituality, being untouched by the things of the world. They are called in Sanskrit Brahmavadinis, the speakers and revealers of Brahman.

When Sankaracharya, the great commentator of the Vedanta, was discussing philosophy with another philosopher, a Hindu lady, well versed in all the Scriptures, was requested to act as a judge.

It is the special injunction of the Vedas that no married man shall perform any religious rite, ceremony, or sacrifice without being joined in by his wife; the wife is considered a partaker and partner in the spiritual life of her husband; she is called, in Sanskrit, Sahadharmini, "spiritual helpmate."

In the whole religious history of the world a second Sita will not be found. Her life was unique. She is worshipped as an incarnation of God. India is the only country where prevails a belief that God incarnates in the form of a woman as well as in that of a man.

In the Mahabharata we read the account of Sulabha, the great woman Yogini, who came to the court of King Janaka and showed wonderful powers and wisdom, which she had acquired through the practice of Yoga. This shows that women were allowed to practice Yoga.

As in religion, Hindu woman of ancient times enjoyed equal rights and privileges with men, so in secular matters she had equal share and equal power with them. From the Vedic age women in India have had the same right as men and they could go to the courts of justice, plead their own cases, and ask for the protection of the law.

Those who have read the famous Hindu drama called Shakuntala know that Shakuntala pleaded her own case and claimed her rights in the court of King Dushyanata. Similar instance are mentioned in the 10th book of the Rig Veda. As early as 2000 B.C. Hindu women were allowed to go to the battlefields to fight against enemies. Her husband in search of robbers sent Sarama, one of the most powerful women of her day. She discovered their hiding place and then destroyed them. Regarding this as the highest dharma of all four castes, husbands, though weak, must strive to protect their wives. His own offspring, character, family, self, and dharma does one protect when he protects his wife scrupulously. The husband should engage his wife in dharma, the collection and expenditure of his wealth, in cooking food for the family, and in looking after the necessities of the household....

A father protects his daughter in childhood, a husband protects his wife in youth, and the sons protect their mother in old age. The father who does not give away his daughter in marriage at the proper time is censurable; censurable is the husband who does not approach his wife in due season; and after the husband is dead, the son, verily is censurable, who does not protect his mother. Even against the slightest provocations should women be particularly guarded; for unguarded they would bring grief to both the families.

Motherhood is considered the greatest glory of Hindu women. The Taittiriya Upanishad teaches, "Matridevo bhava"- "Let your mother be the god to you."

Hindu tradition recognises mother and motherhood as even superior to heaven. The epic Mahabharata says, "While a father is superior to ten learned priests well-versed in the Vedas, a mother is superior to ten such fathers, or the entire world."

Hinduism offers some intriguing and unique examples of strong women in the form of Goddesses. Two thousand years ago Saint Trivalvular observed: "What does a man lack if his wife is worthy? And what does he possess if she is lacking worth?" There is more respect in the Hinduism for women and for their role in society.

In many philosophical texts God is referred to a Tat, meaning it and that God is beyond gender. And, one would find a comparable Goddess for each God. Further, we know for a fact that ancient India was permissive; women could have multiple husbands, widows could remarry, divorce was permitted for incompatibility or when estranged.

The names of Gargi and Maitreyi are too well known as great scholars of Vedic scriptures. We have statements like, "This hymn must be recited by the wife," in the Sroutasutras, which clearly endorse the eligibility of women to the study of the Vedas. The Ramayana describes the performance of Sandhya and Havana by Kausalya and Sita. The wife was a regular participant in the sacrificial offerings of the husband. (Rigveda I-122-2; 131-3; III-53-4-6; X-86-10 etc.). Gobhila Gruhya Sutras state that the wife should be educated to be able to take part in sacrifices.

Woman in the role of wife occupies a position of pre-eminence in ancient Hindu tradition. The Hindus from the Vedic times believed in dual worship Shiva with Sakti, Vishnu with Lakshmi, Rama with Sita, and so on.

In this dual worship, the names of Radha and Sita get precedence over the names of their companions Krishna and Rama. This happens to be true of Goddess Saraswati and her husband Lord Brahma. Lord Shiva appears united in a single body with Sakti, his spouse; he at the right side and she at the left, in a manifestation known as Ardhanariswara, the half-man, half-woman incarnation of God. Each of the three principal Gods Brahma the Creator, Vishnu the Protector and Shiva the Destroyer in the Hindu pantheon, is accompanied by a Sakti, which is both his female double and his power of manifestation.

The Rig Veda too places woman on a high pedestal of sublimity: Yatr nariyastu poojayante ramante tatr devah, where woman is worshipped, Gods preside there. Women must be honoured and adorned by their father, brothers, husbands, and brother-in-law who desire great good fortune. Where women, verily are honoured, there the gods rejoice; where, however, they are not honoured, there all sacred rites prove fruitless. Where the female relations live in grief, that family soon perishes completely; where, however, they do not suffer from any grievance that family always prospers.

Women, who once enjoyed an honoured position and are found in the Upanishads conversing freely with men contributing an active role in the society. Young girls led free lives and had a decisive voice in the selection of their husbands. On festive occasions and at tournaments (samana) girls appeared in all their gaiety. In certain Hindu castes the line of inheritance is from mother to (eldest) daughter, and marriage is a "visiting" relationship. Naturally, women were more independent and free in every respect. Ladies did not lead a secluded life like that of their descendants in later times. Several hymns of the Rig Veda were composed by female Rishis (sages). Young ladies of the time had a voice in their marriage. "The woman who is of gentle birth and of graceful form," so runs a verse in the Rig Veda, "selects among many of her loved one as her husband."

Numerous case of Svayamvara, that is, of ladies selecting their own husbands, is mentioned in the Mahabharata and other works. There is sufficient evidence to show, that widow marriage was allowed, and that the Sati was unknown in the Vedic period.

"Rise up woman," so runs a text of the Rig Veda (X, 18.8) "thou art lying by one whose life is gone, come to the world of the living, away from thy husband, and become the wife of him who holds thy hand and is willing to marry thee."

Every hymn of the Rig-Veda is attributed to a rishi. Though the majority of these hymns were the work of male Rishis, the Rig-Veda contains hymns that were revealed by women seers also. The latter were called rishikas and brahmavadinis...

The brahmavadinis were products of educational discipline of brahmacarya, for which women were also eligible. The Rig-Veda (V, 7, 9) refers to young maidens completing their education as brahmacharinis and then gaining husbands... Rv. iii (55, 16) mentions unmarried learned and young daughters who should be married to learned bridegrooms.

It is, therefore, no wonder that the wife enjoyed with her husband full religious rights and regularly participated in religious ceremonies with him. In fact, the performance of such ceremonies would be invalid without the wife joining her husband as his full partner. Some grammatical passages show that women had other careers open to them apart from a mere literary career.

Some incidents of sati and rash of "dowry murders" have made headlines not only in India, but all around the world, and have focused attention to women's issues in India. In the wake of the discussion it emerged that Indian women's problems are not only problems of Hindu women or problems caused by traditional Hinduism. Media paints India as a dangerous place. But if statistics can be trusted, a study by Hindus against the Abuse of Women presented at the Second International Conference on Bride Burning and Dowry Deaths in India puts USA in the lead of familial femicide. The study says excessive need for control and greed may be the underlying causes, not cultural or religious factors.

The commotion about the sati was just one expression of the colonial mind-set of the ruling class. At one time, most such efforts were closely associated with attempts to justify the

British rule in India. The Westernised who controlled the media, either directly or indirectly made news exhibiting themselves as the protectors of Sati and dowry, a cultural projection of a new form of internal colonialism.

Self-burning of widows was not sanctioned by the Vedic religion, but was due to other causes. Some say that, when the Muslim conquered India, they treated the widows of the soldiers so brutally that the women preferred death, and voluntarily sought it. It is often said that the "British government" has suppressed Sati; but the truth is, that the initiatives in this direction was taken by the noble Hindu, Raja Ram Mohan Roy, who was, however, obliged to secure the aid of the British Government in enforcing the ideas, because India was a subject nation.

The educated classed among the Hindus had strongly protested against this inhuman custom, but as it could not be done without the official help, appeal was made to the then Viceroy, Lord Bentinck, a law against Sati was then passed.

In Hinduism four Vedas, Bhagvad Gita and the two puranas Ramayana and Mahabharata are considered to be the supreme. All others are just commentaries, explanatory notes or stories written by individuals. As commentaries written on the Constitution of India cannot override the articles of the Constitution of India, similarly, commentaries or explanations on Vedas by individuals cannot supersede richas of Vedas or the Ramayana or Gita.

In the Ramayana, everyone knows that after the death of King Dasharatha, his wives were never asked to step into the pyre of Dasharatha. Rather, they lived in family with full honour and Rama always bowed his head before his widowed mothers with full respect. In the Mahabharata, Kunti, mother of the Pandavas did not commit sati. Thus, there is no command in the Ramayana, Mahabharata or in Gita to commit sati.

The Hindu Woman as Wife

Of the ideal woman of the religious orders the West today has very little notion. Teresa and Catherine are now but high-sounding names in history; Beatrice, a true daughter of the Church, is beloved only of the poets; and Joan of Arc, better understood, is rightly felt to be by birth the nun, but by genius the knight. Yet without some deeper sense of kindred with these it will be hard to understand a Hindu marriage, for the Indian bride comes to her husband much as the Western woman might enter a church. Their love is a devotion, to be offered in secret. They know well that they are the strongest influence, each in the other's life, but before the family there can be no assertion of the fact. Their first duty is to see that the claims of others are duly met, for the ideal is that a wife shall, if that be possible, love her husband's people as she never loved her own; that the new parents shall be more to her than the old; that she can bring no gift into their home so fair as a full and abundant daughterhood and a confirmation of their supreme place in their son's love. Both husband and wife must set their faces towards the welfare of the family. This, and not that they should love each the other before all created beings, is the primal intention of marriage.

Yet for the woman supreme love also is a duty. Only to the man his mother must stand always first. In some sense, therefore, the relation is not mutual. And this is in full accordance with the national sentiment, which stigmatises affection that asks for equal return as "shop keeping." When her husband is present or before honoured guests the young wife may not obtrude herself on the attention of her elders. She sits silent, with veil down, plying a fan or doing some little service for the new mother. But through the work of the day she is a trusted helpmeet, and the relation is often very sweet. Nothing is so easy to distinguish as the educational impress of the good mother-in-law. Dignity, with gaiety and freedom, is its great feature.

The good breeding of the Hindu woman is so perfect that it is not noticed till one comes across the exception—some spoilt child, perhaps, who, as heiress or beauty has been too much indulged; and her self-assertiveness and want of restraint, though the same behaviour might seem decorous enough in an English girl of her age, will serve as some measure for the real value of the common standard.

It is not merely in her quietness and modesty, however, that the daughter-in-law betrays good training. She has what remains with her throughout life—a savour faire that nothing can disturb. I have never known this broken; and I saw an extraordinary instance of it when a friend, the shyest of orthodox women, consented to have her photograph taken for one who begged it with urgency. She stipulated, naturally, that it should be done by a woman.

But this was found to be impossible. "Then let it he an Englishman," she said with a sigh, evidently shrinking painfully from the idea of a man, yet feeling that the greater the race-distance the less would be the impropriety. The morning came, and the Englishman arrived, but in the Indian gentle-woman who faced him there was no trace of self-consciousness or fear. A superb indifference carried her through the ordeal, and would have been a sufficient protection in some real difficulty. All the sons of a Hindu household bring their wives home to their mother's care, and she, having married her own daughters into other women's families, takes these in their place.

There is thus a constant bubbling of young life about the elderly woman, and her own position becomes a mixture of the mother-suzerain and lady abbess. She is well aware of the gossip and laughter of the girls amongst themselves, though they become so demure at her entrance. Whispering goes on in corners and merriment waxes high even in her presence, but she ignores it discreetly, and devotes her attention to persons of her own age. In the early summer mornings she smiles indulgently to find that one and another slipped away last night from her proper sleeping-place and betook her to the roof, half for the coolness and half for the mysterious joys of girls' mid-night gossip.

The relationship, however, is as far from familiarity as that of any kind and trusted prioress with her novices. The element of banter and freedom has another outlet, in the grandmother or whatever aged woman may take that place in the community house. Just as at home the little one had coaxed and appealed against the decisions of father or mother to the ever-ready granddame, so, now that she is a bride, she finds some old woman in her husband's home who has given up her cares into younger hands and is ready to forego all responsibility in the sweetness of becoming a confidante. One can imagine the rest.

There must be many a difficulty, many a perplexity, in the new surroundings, but to them all old age can find some parallel.

Looking back into her own memories, the grandmother tells of the questions that troubled her when she also was a bride, of the mistakes that she made, and the solutions that offered. Young and old take counsel together, and there is even the possibility that when a mother-in-law is unsympathetic, her own mother-in-law may intervene on behalf of a grandson's wife. Before the grandmother, therefore, there is none of that weight of reverence which can never be lightened in the mother's presence. Even the veil need not be dropped. The familiar "thou" take the place of the stately "you," and there is no respect shown by frigid reserve.

Long ago, when a child's solemn betrothal often took place at seven or eight years of age, it was to gratify the old people's desire to have more children about them that the tiny maidens were brought into the house. It was on the grandmother's lap that the little ones were made acquainted; it was she and her husband who watched anxiously to see that they took to each other; and it was they again who petted and comforted the minute grand-daughter-in-law in her hours of home sickness. Marriage has grown later nowadays, in answer amongst other things to the pressure of an increasing poverty, and it does not happen so often that an old man is seen in the bazaar buying consoling gifts for the baby brides at home. But the same instinct still obtains, of making the new home a place of choice, when between her twelfth and fourteenth year—the girl's age at her first and second marriages—the young couple visits alternately in each other's families.

The Hindu theory is that a long vista of common memory adds sweetness even to the marriage tie, and whether we think this true or not, we have all known happy marriages on such a basis. But about the mutual sentiment of old and young there can be no theory, because there is no possibility of doubt. In all countries in the world it is recognised as amongst the happiest things in life. The reminiscence of Aruba, one of the heroes of the great War-Epic, gives us the Indian explanation of this fact. "I climbed on his knee," he says, speaking of the aged knight Bhishma, head of his house, "all hot and dusty from my play, and flinging my arms about his neck, I called him 'Father.'" "Nay, my child," he replied, as he held me to his breast, "not thy father but thy father's father!" With each generation, that is to say, the tie has deepened and intensified.

In all cases where one or two hundred persons live under the same roof, a complex etiquette grows up, by which gradations of rank and deference is rigidly defined. Under the Hindu system this fund of observation has so accumulated that it amounts now to an accomplished culture—a completed criticism of life—rich in quaint and delightful suggestions for humanity everywhere. We may not know why a mother's relatives are apt to be dearer than a father's, but the statement will be approved as soon as made.

It has not occurred to us that our relations to an elder sister and a younger are not the same: in India there is a different word for each, for whole worlds of sweetness lie a world apart in one name and the other to the Hindu mind. Yet a cousin is constantly called brother or sister, the one relation being merged entirely in the other. The mere use of a language with this degree of definiteness implies an emotional training of extraordinary kind. It is, of course, best suited to natures of great richness of feeling. In these, sentiment is developed in proportion to expression, and the same attitude that makes every one in the village "Aunt" or "Uncle" to the children, produces an ultimate sense of kinship to the world.

This is perhaps the commonest characteristic of Hindu men and women; shy at first, and passive to slight stimulus, as are all great forces, when once a relationship is established, they believe in it absolutely, blindly; are ready to go to the uttermost in its name; and forget entirely all distance of birth or difference of association. The weak point in the system appears when it has to deal with the harder, more arid class of natures. In these there is less inner response to the outer claim, expressions of difference, therefore, become less sincere and more abject? This is but a poor preparation for the open air of the modern world, where seniority, sanctity, and rank have all to be more or less ignored, and man stands face to face with man, free and equal so far as the innate manhood of each can carry. But such persons—though, naturally enough, they cluster round the powerful foreigner as moths about a lamp—are the failures of Hinduism, not its types, and they are very few. In a perfected education, Western ideals of equality and struggle would present themselves to these for their choosing, while far away in Europe, maybe, hearts born too sensitive for their more rudimentary emotional surroundings would be thankful in turn to find life made richer by Indian conceptions of human relationship.

In a community like that of the Hindu home—as in all clan-systems—the characteristic virtue of every member must be a loyal recognition of common duties and dangers. And this is so. The wife who refused to share her husband's obligation to a widowed sister and her children was never known in India. Times of stress draw all parts of the vast group together; none of the blood can cry in vain for protection and support: even a "village-connection" (*i.e.*, one who is kin by association only) finds refuge in his hour of need. This great nexus of responsibility takes the place of workhouse, hospital, orphanage, and the rest. Here the lucky and the unlucky are brought up side by side. For to the ripe and mellow genius of the East it has been always clear that the defenseless and unfortunate require a home, not a barrack.

Into this complex destiny the bride enters finally, about her fourteenth year. Till now she has been a happy child, running about in freedom, feet shod and head bare, eating and drinking what she would. Till now, life has been full of indulgences—for her own parents, with the shadow of this early separation hanging over them, have seen no reason for a severity that must bring in its train an undying regret. From the moment of her betrothal, however, the girl's experience gradually changes. Just as the young nun, if she runs to find her thimble, will be sent back to bring it "more religiously," so about the newly married girl there grows a subtle atmosphere of recollectedness.

The hair is parted, no longer childishly brushed back; and at the parting—showing just beyond the border of the veil with which her head now is always covered—appears a touch of vermilion, put there this morning as she dressed in token that she wished long life to her husband; much as one might, in taking up a fan, blow a kiss from its edge to some absent beloved one. The young wife's feet are unshod, and the gold wedding bracelet on the left wrist, and a few ornaments appropriate to her new dignity, supply the only hint of girlish vanity. But she has more jewels.

These that she wears daily are of plain gold, more or less richly worked, but on her wedding night she wore the siti, or three-lined coronal, set with gems, and arms and neck were gay with flashing stones. All these were her dower, given by her father to be her personal property, and not even her husband can touch them without her consent, though he will add to them occasionally at festive moments. She will wear them all now and again, on great occasions, but meanwhile the silver anklets and the golden necklet and a few bangles are enough for daily use.

The girl knows her right to her own ornaments quite well, and the world will never hear how often the wife or the mother has hastened to give up the whole of this little resource in order that son or husband might weather a storm or receive an education. The one thing from which she will never part, however, unless widowhood lays its icy hand upon her life, is that ring of iron covered with gold and worn on the left wrist, which is the sign of the indissoluble bond of her marriage—her wedding-ring in fact.

With all the shyness of the religious novice comes the girl to her new home. Its very form, with its pillared courtyards, is that of a cloister. The constant dropping of the veil in the presence of a man, or before a senior, is the token of a real retirement, the sacrament of an actual seclusion, within which all the voices of the world lose distinctness and individuality, becoming but faint echoes of that which alone can call the soul and compel the eager feet.

For India has no fear of too much worship. To her, all that exists is but a mighty curtain of appearances, tremulous now and again with breaths from the unseen that it conceals. At any point, a pinprick may pierce the great illusion, and the seeker become aware of the Infinite Reality beyond. And who so fitted to be the window of the Eternal Presence as that husband, who is at once most adored and loved of all created beings?

For there is a deep and general understanding of the fact that only in its own illumination, or its own feeling, can the soul find its highest individuation. To learn how she can offer most becomes thus the aim of the young wife's striving. All her dreams are of the saints—women mighty in renunciation: Sita, whose love found its richest expression in the life-long farewell that made her husband the ideal king; Sati, who died rather than hear a word against Shiva, even from her own father; and Uma, realising that her love was given in vain, yet pursuing the more eagerly the chosen path. "Be like Savitri," was her father's blessing, as he bade her the bridal farewell, and Savitri—the Alcestris of Indian story—was that maiden who followed even Death till she won back her husband's life.

Thus wifehood is thought great in proportion to its giving, not to its receiving. It would never occur to any one, in writing fiction, or delineating actual character, to praise a woman's charms, as we praise Sarah Jennings', on the score that she retained her husband's affection during her whole life. A good man, says the Hindu, does not fail his wife, but, apart from this, coquetry and vanity, however pleasing in their form, could never dignify marriage.

Lifelong intimacy, to be beautiful, must boast deeper foundations—the wife's love, daring all and asking for no return; the mother's gentleness, that never changes; the friend's unswerving generosity. To the grave Oriental there is something indecorous in the discussion of the subject on any but this highest basis. And yet Persia, the France of Asia, must have been a perpetual influence towards romanticism in Hindu life. There is said to be no love poetry in the world so impassioned as the Persian. The famous verse:

Four eyes met. There were changes in two souls.
And now I cannot remember whether he is a man and I a woman,
Or he a woman and I a man. All I know is,
There were two: Love came, and there is one...

We must believe completely representative of its spirit. The Persian language, however, has only touched India through the Court of Delhi and through letters. It has been the possession of the Indo-Mohammedan and of any man here and there who took the time and trouble to master its literature; but the world of Hindu womanhood has remained probably as remote from it as though it belonged to another planet.

This is not true to the same extent of the romantic aspect of Christianity. The letters taught in English schools result very much in novel-reading, and an indigenous school of fiction has grown up, in the form of books and magazines, which is likely to modify popular ideas on this subject profoundly. Meanwhile, and for long to come, it remains true that according to Hindu notions, the eyes of bride and bridegroom are to be directed towards the welfare of the family and not of themselves, as the basis of society: it is the great springs of helpfulness and service, rather than those of mutual love and romantic happiness that marriage is expected to unloose. Selfish wives and jealous husbands there must be, as among all peoples. But it is a fact, nevertheless, that here the absolute stainlessness of the wife is considered but preliminary to the further virtue demanded of her, the sustaining of the honour of her husband's house.

With this clue it becomes easy to understand even what the West considers to be the anomalies of Hindu custom—the laws regarding rare cases of polygamy and adoption. For it is legally provided that if a woman remain childless her husband may after seven years, and with her permission, take a second wife, in the hope of gaining a son to succeed to his place. On the European basis of individualism, the permission would probably be impossible to obtain; but with the Eastern sense of family obligation, this has not always been so, and I have myself met the son of such a marriage whose story was of peculiar interest. The elder wife had insisted that the time was come for the alternative to be tried, and had herself chosen the speaker's mother as the most beautiful girl she could find, for the husband.

The marriage once over, she made every effort to make it a success, and welcomed the new wife as a younger sister. Not only this, but when the son was born, such was her tenderness that he was twelve years old before he knew that she was not his mother. After her death, however, the younger wife became head of the house. Amongst the children to be fed, there were degrees of kindred, certain adopted orphans, two or three cousins, and himself. He was the eldest of all, and protested loudly that he came in last and his cousins only second, for his mother's attentions. "Nay, my child," she answered, with a Hindu woman's sweetness and good sense, "if I desired to neglect thee, I could not do it. Is it not right, then, first to serve those who have no protection against me?"

The family life which such a story discloses is singularly noble, and it is not necessary to suppose that polygamy entailed such generosities oftener than we find monogamy do amongst ourselves. In any case, the same tide that brings in individualism has swept away this custom; and whereas it never was common it is now practically obsolete, except for princes and great nobles, and even amongst these classes there are signs of a radical change of custom.

"Where women are honoured, there the gods are pleased: where they are dishonoured, religious acts become of no avail." "In whatever family the husband is contented with his wife, and the wife with her husband, in that house will good fortune assuredly abide." Few books offer such delights to their readers as that known as the "Laws of Manu."

It is in no sense a collection of Acts of Parliament, for the one attitude throughout is that of the witness, and the hastiest perusal shows that it represents the growth of custom during ages, and is in no sense the work of a single hand. This is indeed its first and most striking beauty. As must be, of course, it often happens that the superstition of a habit is stated as gravely as its original intent, but rarely so as to obscure that first significance, or leave it difficult of restoration, and from cover to cover the book throbs with the passion for justice, and the appreciation of fine shades of courtesy and taste, clothed in calm and judicial form. Especially of this type are those dicta on the rights of women, which are household words in Indian homes. We all know the reaction of the written word on life.

Fact once formulated as scripture acquires new emphasis, a certain occult significance seems to attach to it, and the words, "it is written" become terrible enough to affright the devil himself. In this way the fear of a feminine curse has become a superstition in India, and I have seen even a low-class mob fall back at the command of a single woman who opposed them. For is it not written in the book of the law that "the house which is cursed by a woman perishes utterly, as if destroyed by a sacrifice for the death of an enemy?"—strange and graphic old phrase, pregnant of woe!

It is evident then that the laws of Manu are rather the unconscious expression of the spirit of the people than a declaration of the ideals towards which they strive. And for this reason they would afford the most reliable foundation for a healthy criticism of Indian custom. The conception of domestic happiness which they reveal is very complete, and no one who has seen the light on an Indian woman's face when it turns to her husband—as I have seen it in all parts of the country—can doubt that conception is often realised in life.

For if the characteristic emotion of the wife may be described as passionate reverence that of the Hindu husband is certainly a measureless protection. If we may presume to analyse things as sacred as the great mutual trusts of life, it would seem that tenderness is the ruling note of the man's relation. Turning as he does to the memory of his own mother for the ideal perfection, there is again something of motherhood in what he brings to his wife. As a child might do, she cooks for him, and serves him, sitting before him as he eats to fan away the flies. As a disciple might, she prostrates herself before him, touching his feet with her head before receiving his blessing. It is not equality. No. But who talks of a vulgar equality, asks the Hindu wife, when she may have instead the unspeakable blessedness of offering worship?

And on the man's side, how is this received? Entirely without personal vanity. The idea that adoration is the soul's opportunity has sunk deep into the life of the people. And the husband can recognize his wife's right to realise her highest through him without ever forgetting that it is her power to love, not his worthiness of love that is being displayed. Indeed, is not life everywhere of one tint in this regard? Does anything stir our reverence like an affection that we feel beyond our merit?

It is often glibly said that this habit of being served spoils the Indian man and renders him careless of the comfort of others. I have never found this to be so. It is true that Indian men do not rise when a woman enters, and remain standing till she is seated. Nor do they hasten to open the door through which she is about to pass. But then it is not according to the etiquette of their country to do these things. With regard to the last point, indeed, their idea is that man should precede woman, maintaining the tradition of the path-breaker in the jungle; and one of the most touching incidents in the national epic of heroic love is Sita's request to go first along the forest paths, in order to sweep the thorns from her husband's path with the end of her veil. Needless to say, such a paradox is not permitted.

Thus, honour for the weaker is expressed in one way in England and quite otherwise in Hindustan, but the heart of conduct is the same in both countries. The courtesy of husbands to their wives is quite unfailing amongst Hindus.

"Thou shalt not strike a woman, even with a flower," is the proverb. His wife's desire for companionship on a journey is the first claim on a man. And it is very touching to notice how, as years go on, he leans more and more to the habit of addressing her as "O thou, mother of our son!" and presenting her to new corners as "my children's mother," thus reflecting upon her his worship of motherhood.

In early manhood he trusts to her advice to moderate the folly of his own rasher inclinations; in old age he becomes, as everywhere in the world, more entirely the eldest of her bairns, and she more and more the real head and centre of the home. But always she remains as she was at the beginning, Lakshmi, her husband's Goddess of Fortune.

In those first days he ate from no hand but his mother's or hers; and one of her devotions was the fast, not broken till he had eaten and their talk was over, though her evening meal might in this way be delayed till long past mid-night. Now, with the responsibilities of her household upon her, she feeds a whole multitude before she takes her own turn, and still the mutual pact of soul and soul has not been broken by the strife of "rights." These two have all these years been each other's refuge against the world. And not once have they felt so separated as to offer thanks, or speak, either of the other, by name, as if head and hand could be different individuals!

On that first bridal evening, the little bride was borne before her young husband, and they were told that the moment was auspicious for their first shy look. Then the old Vedic fire was called to witness their rites of union; the girl flung the garland of flowers about the neck of her bridegroom, in exquisite symbolism of the bond that was to hold them; and finally they took seven steps together, hand in hand, while the priest chanted appropriate texts for each stage of life.

Such was their wedding. Since then, the rights of one have been the rights of the other; joys, griefs, and duties have been held in common. Till now, if the bride of that distant night be entirely fortunate, the prayer of her childhood is fulfilled to her in the end of her days, that prayer that said:

From the arms of husband and sons,

When the Ganges is full of water,

May I pass to the feet of the Lord?

It has seemed to me in watching Hindu couples that they were singular in the frequent attainment of a perfect intimacy. To what is this due? Is it the early association, or the fact that courtship comes after marriage, not before? Or is it the intense discipline of absolute reserve in the presence of others? The people themselves, where their attention is called to it, attribute the fact to child-marriage. I remember asking a friend of my own, a man of wealth and cultivation, orthodox and childless, "If you could put away personal considerations, and speak only from the outside, which you think better in the abstract, our marriage-system or yours?"

He paused, and answered slowly, "I think—ours; for I cannot conceive that two people could grow into each other, as my wife and I have done, under any other." Amongst the luxuries of the West I have sometimes thought that the deepening of the human tie was proportionate to simplicity of surroundings. A people to whom all complexity of externals is impossible must live by thought and feeling, or perish in the wilderness.

But whatever be the truth on this point, I have seen clearly and constantly that the master-note by which the Hindu woman's life can be understood in the West is that of the religious life. This is so, even with the wife.

Cloistered and veiled, she devotes herself to one name, one thought, yet is never known to betray the fact, even as the nun steals away in secret to kneel before the Blessed Sacrament. The ideal that she, like the nun, pursues, is that of a vision which merges the finite in the infinite, making strong to mock at separation, or even at change.

And the point to be reached in practice is that where the whole world is made beautiful by the presence in it of the beloved, where the hungry are fed, and the needy relieved, out of a joyful recognition that they wear a common humanity with his; and where, above all, the sense of unrest and dissatisfaction is gone for ever, in the overflowing fullness of a love that asks no return except the power of more abundant loving.

□□□